Foundations of Microprogramming

ARCHITECTURE, SOFTWARE, and APPLICATIONS

Ashok K. Agrawala

Department of Computer Science
University of Maryland
College Park, Maryland

Tomlinson G. Rauscher

Advanced Development Department
NCR Corporation
Cambridge, Ohio

Academic Press, Inc.

NEW YORK SAN FRANCISCO LONDON 1976
A Subsidiary of Harcourt Brace Jovanovich, Publishers

ACADEMIC PRESS, INC.
111 Fifth Avenue, New York, New York 10003

United Kingdom Edition published by
ACADEMIC PRESS, INC. (LONDON) LTD.
24/28 Oval Road, London NW1

Library of Congress Cataloging in Publication Data

Agrawala, Ashok K
        Foundations of microprogramming

        (ACM monograph series)
        Bibliography: p.
        1.   Microprogramming.   I.   Rauscher, Tomlinson G., joint
author.   II.   Title.   III.   Series: Association for
Computing Machinery. ACM monograph series.
QA76.6.A35   001.6'42   75-37656
ISBN 0-12-045150-6

Foundations of
Microprogramming

ACM MONOGRAPH SERIES

Published under the auspices of the Association for
Computing Machinery Inc.

Editor ROBERT L. ASHENHURST *The University of Chicago*

To
Radhika and Suki

Contents

ERRATA
FOUNDATIONS OF MICROPROGRAMMING
By Ashok K. Agrawala and Tomlinson G. Rauscher

Page 32. The upper right-hand quadrant of Figure 1.5-1 should be shaded as follows:

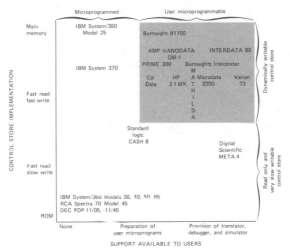

Page 36. Delete the words "OUTPUT INTERRUPT" and the dashed line beside them at the top of the page.

Page 216. The continued portion of Figure 6.2-4 at the top of the page should appear as follows:

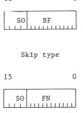

Pages 263–268. Delete the right-hand column headed "References" on these pages.
Page 348. Delete the figure legend beginning "Fig. 5."
Page 384. Delete the number 123 from the upper right-hand corner of Figure 8.7-1.
Page 408. Delete the vertical line following "Generation" in two places.

Preface

The purpose of this book is to define, describe, and illustrate the foundations and current trends in microprogramming. Because the emergence of *user* microprogrammable computers is responsible for significant activity in this field, the book covers this topic extensively. The level of presentation highlights the architectural, software, and applications aspects of microprogramming without becoming mired in intricate details. Descriptions of current developments are intended to provide examples, illustrate capabilities, and show alternatives with the expectation that they will provoke thought, provide insight, and indicate directions for new developments.

Microprogramming is receiving new interest with the development of fast writable memories for microprogram residence, and the subsequent marketing of several user microprogrammable computers. Whereas previous developments of read—only memories provided manufacturers with the capability to microprogram machine language instruction sets, recent developments have facilitated new techniques, implementations, and applications for users.

The book is intended for a wide audience and can be used in a variety of ways. Chapter 1 introduces microprogramming concepts. This chapter presents background material, develops a general definition of microprogramming and its characteristics, provides an easy to understand example, and compares microprogramming with programming and microprocessors. An elementary understanding of machine languages and computers is helpful in reading the chapter. In describing the fundamental concepts of microprogramming, Chapter 1 presents microprogramming from a slightly different but more general viewpoint than the classical approach. The sections on programming, microprogrammability, and microprocessors should provide some new insights as all these subjects are seldom considered in microprogramming presentations.

Microprogramming has borrowed heavily from the areas of computer architecture and software, and should be regarded as another level in a system hierarchy. There is little underlying theory to microprogramming but there are basic concepts; these concepts are described in Chapter 2 on architectural characteristics and in Chapter 3 on microprogramming languages and support software. For those new in the field these chapters define the characteristics that will be illustrated by the developments described in Chapters 4-7. Although the principles discussed in Chapters 2 and 3 should be well known to those familiar with microprogramming, they are often confused in the literature. Thus Chapters 2 and 3 separate and clarify the issues involved in microprogramming architecture and software. The student and practitioner should be well aware of the distinction and interrelationships among these concepts.

Chapters 4-7 present contemporary developments of user microprogrammable computer systems and microprogramming languages. The computers are primarily commercially available systems, and many are fairly inexpensive. The computers are described through the characteristics discussed in earlier chapters using the terminology developed in those chapters. The architecture diagrams have generally been drawn in the same format; common components have been placed in the same relative locations for each machine. These diagrams show the logical structure of the computers; we are not overly concerned with the engineering aspects of these designs. An attempt has been made to avoid a favored treatment of any machine. Our biases are reserved for the last chapter of the book.

In reading the machine descriptions, an interesting exercise is to determine the characteristics that a machine demonstrates well, or the degree to which various characteristics are in evidence. Example microprograms have been included for most of the computers and have been explained carefully in an effort to illustrate current microprogramming characteristics. Whereas the manufacturers of most of the computers discussed agree with our descriptions, the descriptions are not to be construed as operating specifications nor as commitments to specifications. Although software developments have been largely experimental, the same comments apply.

A number of applications of microprogramming are described in Chapter 8, which surveys practical applications that are in wide use and also applications investigated primarily as research projects but which may come into common use in the future. Chapters 4-8 present a significant accumulation of information on the current state of microprogramming, and should serve as a handy reference to computer professionals.

The annotated bibliography at the end of each chapter should be helpful in further exploring the ideas presented in the book.

In Chapter 9 we try to provide a perspective on microprogramming systems by summarizing past, present, and future trends.

We believe the book is well suited for a short seminar on microprogramming or as an introduction to microprogramming in a course on computer architecture. This book could also serve as a primary text for a graduate course on microprogramming. In that case the bibliographies serve as a guide to topics to be studied in more detail.

This book evolved from work begun early in 1973. An early short report which summarized some parts of this work was published in the *IEEE Transactions on Computers* in August 1974.* This book, which incorporates many new developments, is a significantly expanded and updated report on this work.

*A.K. Agrawala and T.G. Rauscher, Microprogramming: perspective and status, IEEE Trans. on Comp., Vol. C-23, No. 8, Aug. 1974, pp. 817-837.

Acknowledgments

The assistance of many people helped make this book possible. We are especially grateful to those who provided information on computers and micro-programming languages: Mr. Ron Compton and Mr. Norman Compton, Standard Logic Inc.; Dr. Wayne Wilner, Burroughs Corporation; Mr. Han Park and Mr. Bill Dallenbach, Hewlett-Packard Company; Mr. Richard Caveny, Digital Scientific Corporation; Mr. W. David Elliott, Naval Research Laboratory; Mr. Paul Anagnostopoulos, Brown University; Mr. Frank Ferraro, INTERDATA Incorporated; Mr. Cliff Roebuck, Microdata Corporation; Mr. Ken Omohundro, California Data Processors; Mr. Steven Andleman and Mr. James Coffey, PRIME Computer Inc.; Mr. Bob Mahoney, Mr. Ed O'Neil, and Mr. Angus McLagan, Varian Data Machines; Mr. Jack Lynch and Dr. Earl Reigel, Burroughs Corporation; Mr. Joel Herbsman and Dr. John Hale, NANODATA Corporation; Mr. William Lidinsky, Argonne National Laboratory; Dr. Bruce Shriver, Dr. Ted Lewis, Mr. L. Phillip Caillouet, Jr., Mr. Allan Lang, and Mr. Les Waguespack, University of Southwestern Louisiana; Dr. Richard Eckhouse, Jr., Digital Equipment Corporation; Mr. Clinton W. Parker II, University of Maryland. The photograph in Figure 1.2-2 is courtesy of Hewlett-Packard. The Association for Computing Machinery and The Institute of Electrical and Electronics Engineers graciously permitted reproduction of several figures from their publications.

Finally, we would like to thank our colleagues in the Department of Computer Science and the Computer Science Center of the University of Maryland for their encouragement and support during this work.

Foundations of Microprogramming

CHAPTER 1

INTRODUCTION TO MICROPROGRAMMING CONCEPTS

1.1 Basic Computer Organization

A digital computer is functionally organized into the four basic sections shown in Figure 1.1-1. The input/output (I/O) section maintains communication between the computer and its environment. It accepts information from devices (card readers, teletypes, tape drives, etc.) and converts it to a form

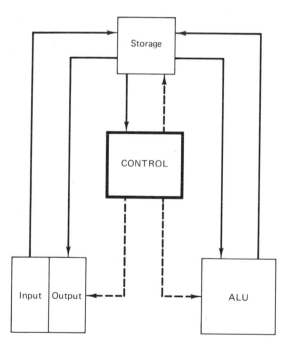

Figure 1.1-1 Functional organizaton of a digital computer.

suitable for use by the rest of the computer; it also transforms internal information into a form suitable for external use or storage (printed reports, magnetic tapes, microfiche, etc.). The storage section, often called the memory or main memory, provides a place to store information, such as data and programs. The arithmetic and logic unit (ALU) transforms data by performing arithmetic and logical operations, such as addition, subtraction, comparison, shifting, logical and, and logical or. These sections operate under the command of the control section which controls the operations of the various sections and directs the flow of information among them via several links (data paths).

The information utilized in the operation of a digital computer, almost always represented in binary form, comprises two basic types - control information and data. While this dichotomy provides a useful classification, the two types of information are distinguishable inside a computer only by the separate links (paths) for them. Control information, generated by the control section, controls the operations of the I/O, storage, and ALU sections and also the future operation of the control unit itself. Physically, control information effects operations with binary signals; these signals stimulate the circuits which constitute the various sections. As these circuits must be activated at specific instants in time, the temporal characteristics of control information generation are important.

The information not treated as control information in a computer may be considered data. While data are generally represented in binary form, they may represent a variety of types - integer numbers, character strings, digitized images, etc. So called "machine language instructions" are a special type of data that is used by the control section to determine the proper generation of control signals to effect a program. Although some computers utilize data paths that transfer only machine language instructions, in most computers, machine language instructions and other types of data stored in memory are indistinguishable.

A computer may be viewed as an automatic data processing machine which has the capability to perform a variety of operations (transformations) on different types of data. For each operation there is typically a machine language instruction. A sequence of machine language instructions, i.e., a program, can thus effect a complex task when executed by the computer hardware.

1.1.1 Basic Hardware Resources

Each section of a computer can perform a variety of operations, and the actual repertoire depends on the hardware which implements the section. There are three basic types of hardware units:

1. Transformation units are hardware units which perform specific transformations or operations on data. To perform the addition operation, for example, there is a hardware adder unit which accepts two data items as input, treats these inputs as numbers, performs the addition, and makes the result available as output. Modern computers contain a large number of such hardware transformation units; however, the complexity of the circuits and hence the time required to perform the operations may vary greatly.

2. Storage elements are hardware units capable of retaining information over a period of time. Once information is assigned to a storage element, it remains there until it is replaced by new information. Storage elements have fixed sizes (lengths) measured by the number of bits of information they store. Common examples of storage elements are registers, which

3

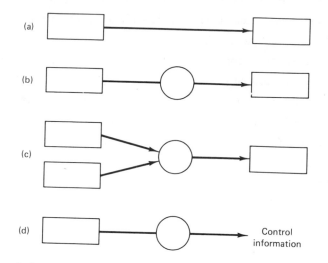

Figure 1.1-2 Primitive computer operations: (a) move operation, (b) unary operation, (c) binary operation, (d) convert operation. The rectangles represent storage units (registers), the lines repesent data and control paths, and the circles represent hardware transformation units.

may consist of several flip-flops, and words in main memory, which often comprise several magnetic cores.

3. Links are paths which transfer information among storage and transformation units. As this information may be data or control information, links may be further classified as data paths and control paths. Physically a link is simply a "wire" that can route one bit of information at a time; however, a link is often considered to be a group of such wires that transfer information from one unit to another. The number of wires in a group, and hence the number of bits that can be simultaneously transferred, is called the width of the link.

A computer can thus be described in terms of its transformation units, storage elements, and links.

4

1.1.2 Control of Primitive Operations

A computer effects primitive operations by connecting its hardware transformation units, storage units, and links in a variety of combinations. As illustrated in Figure 1.1-2 the basic types of primitive operations are

1. move operations,
2. unary operations,
3. binary operations, and
4. convert operations.

A move operation transfers information from one storage element to another via a link. In a unary operation, a hardware transformation unit receives information from a storage element via a link, the hardware transformation unit transforms the input information creating a result, and finally a storage element receives the result via a link. In a binary operation, the hardware transformation unit receives information from two storage elements over two links before the operation is performed and the result is transferred to a destination. Operations with three and more inputs are possible but not common. A convert operation works much like a unary operation, however, unlike the other primitive operations, the convert operation transforms data into control information.

Performing these primitive operations requires some control. A move operation requires a control signal to activate a link. If the selected link connects several source storage elements and several destination storage elements, then a specific source storage element and a specific destination storage element must be selected. The amount of information required to make unique selections depends on the number of

5

storage elements and links. A unary operation additionally requires the selection of a hardware transformation unit and a link over which to transfer its result to the destination storage element. A binary operation additionally requires the selection of another input storage element and link.

A common characteristic of these primitive operations is that they require minimal sequential control. In a move operation the selection of the source storage element, the link, and the destination storage element may be simultaneous because the transfer of information is essentially instantaneous. For unary and binary operations there may be a short time delay caused by the hardware transformation unit, so that the activation of the output link and storage element may follow the activation of the input link and storage element. Primitive operations can, therefore, generally be completed in one or two phases (basic clock cycles).

1.1.3 Generation of Control Information

Computers are required to perform complex operations; however, due to the variety and cost involved, such operations are seldom implemented as primitive operations. Computers therefore perform sequences of primitive operations to effect complex operations. Multiplication and division, for example, may be effected by sequences of primitive operations such as addition, subtraction, and shifting.

One method of implementing a complex operation is to design a sequential logic circuit which generates in sequence the control information (signals) to activate the primitive operations which constitute the complex operation. As the sequence of primitive operations required for each complex operation is different, each complex operation the computer is to perform requires a sequential logic circuit. For a general purpose computer with a comprehensive set of complex operations, there will be a large number of such sequential logic circuits, and as a result the computer will have a very complex control unit. As the sequential logic circuits that effect the complex operations may have common subsequences of primitive operations, two or more sequential logic circuits may be combined. While such minimization reduces the amount and cost of hardware, it further complicates the organization of the control unit.

For some time all computers used this technique of implementing complex operations by sequential logic circuits. The complex operations are called machine language instructions or simply machine instructions, and more complex functions are performed by a sequence of machine language instructions, i.e., a machine language program. The sequence of machine language instructions that constitute a program reside in the computer memory. The machine instructions are individually fetched from the memory into the control unit and converted (i.e., decoded) into control information that activates a sequential logic circuit, which in turn activates the primitive operations that constitute the machine instruction. Figure 1.1-3 illustrates this process of executing machine language instructions. With such a hardwired implementation, a computer can perform only those operations in its repertoire of machine language instructions, i.e., the computer can perform only those operations for which it has a sequential logic circuit that sequentially executes the primitive operations which effect a machine language instruction.

Microprogramming is an alternative method of implementation that can reduce the complexity and inflexibility of the control unit. This method of implementation is based on the observations that a complex operation is completely

7

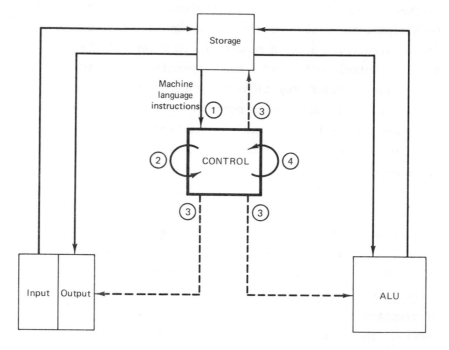

Figure 1.1-3 Executing machine language instructions in a hardwired implementation; Legend: Solid Line, Data; Dashed Line, Control Information.

Step 1.   Under command of the control unit, the next machine language instruction is fetched from main memory into an instruction register.

Step 2. The control unit converts the machine language instruction (decodes it) into control information.

Step 3. The generated control signals select the sequential logic circuits that effect the machine language instructions. A sequential logic circuit effects a sequence of primitive operations of the type in Figure 1.1-2.

Step 4. The control unit prepares for fetching the next machine language instruction, e.g., it updates the instruction counter.

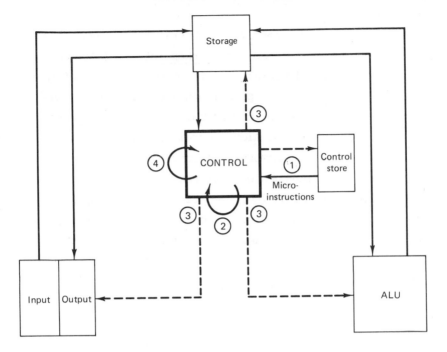

Figure 1.1-4   Executing   microoperations   on   a
microprogrammed machine; Legend: Solid Line, Data; Dashed Line,
Control Information.

Step 1. Under command of the control unit, the next
        microoperation (or microinstruction) is fetched from
        control store into a microinstruction register.
Step 2. The control   unit   converts   the   microoperation   into
        control information.
Step 3. The generated   control signals stimulate   the   hardware
        resources indicated in the microoperation.
Step 4. The control   unit   prepares   for   fetching   the   next
        microoperation, e.g.,   it   updates the microinstruction
        counter.

9

specified by a sequence of primitive operations, and that storage elements may be used to store information about primitive operations directly. Each primitive operation may be represented in storage as a microoperation* (also called a microorder or an elementary order) which contains information to specify the primitive operation uniquely. The storage unit which contains microoperations is called a control store (also called control memory or microprogram memory) and is usually separate from the main memory. A complex operation** can thus be represented as a sequence of stored microoperations, i.e., a microprogram or microroutine. Executing a complex operation now reduces to executing a microprogram in much the same way that a hardwired implementation executes a machine language program, viz., by executing the microoperations in sequence. Executing a microoperation thus involves the control unit fetching it and generating the control signals required to activate the primitive operation corresponding to the microoperation. Using generated control signals to activate primitive hardware resources directly contrasts with the hardwired execution of machine language instructions, where generated control signals typically activate sequential logic circuits which in turn activate the primitive hardware resources. As illustrated in Figure 1.1-4, the execution of a microoperation requires a fetch–decode–execute sequence. Since microoperations correspond to primitive computer operations, this fetch–decode–execute sequence is a very simple task compared to the hardwired fetch–decode–execute phases for machine language instructions. A computer is thus microprogrammed if the instructions it

---

* A microinstruction, which consists on one or more micro-operations, is a more general concept and will be discussed subsequently.
** Complex operations or machine instructions are sometimes called macroinstructons to distinguish them from microinstructions. We do not use this terminology because it conflicts with the more common use of "macro" as a parameterized assembler language routine.

directly (by hardware) fetches, decodes, and executes correspond to the primitive operations the machine can perform. Note that this notion includes the more specific definition of microprogramming as an alternative implementation of a machine language instruction set.

1.2 Evolution of Microprogramming

The basic concepts of microprogramming described in the previous section were discussed by Professor Maurice V. Wilkes of the University of Cambridge as early as 1951 [Wilkes 1951]. Noting that "it is in the control section of electronic computers that the greatest degree of complexity generally arises,"* Wilkes's objective in introducing microprogramming "was to provide a systematic alternative to the usual somewhat ad hoc procedure used for designing the control system of a digital computer."**

Although microprogramming received some attention during the 1950's,*** it was not used commercially on a significant scale until the mid 1960's when IBM employed microprogrammed implementations in most of the models of the System/360 [Fagg 1964]. This delay can be traced directly to memory technology. As noted in the previous section, a computer performs a fetch–decode–execute sequence to effect a microinstruction. This sequence involves referencing a memory that contains microinstructions before directing the hardware resources to perform the operation. Although the execution of the primitive microoperation proceeds at the speed of sequential logic circuits, until the 1960's memory technology was significantly slower than logic speeds. With that

*Wilkes, 1953.
**Wilkes, 1969, p. 139.
***See, for example, the surveys of Wilkes [1969] and Husson [1970].

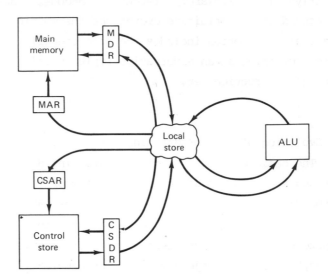

Figure 1.2-1 Simplified organization of a microprogrammed computer. Control store holds microinstructions. The CSAR (control store address register) addresses the control store. The CSDR (control store data register) contains microinstructions read from or into control store. Main memory, which contains data and "machine" language instructions, is addressed by the MAR (memory address register). The MDR (memory data register) contains data read from or into main memory. Local store usually contains fast registers and connecting data paths. The ALU (arithmetic and logic unit) performs operations on data stored in local store registers.

technology the simplicity and flexibility offered by microprogramming was much more than offset by the tremendous overhead of a memory access for each microinstruction. It was only with the availability of faster memories that substantial efforts toward microprogrammed implementations began.

The first memory technology developments that influenced microprogramming were a variety of types of read only memory (ROM) also called read only storage (ROS).* Such ROMs served as control stores in the first microprogrammed machines. The microprograms stored in the ROM control stores were used to perform machine language instructions. Machines which used ROM control stores to execute a single set of machine language instructions were "microprogrammed" by the manufacturer, and their microprogrammed nature was invisible to the user. The recent development of fast read/write semiconductor memories has provided new capabilities in implementing machines by microprogramming. Many computers use such fast read/write memories as control stores whose microinstructions interpret machine language instruction sets, but, some computers permit users to access and modify the control store; users can, therefore, develop and insert their own microprograms into control store. A number of such "microprogrammable" computers will be discussed in detail in Chapters 4 through 6.

Microprogramming was proposed and continues to be used mainly as an alternative method for implementing machine language instructions. However, with continued developments in hardware technology, the concept of microprogramming has evolved to connote a more general notion than an alternative method for implementing machine language instructions. To illustrate this, consider the very simplified organization of a microprogrammable computer shown in Figure 1.2-1. In such a machine a microinstruction controls the operation of various primitive resources** of a computer - main memory and local store registers (both general and special purpose), arithmetic and logic units (ALUs), data paths, etc. The microinstructions

---

*Husson [1970] provides a detailed discussion of ROMs.
**Note that the concept of a primitive hardware resource continually changes with the development of new circuits and technologies.

are stored as words in a control store that is traditionally (but not necessarily) separate from main memory. The execution of a microinstruction involves selecting the microinstruction at the address specified by the <u>control</u> <u>store</u> <u>address</u> <u>register</u> (CSAR), reading the microinstruction into the <u>microinstruction</u> <u>register</u> (MIR) (sometimes called the <u>control</u> <u>store</u> <u>data</u> <u>register</u> – CSDR), updating the CSAR to address the next microinstruction, and performing the primitive operations requested by the microinstruction in the MIR. By repeating this process a sequence of such microinstructions, i.e., a microprogram, can be executed.

While microprograms contain information that controls hardware at a primitive level, they are stored in a memory and are executed as stored programs. This gives microprogramming a software as well as a hardware flavor so the appellation "firmware," "a term to designate microprograms resident in the computer's control memory,"* is most appropriate. With such a software influence microprogramming may be considered independently from machine languages; indeed, the brief description in the previous paragraph of the operation of a microprogrammable computer makes no reference to machine language instructions.

Figure 1.2-2 is a photograph of a contemporary microprogrammable computer, the Hewlett-Packard HP21MX described in Section 5.2. It is presented here to illustrate the physical appearance of a machine.

1.3 An Example – Simple Microprogrammable Machine

In order to provide a more detailed understanding of microprogramming and microprogrammable computers and to provide a basis for later definitions and concepts, we consider in some

*Opler, [1967], p. 22.

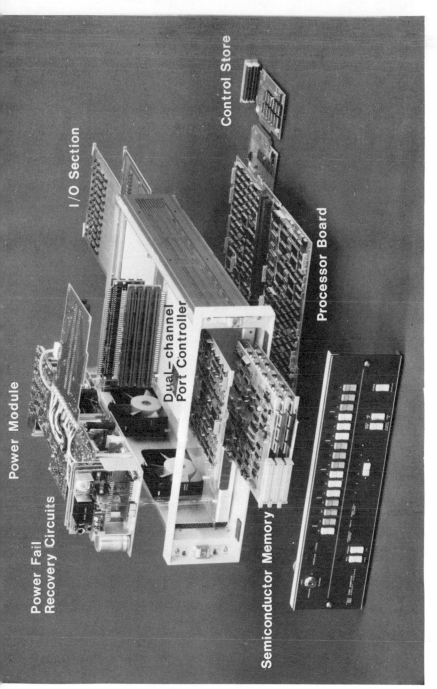

Power Module

Power Fail
Recovery Circuits

I/O Section

Control Store

Dual-channel
Port Controller

Processor Board

Semiconductor Memory

Figure 1.2-2

15

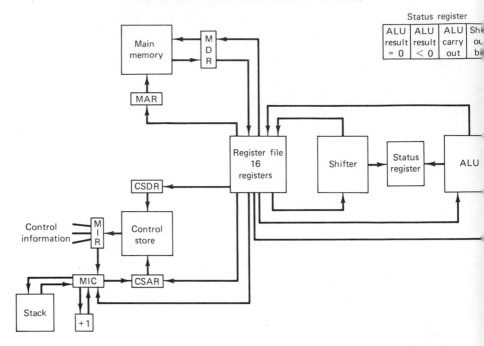

Figure 1.3-1 Organization of a simple microprogrammable machine (SMM).

detail the organization and operation of a simple microprogrammable computer. Figure 1.3-1 illustrates the organization of our simple microprogrammable machine (SMM). Figure 1.3-2 lists the microoperations, i.e., the primitive operations, that the SMM can perform. Assume, for the present, that in this machine each microinstruction performs one primitive operation. The execution of a microinstruction, however, may depend on the conditions indicated by the status register.

Consider the process of implementing machine language instructions on the SMM. Assume that the main memory of SMM

Simple Register Transfer Operations

        MAR <- GPR

        MDR <- GPR

        GPR <- MDR

        CSDR <- GPR

Transformation Operations

        GPR <- shifted GPR

          The shift direction and type are indicated by the operation,

          and the shift amount is specified by the operation or in a GPR

        GPR <- GPR binary operation GPR

        GPR <- unary operation GPR

          The ALU performs the operations: addition, addition with

          carry, subtraction, logical and, logical or, and

          logical complement (not), and sets the status register

Sequencing Operations

        MIC <- GPR

        MIC <- MIR   (or part of the MIR)

        Push MIC onto stack

        Pop stack to MIC

Memory Operations

        READ Main Memory

          Main memory addressed by MAR -> MDR

        WRITE Main Memory

          MDR -> main memory addressed by MAR

        CSAR <- GPR and READ control store into CSDR

        CSAR <- GPR and WRITE from CSDR into control store

Figure 1.3-2. SMM microoperations.

contains "machine language" programs. The machine language instructions are two address instructions having the format specified in Figure 1.3-3. Some typical machine language instructions are shown in Figure 1.3-4. The words in the main memory, the registers in the register file, and the MDR in the SMM are all 32 bits wide.

The first step in performing a machine language instruction, like a microinstruction, is to fetch the instruction from the main memory and then decode it, i.e., break it into its constituent parts and determine their meaning. The sequence of microinstructions shown in Figure 1.3-5 performs the fetch and decode for our simple machine language for SMM. As can be seen from this sequence, Register 14 serves as the instruction counter and contains the main memory address of the next instruction to be executed. Register 15 is used as the instruction register which holds the machine language instruction being executed. The decoding in this machine is simplified by using the numeric value of the OPCODE as the control store address. At the end of executing the sequence of microinstructions in Figure 1.3-5, the MIC contains the value specified by the opcode of the instruction in register 15. For example, if the machine instruction were a multiply instruction the MIC would contain the number 2. The next microinstruction executed will be from the control store location 2. By placing a branch operation at location 2 which effects a branch to the routine for executing the multiply instruction, the execution of the machine language instruction can be completed. Control store location 2 will thus have the microinstruction for branching to the microinstruction at control store location 83. The locations 0 to 63 of the control store contain branch operations and help simplify the decoding of the machine instructions.

Op code	Address in MM of first operand	Address in MM of second operand

6 bits 13 bits 13 bits

Figure 1.3-3 Format of SMM machine language instructions.

Op Code Value

(in decimal)	Representation	Meaning
0	ADD A,B	(A) <- (A) + (B)
1	SUB A,B	(A) <- (A) - (B)
2	MPY A,B	(A) <- (A) x (B)
3	MOVE A,B	(B) <- (A)
4	MOVE constant,B	(B) <- constant
5	GO TO constant address	(Instruction counter) <- constant address
6	IF ZERO GO TO constant address	If zero bit in the status register is set then (instruction counter) <- constant address
7	GO TO INDIRECT A	(Instruction counter) <- (A)
8	MOVE INDIRECT A,B	((B)) <- (A)

Figure 1.3-4. Some typical SMM machine language instructions.
Comments: A and B are names of memory addresses;
(X) means contents of word at address X;
<- means is replaced by.

19

Address of Microinstruction	Microinstruction	Comments
64	MAR <- R14	Fetch next
65	READ	instruction
66	R15 <- MDR	into R15
67	R13 <- R15 RS 26	Put op code into R13
68	R12 <- R15 LS 6	Put address of first
69	R12 <- R12 RS 19	operand into R12
70	R11 <- R15 LS 19	Put address of second
71	R11 <- R11 RS 19	operand into R11
72	R14 <- R14 + 1	Update instruction counter
73	MIC <- R13	Go to decode microroutine

Figure 1.3-5 SMM microprogram to fetch and decode machine language Instructions.

The sequence of microinstructions to perform the multiply instruction, shown in Figure 1.3-6, would be stored starting at address 83 in the control store. The last instruction in this sequence is a branch instruction to branch back to the fetch sequence. The microroutine in Figure 1.3-6 is thus similar to a subroutine. Other machine language instructions are effected in a similar manner. Combining these routines results in a microprogram that performs all the machine language instructions shown in Figure 1.3-4. Such a microprogram is shown in Figure 1.3-7.

While the execution of machine language instructions was the original application of microprogramming, it should be clear that microprogramming can be used directly in the more general problem solving sense without using the traditional machine language instructions. Consider, for example, the type of programming. Microprogramming, however, has the connotation of being an extremely difficult process that can be done only by select individuals who have detailed knowledge of the design and operation of logical circuits. It has been said that

> a microprogrammer must have a thorough knowledge and understanding of every ... function, every data path, every gate, and the amount of parallelism that exists in the system. He must be familiar with every in-gate and every out-gate associated with every piece of hardware, the timing pulses and the gates affected by each pulse, and the relationship between CPU clocks and the main storage, the local storage, and all other units of hardware in the system.

The unfortunate perpetuation of such misrepresentations in the literature and the production of machines that are difficult to microprogram have led Rosin to define microprogramming as "the implementation of hopefully reasonable systems through interpretation on unreasonable machines!"* It should be evident that this connotation of microprogramming is not inherent in the basic concept but merely an accident of historical development.

While microprogramming is a type of programming, there are some characteristics of microprogramming that distinguish it from the ordinary concept of programming. These include the following.

1. the level of control - microinstructions exercise direct control over primitive hardware resources, while programs manipulate user defined data structures. In microprogramming the problem of moving data between levels in the memory hierarchy may become acute.

2. the repertoire of instructions - the set of microoperations is generally small, while the set of program operations can be large and natural.

*Rosin, [1973].

21

Address of Microinstruction	Microinstruction	Comments
83	MAR <- R12	Fetch first
84	READ	operand
85	R2 <- MDR	into R2
86	MAR <- R11	Fetch second
87	READ	operand
88	R3 <- MDR	into R3
89	R1 <- 0	Initialize R1 for product
90	R4 <- 16	Initialize R4 for counting
91	R3 <- R3 RS 1	Multiply R2 by
92	IF shiftout = 0 GO TO 94	R3 using a shift and add
93	R1 <- R1 + R2	algorithm
94	R2 <- R2 LS 1	and put
95	R4 <- R4 - 1	the result
96	IF NOT ZERO GO TO 91	into R1
97	MDR <- R1	Write result into
98	MAR <- R12	memory at address
99	WRITE	of first operand
100	GO TO 64	Branch to instruction fetch microroutine

Figure 1.3-6 SMM microprogram to multiply 2 sixteen bit numbers.

Address of Microinstruction	Microinstruction	Comments
	Branch to instruction execution microprograms	
0	GO TO 101	ADD
1	GO TO 111	SUB
2	GO TO 83	MPY
3	GO TO 121	MOVE
4	GO TO 126	MOVE constant
5	GO TO 130	GO TO
6	GO TO 132	Conditional GO TO
7	GO TO 134	GO TO Indirect
8	GO TO 138	MOVE Indirect
	.	
	.	
	.	
	Instruction fetch and decode microprogram	
64	MAR <- R14	Fetch next
65	READ	instruction
66	R15 <- MDR	into R15
67	R13 <- R15 RS 26	Put op code into R13
68	R12 <- R15 LS 6	Put address of first
69	R12 <- R12 RS 19	operand into R12
70	R11 <- R15 LS 19	Put address of second
71	R11 <- R11 RS 19	operand into R11
72	R14 <- R14 + 1	Update instruction counter
73	MIC <- R13	Go to decode microroutine
	.	
	.	
	.	
	MULTIPLY microprogram	
83	MAR <- R12	Fetch first

23

84	READ	operand
85	R2 <- MDR	into R2
86	MAR <- R11	Fetch second
87	READ	operand
88	R3 <- MDR	into R3
89	R1 <- 0	Initialize R1 for product
90	R4 <- 16	Initialize R4 for counting
91	R3 <- R3 RS 1	Multiply R2 by
92	IF shiftout = 0 GO TO 94	R3 using a shift and add
93	R1 <- R1 + R2	algorithm
94	R2 <- R2 LS 1	and put
95	R4 <- R4 - 1	the result
96	IF NOT ZERO GO TO 91	into R1
97	MDR <- R1	Write result into
98	MAR <- R12	memory at address
99	WRITE	of first operand
100	GO TO 64	Branch to instruction fetch microprogram

ADD micropogram

101	MAR <- R11	Fetch second
102	READ	operand
103	R2 <- MDR	into R2
104	MAR <- R12	Fetch first
105	READ	operand
106	R3 <- MDR	into R3
107	R3 <- R3 + R2	Add operands
108	MDR <- R3	Write result into
109	WRITE	first operand location
110	GO TO 64	Branch to instruction fetch microprogram

SUBTRACT microprogram

111	MAR <- R11	Fetch second
112	READ	operand
113	R2 <- MDR	into R2
114	MAR <- R12	Fetch first

115	READ	operand
116	R3 <- MDR	into R3
117	R3 <- R3 - R2	Subtract operands
118	MDR <- R3	Write result into
119	WRITE	first operand location
120	GO TO 64	Branch to instruction
		fetch microprogram

MOVE A to B microprogram

121	MAR <- R12	Fetch first operand
122	READ	into MDR
123	MAR <- R11	Move address of second
		operand to MAR
124	WRITE	Write first operand into second
125	GO TO 64	Branch to instruction
		fetch microprogram

MOVE constant to B microprogram

126	MDR <- R12	Move first operand (literal) to
		MDR
127	MAR <- R11	Move address of second operand to
		MAR
128	WRITE	Write first operand into second
129	GO TO 64	Branch to instruction
		fetch microprogram

GO TO constant address microprogram

130	R14 <- R12	Move address to instruction
		counter
131	GO TO 64	Branch to instruction
		fetch microprogram

IF ZERO GO TO constant address
                         microprogram

132	IF ZERO GO TO 130	If status register zero bit is
		set,
		go to 130 to perform go to
133	GO TO 64	Branch to instruction
		fetch microprogram

GO TO INDIRECT A microprogram

25

```
134          MAR <-   R12          Read first operand
135          READ                   into MDR
136          R14 <- MDR            Assign first operand to
                                   instruction counter
137          GO TO 64             Branch to instruction
                                   fetch microprogram
```

                    MOVE INDIRECT microprogram

```
138          MAR <- R12           Read first
139          READ                  operand
140          R3 <- MDR             into R3
141          MAR <- R11           Read second
142          READ                  operand
143          R2 <- MDR             into R2
144          MAR <- R2            Move second operand to MAR
145          MDR <- R3            Move first operand to MDR
146          WRITE                Write first operand at location
                                   specified by second operand
147          GO TO 64             Branch to instruction
                                   fetch microprogram
```

Figure 1.3-7. SMM microprogram to perform the instructions in Figure 1.3-4.

Comments:The microprograms to perform the various instructions were designed for simplicity rather than for efficiency of space or time. machine language instruction set and the microprograms to interpret could easily be expanded.

```
C
C FORTRAN ROUTINE TO SORT AN ARRAY OF ONE HUNDRED INTEGERS
C   INTO ASCENDING ORDER
C
C DATA STRUCTURES
C   THE INTEGERS ARE STORED IN AN ARRAY CALLED LIST
C   TEMP IS A VARIABLE TO TEMPORARILY HOLD A VALUE
C            WHEN INTERCHANGING TWO ELEMENTS IN THE ARRAY
C   I AND J ARE LOOP INDICES
C
C DECLARATIONS
C      INTEGER LIST(100),TEMP,I,J
C
C ALGORITHM
C   FIND THE SMALLEST NUMBER (BY COMPARING THE FIRST
C          NUMBER TO THE REMAINING 99)
C          AND PUT IT IN LIST (1)
C   FIND THE NEXT SMALLEST NUMBER (BY COMPARING THE
C          SECOND NUMBER TO THE REMAINING 98)
C   REPEAT THIS PROCESS 97 MORE TIMES
C
       DO 2000 I=1,99
          K=I+1
          DO 1500 J=K,100
             IF(LIST(I).LT.LIST(J))GO TO 1500
             TEMP=LIST(I)
             LIST(I)=LIST(J)
             LIST(J)=TEMP
 1500     CONTINUE
 2000  CONTINUE
C
C
```

Figure 1.3-8 Fortran routine to sort an array of 100 integers into ascending order.

```
              .
              .
      WORKING-STORAGE SECTION.
      77  I        PICTURE IS 999.
      77  J        PICTURE IS 999.
      77  K        PICTURE IS 999.
      77  TEMP     PICTURE IS 9(10).
      01  IN-TABLE.
          02  LIST   PICTURE 9(10) OCCURS 100 TIMES.
              .

              .
      PROCEDURE DIVISION.
      RUNNER.
              .

              .
          PERFORM SORT-TABLE VARYING I FROM 1 BY 1 UNTIL I > 99.
              .

              .
      SORT-TABLE.
          ADD 1, I GIVING K.
          PERFORM INNER-LOOP VARYING J FROM K BY 1 UNTIL J > 100.
      INNER-LOOP.
          IF LIST (I) NOT LESS THAN LIST (J) PERFORM INTERCHANGE.
      INTERCHANGE.
          MOVE LIST (I) TO TEMP.
          MOVE LIST (J) TO LIST (I).
          MOVE TEMP TO LIST (J).
```

Figure 1.3-9 COBOL routine to sort an array of 100 integers into ascending order.

Address of Microinstruction	Microinstruction	Comments
0	R2 <- 1	Initialize R2 (variable I)
1	R7 <- R2 + R1	Fetch LIST(I) from
2	MAR <- R7	main memory and
3	READ	put it
4	R5 <- MDR	into R5
5	R3 <- R2 + 1	Initialize R3 (variable J)
6	R8 <- R3 + R1	Fetch LIST(J) from
7	MAR <- R8	main memory and
8	READ	put it
9	R6 <- MDR	into R6
10	R9 <- R5 - R6	Compare
11	IF <0 GO TO 19	R5 to R6
12	MAR <- R7	and interchange
13	MDR <- R6	them
14	WRITE	in
15	MAR <- R8	main memory
16	MDR <- R5	if
17	WRITE	necessary
18	R5 <- R6	
19	R3 <- R3 + 1	Increment J and see if
20	R9 <- R3 - 100	we have examined
21	IF <0 GO TO 6	elements I+1 - 100
22	R2 <- R2 + 1	Increment I
23	R9 < R2 99	test for
24	IF <0 GO TO 1	completion

Figure 1.3-10 SMM microprogram to sort an array of 100 integers into ascending order.

29

1.4 Microprogramming and Programming

Before describing similarities and differences between microprogramming and programming, it is appropriate to review some common programming terminology. A <u>translator</u> is a program that converts a high level representation of a program into a low level representation. For example, a COBOL compiler is a program that translates COBOL programs into machine language programs. An <u>interpreter</u> is a program that performs the instructions of another program. It differs from a translator in that it produces results directly while a translator produces a representation of a program that must be interpreted by a program or directly executed by a machine to produce results. A <u>simulator</u> is an interpreter in which the interpreted instructions are machine language instructions for some machine (real or pretend).

As microinstructions are stored in a memory and executed as stored programs, microprogramming is a type of programming as the name implies. It is therefore possible, at least in theory, to translate high level representations of programs into microprograms, to microprogram interpreters, and to microprogram simulators. Indeed, the most common use of microprogramming is to interpret machine language instructions. Such a microprogrammed simulator, called an <u>emulator</u>, was illustrated in Figure 1.3-7. The subject of emulation will be discussed in detail in Section 8.2.

With the availability of microprogrammable computers, the programming aspects of microprogramming have become more evident. The examples of microprograms in the previous section should reinforce this concept of microprogramming as another

3. parallelism – machines may allow simultaneous execution of several microoperations.

4. control store – microprograms are generally stored in a special storage unit which is very fast, therefore expensive, and hence a limited resource.

Microprogramming may be viewed as a specific type of programming which, owing to differences such as those listed previously, has a peculiar set of problems, applications, and implications.

1.5 Microprogrammability

Before microprogramming a computer for a specific application such as interpreting a machine language instruction set, one must become familiar with the computer's organization. In discussing the SMM, for example, we examined the various storage units, transformation units, links, microoperations, etc. Equipped with such information, one prepares a microprogram for a computer by first writing it in some representation and translating it into a binary representation which the machine can interpret. The binary microprogram must then be physically put into the control store for execution. The microprogrammability of a computer is characterized by

1. the software facilities for writing, translating, and debugging microprograms, and

2. the hardware facilities for changing the contents of control store.

Microprogrammability thus deals with both the hardware and

31

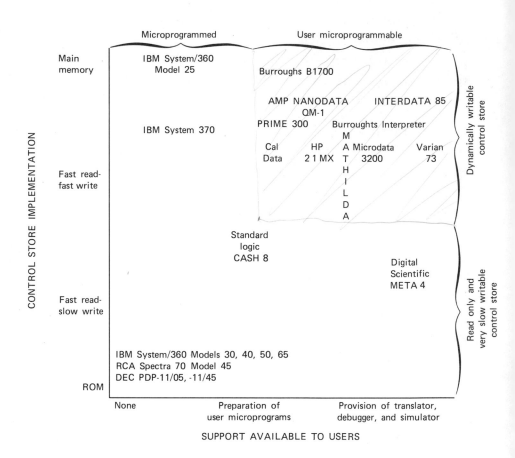

Figure 1.5-1 Microprogrammability.
Relative microprogrammability is the distance from the origin
to the machine. The shaded area represents dynamically user
microprogrammable computers.

software aspects of a system. The microprogrammability aspects
of several computer systems are summarized in Figure 1.5-1.*

* Figure 1.5-1 is not intended to be an exact evaluation of
different systems; its intent is to illustrate our view of
relative capabilities in this two-dimensional space.

A few types of software support are available for writing, translating, and debugging microprograms, but the quality of such support varies widely among systems. Many systems provide a translator which takes representations of microprograms and converts them into forms that are amenable to direct execution by the machine. Types and examples of microprogramming languages are discussed in detail later in the book. Since microprograms, like programs, seldom run properly when first executed, many systems provide simulators and debuggers to assist in the development of correct microprograms. Debuggers allow the user to interact with and monitor the execution of a microprogram as it is being run on the machine. Simulators usually run on a different machine and simulate the actions of the machine for which the microprograms were written. Systems which provide users with such support software for developing microprograms are called user microprogrammable.

The variety of types of memories used to implement control stores provides a wide range of microprogramming capabilities. For some time the most prevalent type of control store was read only memory (ROM) because it was relatively cheap and fast when compared to other memories. While a variety of technologies were used for ROMs, microprograms in such control stores could not be changed once they had been entered. Such control stores were ideal for machines in which microprograms had a fixed function, such as interpreting a fixed machine language. With fast read - slow write control stores, such as the programmable read only memory (PROM), microprograms may be changed, but the process may be relatively slow, requiring several seconds or minutes. These devices are finding more and more applications in microprogramming as the cost and speed of new developments continue to improve. More flexibility is offered by computers which use fast read - fast write memories for control store.

33

Access speeds for these memories often matches the basic processor clock cycle; 200 n sec and less are common. Write speeds may be slightly slower, but they are generally of the same order of magnitude as read speeds so that new microprograms may be loaded into control store dynamically. In some machines main memory itself may serve as control store. Although this scheme provides flexibility it is too slow for many applications. Computers in which the control store is writable at electronic speeds are called dynamic microprogramming systems.

A brief historical classification provides insight into the microprogrammability characteristic of computers. Owing to the very high cost of fast memories, most of the computers built in the early 1960's employed hardwired control. The CDC 6600 and UNIVAC 1108 are typical examples. The implementation of the IBM System/360 architecture, however, spans a sector of the microprogrammability spectrum. In the 360 series, the Model 75, a high performance machine, employed conventional logic to implement control functions because available ROM was not fast enough. The Model 85 used hardwired logic to control instruction fetch and microprograms to control instruction execution. Models 65, 50, 40, and 30 used various types of ROMs to store microprograms. The RCA Spectra 70 Model 45, whose architecture is essentially identical to that of the 360, also implemented control by ROM resident microprograms. Microprograms that controlled the System/360 Model 25 resided in main core storage; since they could be read from cards, the Model 25 was one of the first commercial machines with writable control store. Typical of the IBM System/370 models is the 145 in which microprograms are loaded from an external device, e.g., a "floppy" disk, into a writable control store, from where they are subsequently executed. While the 370 computers execute microprograms from a writable control store, they characterize this group of computers in concealing the microprogrammed implementation from the user. User microprogramming is not supported so these machines are designated as microprogrammed, but not microprogrammable. Just as the architectures of minicomputers varies over a wide range, so the implementations of control in minicomputers cover almost the entire microprogrammability spectrum. Many manufacturers do not utilize microprogramming in their computers. Several machines, e.g., the DEC PDP 11 series, the Interdata 80, and the PRIME 200, utilize maufacturer supplied ROM resident microprograms to interpret machine language programs and do not support user microprogramming. Some minicomputers do permit user microprogramming, and discussions of such machines in Chapters 4 through 6 includes descriptions of their microprogrammability aspects.

1.6 Microprogramming, Microprocessors, and Microcomputers

A significant trend in computer development in the 1970´s has been the use of large scale integration (LSI) to implement computers. The resulting microprocessors are characterized by small size ("computer on a chip"), low prices (a few hundred dollars), short word lengths (usually four or eight bits), limited instruction set and memory capacity, and relatively slow instruction execution times (several microseconds). Microcomputers are integrated packages of microprocessors and support chips; a microcomputer may comprise several types of chips: microprocessor CPU chips to provide control, read only memory (ROM) chips to provide instruction storage, random access chips to provide data storage, and I/O interface chips for attaching external devices. With their small size and low

OUTPUT INTERRUPT

cost, microprocessors and microcomputers have been used primarily as special dedicated devices and as components in a variety of digital products.

Owing to the prefix "micro," it is commonly thought that microprocessors and microcomputers are inherently microprogrammed, i.e., that programming a microprocessor or a microcomputer is microprogramming. This notion is not true; as with minicomputers and large computers, some microprocessors and microcomputers are microprogrammed and some are not. Although the machine language instructions of some microprocessors are implemented by microprograms, few microprocessors permit users to access the control store. The common but erroneous belief that microprocessors and microcomputers are microprogrammed and not programmed in the ordinary sense is probably due to the facts that the word "microprocessor" formerly was used as an abbreviation of "microprogrammable processor" and that few microcomputer manufacturers offer extensive higher level language support for their products.

Annotated Bibliography

1. P. Fagg et al., "IBM System/360 Engineering," 1964 Fall Joint Computer Conference Proceedings, AFIPS Press, Montvale, New Jersey, pp. 205-231.

    Stressing the independence between the architecture of a computer and its physical implementation, this article describes the reasons for using microprogramming in the System/360 and discusses the microprogramming aspects of several System/360 models.

2. H. Falk, "Self-contained Microcomputers Ease System Implementation," IEEE Spectrum, Volume 11 Number 12 (December 1974), pp. 53-55.

     Stressing that microprocessors form the basis for microcomputer systems, Falk describes a microcomputer system as a complex of hardware and software modules, discusses who should and who should not use microcomputer systems, and summarizes thirteen commercial microcomputer systems.

3. S. S. Husson, Microprogramming Principles and Practices, Prentice-Hall, Englewood Cliffs, New Jersey, 1970.

     This first book on microprogramming contains chapters on microprogram control, applications, and control store technology through early 1969. Nearly 400 pages are devoted to descriptions of microprogrammed computers, and four machines (IBM System/360 Model 40, IBM System/360 Model 50, RCA Spectra 70/Model 45, and Honeywell H4200) are studied in great detail. The detailed bibliographies on microprogramming and control stores span the years 1947 to 1969.

4. D. R. Nelson, editor, Computer, Volume 7 Number 7 (July 1974).

     This issue, devoted mainly to microprocessor architecture, includes a paper on present and future microprocessors and an extensive bibliography of microprocessor literature.

5. J. L. Ogdin, "Survey of Microprogrammable Microprocessors Reveals Ultimate Software Flexibility," EDN, July 20, 1974, pp. 69-74.

This survey of four microprogrammable microprocessors (user microprogrammable but not dynamically microprogrammable) from the microprocessor viewpoint reveals some interesting features of commercial microprocessor systems.

6. A. Opler, "Fourth-Generation Software," Datamation, Volume 13 Number 1 (January 1967), pp. 22-24.

   Many of the predictions in this "man's guess about the next generation" of computer systems and the use of microprogramming are beginning to be realized.

7. R. F. Rosin, "Contemporary Concepts of Microprogramming and Emulation," Computing Surveys, Volume 1 Number 4 (December 1969), pp. 197-212.

   Although "contemporary" refers to 1969, this article remains valuable due to the excellent presentations of microprogramming, emulation, hardwired implementations, and their applications. The discussion of research areas provides insight into problems still under study. This article should be read by everyone with the slightest interest in microprogramming.

8. R. F. Rosin, "The Significance of Microprogramming," presented at the International Computing Symposium, Davos, Switzerland, September 1973 (reprinted in SIGMICRO Newsletter, Volume 4 Number 1 (January 1974), pp. 24-39).

   In this paper, Rosin offers "reorientation and redirection of the common perception of microprogramming" by considering the evolution of microprogramming, the evolution in the use of interpretation as an implementation technique, and a set of "rules of thumb" adopted by system designers.

Rosin's assertion that microprogramming has been exploited to hide a multitude of design sins is unfortunately true and will be demonstrated by the machines discussed in Chapters 5 through 7 of this book.

9. G. W. Schultz et al., "A Guide to Using LSI Microprocessors," Computer, Volume 6 Number 6 (June 1973), pp. 13-19.

   In addition to describing the use of microprogramming in microprocessors, this paper compares microcomputers and minicomputers, describes microprocessor applications, and discusses systems development using microprocessors.

10. E. A. Torrero, "Focus on Microprocessors," Electronic Design, Volume 22 Number 18 (September 1, 1974), pp. 52-69.

    This comprehensive article is divided into five sections. The first section surveys the advantages, product range, architectural characteristics, and software support of microprocessor systems. The remaining sections discuss commercially available microcomputer components and systems, new LSI microprocessors, and microprocessor based minicomputers.

11. M. V. Wilkes, "The Best Way to Design an Automatic Calculating Machine," Manchester University Computer Inaugural Conference, Ferranti Ltd., London, 1951, pp. 16-21.

    A cornerstone in the literature, this paper introduces the term microprogramming, illustrates a possible ROM implementation, and discusses its advantages and disadvantages.

12. M. V. Wilkes and J. B. Stringer, "Microprogramming and the Design of the Control Circuits in an Electronic Digital Computer," Proceedings of the Cambridge Philosophical Society, Part 2 Volume 49 (April 1953), pp. 230–238 (reprinted in C. G. Bell and A. Newell, "Computer Structures: Readings and Examples," McGraw–Hill, New York, 1971, pp. 335–340).

    This paper provides a detailed discussion of the concepts outlined by Wilkes in his earlier paper. It includes a description of a machine, its machine language, and the microprogram to interpret the machine language. This well written paper is highly recommended for its insight and historical perspective.

13. M. V. Wilkes, "The Growth of Interest in Microprogramming: A Literature Survey," Computing Surveys, Volume 1 Number 3 (September 1969), pp. 139–145.

    Including a bibliography of 55 papers, Wilkes surveys and comments on the growth of interest in microprogramming and its applications from the early 1950's to the late 1960's.

CHAPTER 2

ARCHITECTURAL CHARACTERISTICS OF MICROPROGRAMMED COMPUTERS

2.1 Introduction

In a simple sense, microprogramming may be considered an alternative method for implementing the architecture of a computer. Computer architecture is defined as the attributes of a computer as seen by the programmer, i.e., the conceptual structure (e.g., registers, memories, arithmetic and logic units, and their logical connections) and the functional behavior (as represented by a machine language instruction set). The architecture of a computer must be distinguished from its implementation which includes the entire set of hardware units, the physical connections among them, and the manner of effecting machine language instructions. With the generalization of the microprogramming concept to include more than a method of implementing machine language instruction sets, it is now necessary to consider architecture at the microprogramming level as well as at the machine language level. Thus microprogramming has evolved from an implementation technique to a subject that merits architectural design considerations in its own right.

In examining the microprogramming level architecture one has to consider the functional components of machines, including the paths and interactions among them, and the design of microinstructions. The design of the functional components and the interactions among them directly influence the

1. One microinstruction
   per word

2. Two microinstructions
   per word

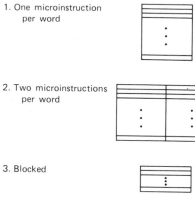

3. Blocked

4. Split

Addresses

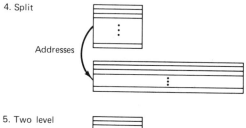

5. Two level

Interprets

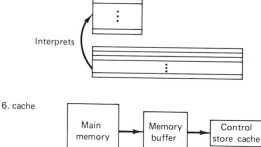

6. cache

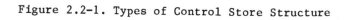

Main memory → Memory buffer → Control store cache

Figure 2.2-1. Types of Control Store Structure

performance and understandability of microprogrammed computer systems. The design of microinstructions must take into account the information that is required to control the hardware components and determine how that information is arranged in a microinstruction word. To illustrate a similarity to the implementation of machine language instructions, the implementation of microinstructions is briefly discussed. The implementation of microinstructions reflects the manner in which hardware effects their execution.

2.2 Hardware Components

2.2.1 Overview of Hardware Components

As illustrated in Figure 1.2-1 the basic functional components of the CPU in a microprogrammed computer are the main memory, control store, arithmetic and logic units (ALUs), local store, and the paths that interconnect these units. For each of these functional units there is a wide variety of designs and implementations; this leads to an even wider variety of machine designs, several of which are commercially available.

2.2.2 Control Store Design

The following factors are manifested in the design of the control store in a microprogrammed computer: structure, size, speed, associated registers, and loading process. Figure 2.2-1 illustrates several types of control store structures.

1. The simplest and most common control store structure is the ordinary memory array in which there is one microinstruction in each control store word. There are several variations of this structure.

43

2. In one form the number of bits in each control store word is increased so that two microinstructions occupy each control store word. The advantage of this scheme is that two microinstructions may be read into the microinstruction register (MIR) simultaneously. This reduces the number of control store references. Although this scheme may be considered an implementation factor, its effect on microinstruction addressing merits its consideration as an architectural feature.

3. In another structure, the control store is divided into blocks (sometimes called pages). In this scheme there are two types of control store addresses – addresses of control store words in the same block as the current microinstruction and addresses of other blocks. As a result of this organization, addresses of other microinstructions in the same block are shorter than in a nonblocked structure.

4. In the split control store structure, control store comprises two distinct storage units which have different word sizes. The storage unit with the shorter word size contains microinstructions which move literal data contained in the microinstruction to one or more machine registers, or initiate the execution of a microinstruction which resides in the other storage unit. The second storage unit has many more bits per word and hence can exercise more control over machine resources.* This split control store scheme requires fewer bits of memory compared to a standard organization when short microinstructions which move data are executed frequently, and when several short microinstructions refer to the same long microinstruction.

5. In a two level control store structure, the microinstructions in the lower level storage unit interpret

* See the discussion of vertical and horizontal microinstructions in Section 2.2.3.

microinstructions in the upper level storage unit much like ordinary microinstructions interpret machine language instructions. This two-level structure permits flexibility in the design of upper level microinstructions as well as in the design of machine language instructions.

6. In the cache control store structure, microinstructions are executed from a small high-speed cache memory even though the entire microprogram resides in a larger and slower memory buffer or in main memory itself. Because the movement of microinstructions to the cache is invisible to the microprogrammer, he need not be concerned with the number of microinstructions in his microprogram.

7. Of course microinstructions may be fetched and executed directly from main memory, so it too may be considered a type of control store. Alternative main memory organization techniques, such as interleaving, paging, and segmentation, are also applicable to the organization of control store.

The size of control store depends on its two dimensions: the number of bits in a word and the number of words in the control store. While such a specification of control store usually implies the number of bits in a microinstruction and the number of microinstructions, the various control store structures described previously alter the usual definition and require special consideration. The number of bits in a microinstruction generally depends on the number of primitive operations (microoperations) the computer can perform, the parallelism involved in executing the microoperations, and the representation of the microoperations. The latter two topics are described in detail in Section 2.2.3. Influencing the selection of microoperations for implementation in a machine are the particular machine language to be implemented, the application for which the machine is to be used, the economic

45

factor of realizing the microoperations in hardware, and perhaps the designers´ ideas of the basic operations needed in a machine to provide a variety of tasks "well" (a universal host machine). For computers in which the sole use of microprogramming is interpreting a fixed machine language, the length of microinstructions may be reduced by techniques such as combining several primitive operations that always appear together in microinstructions and representing them as one microoperation. Common microinstruction lengths of commercially available computers which can be microprogrammed by the user are 16, 24, 32, 48, and 64 bits.* Figure 2.2-2 shows microinstruction lengths on commercially available machines in which the the primary purpose of microprograms was to interpret fixed machine languages, and microprogramming was not intended for users. For microprogrammed computers, the number of words in control store depends on the repertoire of machine language instructions being microprogrammed and on the capabilities of the individual microinstructions. Figure 2.2-2 shows the control store lengths for a few microprogrammed machines. For machines which allow user microprogramming, users generally can purchase as much control store as they want and are limited only by the addressing capability of the microinstructions. In contemporary machines the maximum control store size typically ranges from 256 to 4096 words.

The speed of control store, usually considered to be the time required to read a word from control store into an associated register, may be the limiting factor in the speed of the system. Most simple microoperations (such as register transfers and simple transformation operations like add, subtract, one bit shift, and logical operations) can be executed in less than 50 n sec, with present circuit technology. Because control store access speed is seldom faster

---

* For details of commercially available computers see Chapters 4-6.

Machine	Bits per word of control store	Microin structions per control store word	Number of control store words	Effective control store speed (nsec)	Main memory cycle time (μsec)	Main memory width (bits)
IBM S/360 Model 20	60	3	4096			
IBM S/360 Model 25	16	1	8192[2]	900	1.8	16
IBM S/360 Model 30	55	1	4096	750	1.5	8
IBM S/360 Model 40	56	1	4096	625	2.5	16
IBM S/360 Model 50	90	1	2816	500	2.0	32
IBM S/360 Model 65	100	1	2816	125	.75	64
IBM S/360 Model 85	{108	1	2048[3]	80	1.0[5]	128
	{108	1	512[4]			
IBM S/370 Model 145	32	1	16384[2]	315	.608	64
IBM S/370 Model 155	72	1	8192	115	2.07[5]	128
IBM S/370 Model 165	108	1	2560	80	2.0[5]	64
RCA Spectra 70/Model 45	56	1	2048	480	1.44	16
Honeywell H4200	120	1	2048	125	.75	32

Figure 2.2-2. Some Statistics on Control Store and Main Memory for Computers that are not User Microprogrammable

than 50 n sec, it is often considered the limiting factor and used as a guide for machine speed. While control stores with speeds of less than 100 n sec are available, the cost of these stores has to be balanced against other system resources. The speed of main memory, for example, is usually much slower than the speed of control store. If the execution of microinstructions must continually be delayed while waiting for data from a slow main memory, then a faster control store may not be economically justified. The ratio of main memory cycle time (time required to read and rewrite a word in main memory) to control store speed for machines intended for user microprogramming ranges to the order of 10:1. Statistics for machines not intended to be microprogrammed by users appear in Figure 2.2-2.

As shown in Figures 1.2-1 and 1.3-1, several registers may be associated with control store. The microinstruction counter (MIC) contains the control store address of the next microinstruction to be executed. The control store address register (CSAR) physically addresses the control store and selects the word that will be read from or written into control store. In many computers the MIC and CSAR are merged into a

1. Data from Clapp (1972) and Husson (1970).
2. Control store is not part of main memory.
3. ROM control store is used for machine instruction execution. Fetch and decode are hardwired .
4. Writable control store is intended for microdiagnostics (see Chapter 6).
5. Also has 80-nsec cache.

single register because the CSAR is used primarily to address microinstructions for execution. When data (including microinstructions) are to be read from or written into control store rather than directly executed, the functions of the MIC and CSAR become distinct and necessitate special consideration. The microinstruction register (MIR) holds the microinstruction being executed. The control store data register (CSDR) contains data being read from or written into control store. Control store data registers seldom appear in microprogrammed computers that do not permit general data storage in control store. In performing microinstructions the basic phases of fetch, decode, and execute used in performing machine language instructions are still identifiable. While it may theoretically be possible to overlap the execution phase of one microinstruction with the fetch and decode phases of the next (see Section 2.3), it is common for the MIR to hold a microinstruction during its entire execution, thus preventing parallel operation. Two MIRs may be used to overcome this difficulty. By arranging two MIRs serially, a microinstruction may reside in the first MIR when it is being decoded and in the second MIR when it is being executed. By arranging the two MIRs in parallel, the computer executes microinstructions alternately from them. The association of additional registers with control store facilitates the writing of microprograms and assists in improving processor speed. A stack (last in – first out list) can store microinstruction addresses from the MIC, and thus may be used in microprogram subroutine linkages in the same way stacks are used in machine language programs. This stacking capability not only facilitates writing microprograms, it also provides a simple mechanism for handling interrupts. In some machines the occurrence of a hardware interrupt automatically pushes the CSAR onto the stack, and puts the control store address of an interrupt handling microprogram into the CSAR.

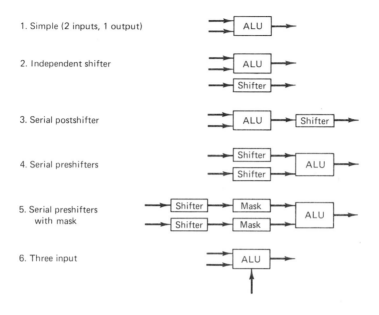

Figure 2.2-3. Types of ALU Structures

Once a microprogram has been written and translated, it is loaded into control store and executed. While the loading capability may be incorporated into a translator, it has been treated historically as a separate process. In many computers the process of loading microprograms into control store is hidden from users. Most computers with ROM control store work this way - users are not given information about the format and preparation of the ROM control stores. Many large computers with writable control store also operate this way - the control store may be loaded by pressing a console switch to initiate reading microprograms from an external device, but users are not given information about the format of microinstructions on the external device nor how to prepare them. In systems which

49

encourage user microprogramming there are a variety of techniques for loading control store and executing microprograms. In some computers, writing into control store is like writing to an I/O device. Other machines allow users to transfer information from main memory to control store via machine language instructions or microinstructions. Because most commercially available microprogrammable computers support a standard machine language instruction set, a part of the control store is often reserved for microprograms dedicated to interpreting the machine language instructions. Users must therefore pay careful attention to control store allocation. Often special instructions are required to transfer control from the standard microprogram that inteprets the machine language to user written microprograms.

2.2.3 Arithmetic and Logic Unit Design

In the design of an arithmetic and logic unit (ALU), the different points of interest are its structure, the repertoire of operations it can perform, the speed of performing these operations, the size of the operands, symmetry, and associated registers.

A variety of ALU structures is shown in Figure 2.2-3. The simplest is the common two input, one output unit that performs simple arithmetic and logical functions like add, subtract, and, or, and not. Many computers employ a shifter unit as well. The shifter may be attached to the output of the ALU providing a postshift capability, or it may be independent of the basic ALU to facilitate parallel operation. Inputs to the ALU may also be routed through shifters to provide a preshift capability. In addition to using shifters, ALUs may contain masking units which select certain bits from the input operands or the result. Another modification on the basic structure is the three input ALU, in which the third input may be a carry from a previous ALU operation. While these are some of the more common ALU organizations it is not difficult to construct more complex ALUs which may combine techniques discussed previously, utilize special purpose transformation units, etc.

The selection of the repertoire of ALU operations reflects the particular machine language the microprograms will interpret, the types of operations indigenous to a particular application, and the repertoires of available ALU integrated circuit chips. In commercially available microprogrammed computers, the repertoire has been influenced most strongly by the machine language instruction set. Often the ALU can perform several of the arithmetic and logic machine language operations directly, and other operations are implemented as combinations of microinstructions. The representation of data is very important in this connection. Data represented in a variety of formats (one's complement, two's complement, floating point, binary coded decimal, etc.) may be difficult to manipulate if the computer's ALU can only handle one representation. The length of operands is another major factor in ALU design. If the operands on which the ALU is to operate are longer than the operands it can physically handle, repetitive time consuming ALU use is necessitated. This is especially important when performing operations like multiply in which the length of the result is greater than the length of the operands. Another factor of concern is the symmetry of the ALU. Problems may arise in performing noncommutative operations like subtraction when different sets of registers serve as left and right inputs. In some application areas, certain operations may be performed frequently enough to warrant their inclusion as microoperations. In general purpose emulation, for example, it is often desirable to have sophisticated shift and mask

51

facilities to assist in instruction decoding.* In signal processing, a large percentage of operations are multiplies, so computers designed for this application usually have fast hardware multipliers, whereas general purpose computers often implement the multiply operation by a microprogrammed sequence of shifts and additions or by a sequence of special multiply steps each of which does both a shift and an addition. Because integrated circuit chips with a fixed repertoire of operations are readily available at low cost, it is often cheaper to use such chips and perform extra operations in microprograms when required, than to design, test, and manufacture a custom ALU.

The speed of performing ALU operations should be chosen to be compatible with the speeds of other system components. With present technology, ALUs can perform simple operations (add, subtract, and, or, not, etc.) on sixteen bit numbers in less than 50 n sec. Special purpose ALUs can perform the multiplication of two sixteen bit operands in less than 200 n sec. In business data processing applications, where many operations are memory-to-memory transfers or simple arithmetic operations and multiply and divide are seldom used, high speed ALUs may not be necessary. In signal processing, however, where many multiplications are required, the speed of a multiply operation may be the determining factor for the processing time.

By associating registers with an ALU, related operations may be facilitated. Conditions that arise in performing operations may be the basis for future decisions in a machine language or microprogram. These conditions include:

* For detailed discussions of these applications see Chapter 8.

1. ALU result equal to zero,
2. ALU result less than zero,
3. a bit lost in shifting,
4. a carry out bit in addition and subtraction, and
5. ALU overflow.

The existence of each of these conditions may be represented by a single binary digit and stored in a separate status register, or the conditions may be combined to form a single status register each of whose bits has a special meaning. The capability to test such registers associated with an ALU provides a useful control mechanism in sequencing through a microprogram. Associated with the ALU in some machines are special input and output registers that are distinct from general purpose local store regiters. Moving data from local store registers to the ALU input registers or from the ALU output register to a local store register then requires special microoperations.

2.2.4 Local Store

Local storage is the set of CPU registers not associated with main memory, control store, or ALUs. These registers serve as fast access storage units for temporarily holding data being transferred among the other three units. As the control store seldom contains variable data, operands for microinstructions generally reside in local store registers. The characteristics of interest in discussing local store include the number, size, use, and organization of the registers.

The purpose of local store registers is to hold information to be routed to another functional unit, hence local store registers generally have very fast read/write times and are usually the most expensive storage media in the system. The number of registers in a computer is thus primarily

53

influenced by expense. The register set seen by the machine language programmer is often smaller than the set of local store registers because some registers serve special purpose functions. If an implementation has few local store registers then some of the registers seen by the machine language programmer may actually be implemented in main memory. Such implementations may affect the time required to execute machine language instructions. A large number of local store registers may enhance the performance of certain algorithms. Another factor influencing the number of local store registers is the problem of addressing them in microinstructions. As the number of local store registers increases, so does the number of bits required to address them. Increasing the number of local store registers may require increasing the length of microinstructions and hence the widening of control store. This has a significant impact on control store cost.

The size (width in number of bits) of local storage registers also depends on cost and the effects of machine languages and applications for which the computer is designed. Because local store serves as an intermediary in communication among the other functional units, it's interface to each of them must be considered. As is usually the case the width of general purpose local store registers is the same as the width of ALU input operands and the width of main memory words.

Local store registers may be used in a variety of ways. In computers that support a machine language, two of these registers are usually dedicated to serve as the instruction counter (program counter, location counter), which contains the main memory address of the next machine language instruction to be executed, and the instruction register, which holds the machine language instruction currently being executed. There are often special functional units associated with these registers – an adder to increment the instruction counter after

54

each machine instruction is executed and a special circuit to assist in decoding the machine language instruction in the instruction register. Such special circuits, which often use ROM tables for instruction lookup, increase the efficiency in performing machine language instructions but usually decrease the machine's flexibility by recognizing only special instruction formats. Other special purpose registers may hold portions of the machine instruction - the operation code, the operand addresses, etc. There may be registers which serve as the sole input or output registers to an ALU. In multiprogramming computers there may be registers which indicate the program status (program status word) and pending interrupts. For generality, several machines contain one or more sets of registers (register files) that may be used for a variety of purposes and are not dedicated to a specific function.

The organization of the local store registers is largely determined by their use. Special purpose registers are seldom directly connected; they are referenced by a limited set of microoperations. These microoperations may have special functional units for their execution. The operations referencing an instruction counter, for example, include incrementing it by one, assigning it an address contained in the instruction register, and a few others. Another example is the bit testing facility associated with interrupt registers. General purpose registers are often grouped together; their addressing may be restricted so that only one may be referenced at any instant in time. To overcome this problem, e.g., when two ALU inputs are requested, some computers provide two register files in which corresponding registers always contain the same value. While special purpose registers are addressed directly (e.g., Increment the Instruction Counter) or implicitly (e.g., Read Next Machine Language Instruction implicitly references the Instruction Register), general purpose registers are often addressed indirectly (e.g., add the register addressed by register 0 to the register addressed by register 1 and store the result in the register addressed by register 2). Local store registers may also be organized as stacks or associative arrays.

2.2.5 Main Memory

Although a large variety of main memory organizations have been designed and implemented, we restrict our attention to those aspects which influence the microprogram level design. Of concern to the microprogrammer are the size of main memory (both length and width) and its access speed.

The length (number of words) of main memory is important because there must be a memory address register (MAR) of sufficient size to address it. The size of the MAR in turn affects other resources, such as the ALU size for computing memory addresses. The width of main memory affects the size of the MDR and local store registers. As mentioned earlier the speed of main memory and its relation to processor speed is a major factor in system performance.

2.2.6 Data Paths

Microprogramming is often considered to be the control of data paths connecting the various functional components in a computer. While such a view is an oversimplification, the size and organization of data paths merits consideration.

Data path size generally reflects the size of registers and functional units which the paths link. In some cases it is economical to use a narrow data path repeatedly to effect a transter of information; in other instances, only a portion of a path may be used.

The number of data paths in a machine affects the flexibility and ease of microprogramming a machine. One approach is to provide several data paths; in the extreme there is a unique path between every pair of hardware resources. This scheme provides flexibility and possible concurrency of data path use, yet it may be prohibitively complex and costly to implement. In the other extreme there is a single bus to which various hardware resources are connected. During the execution of a microinstruction, one resource may put a value on the bus and another resource may use the value on the bus as input. While not as flexible as the previous scheme, it is generally easier to implement. A compromise design, which includes a few busses that allow concurrent transfers, may provide sufficient flexibility when there are only a few functional units.

2.2.7 Summary of the SMM

We now return to our simple microprogrammed machine (SMM) shown in Figure 1.3-1 and examine it in light of the discussions of the present chapter. For simplicity, the common memory array organization was selected as the SMM control store structure. The provision of a separate CSAR and CSDR facilitates writing new microinstructions into control store. The SMM control store was not intended as a general data storage unit so there is no path from the control store to the CSDR. The inclusion of a stack facilitates microprogram subroutine linkages, and the paths from the MIR and general purpose registers to the MIC simplify sequencing among microoperations.

Simplicity and generality were factors that influenced the SMM ALU design. Although the microoperations are few and

57

simple, they are symmetrical since their inputs may be any of the general purpose registers. The separate shifter permits parallel operation, and the use of a special status register provides a conditional testing capability.

The local store is a simple array of sixteen registers which have the same word size as main memory words, machine language instructions, and the memory data register. The large number of data paths between the local store and other SMM units provides direct communication and facilitates parallel operation. Such a general local store scheme might be difficult to implement efficiently, and thus such a structure is not found in commercially available microprogrammable computers.

2.3 Microinstruction Design

2.3.1 Introduction

The design of microinstructions includes the specification of the information that is required to control the hardware resources described in Section 2.2 and how that information is arranged in a microinstruction word. Although the microoperations that a computer can perform are generally determined by its hardware resources, there is a wide range of possible methods for combining microoperations to form microinstructions. Thus a set of microoperations can be represented by a variety of microinstruction repertoires.

2.3.2 The Vertical-Horizontal Characteristic

Of primary interest in the design of microinstructions is the number of hardware resources each microinstruction controls, i.e., the number of microoperations that each microinstruction can execute. In this regard, microinstructions are often classified as vertical or horizontal, although these appellations actually refer to the end points of a broad spectrum of possible designs.

Vertical microinstructions generally represent single microoperations. They often resemble classical machine language instructions comprising one operation and a few operands. As an example, for the SMM in Figure 1.3-1 a repertoire of vertical microinstructions would be the same as the microoperations shown in Figure 1.2-3. Figure 2.3-3 shows a detailed representation of such a vertical microinstruction repertoire. Lengths of vertical microinstructions usually lie in the range of twelve to twenty-four bits.

In contrast to vertical microinstructions are horizontal microinstructions which represent several microoperations that in general are executed concurrently. In the extreme, each horizontal microinstruction controls all the hardware resources in a machine, and microprogramming becomes a matter of selecting which microoperation each resource is to perform during the execution of each microinstruction. Because horizontal microinstructions control multiple resources simultaneously, they typically contain more information than vertical microinstruction and hence have greater length. Horizontal microinstructions with forty-eight or more bits are common. Figure 2.3-4 illustrates a horizontal microinstruction format for the SMM. Note that the determining characteristic between vertical and horizontal microprogramming is the number of simultaneously controlled hardware resources and not the number of bits in the microinstructions.

The one-to-one correspondence between microoperations and microinstructions in vertical microprogramming makes it similar in concept to traditional machine language programming. The relative ease and techniques of this kind of programming apply

(a)

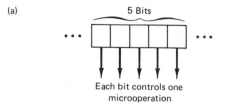

(b)

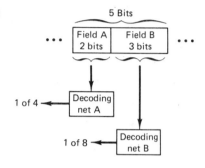

(c)

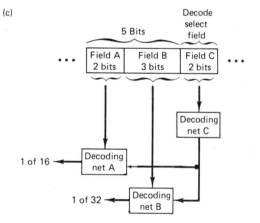

Figure 2.3-1. Microinstruction Encoding

to vertical microprogramming as well. Horizontal microprogramming has the potential advantage of more efficient hardware utilization that results from the capability of each microinstruction to control several resources simultaneously. Developing horizontal microprograms that use resources optimally or efficiently, however, is a difficult problem.

With continuing developments in logic technology and circuit design, the capabilities of single microoperations have been steadily increasing, so what formerly may have been considered several distinct microoperations might now be considered a single microoperation. For this reason, the dividing line between vertical and horizontal microinstructions is not well defined. The microinstructions for several machines have been designed to combine the better features of vertical and horizontal microinstructions. Like vertical microinstructions they are fairly easy to understand, generate, and implement, yet following horizontal microinstructions they may have a limited capability to perform some microoperations simultaneously. Such microinstructions have been designated, somewhat humorously, "diagonal microinstructions."

2.3.3 The Encoding Characteristic

The degree of encoding in a microinstruction word affects the length of a microinstruction and hence is often confused with the vertical-horizontal characteristic. In the simplest microinstruction design, there is no encoding in the representation of microinstructions; each bit represents one microoperation (see Figure 2.3-1a). In this scheme a one appearing in a bit position indicates that a particular microoperation is to be executed. This type of representation is a vestige of Wilkes's original microprogramming proposal, where each microoperation was the opening of a hardware gate, and is little used in contemporary microprogrammable computers.

61

No Encoding	Encoded	Operation
00000001	000	Add
00000010	001	Subtract
00000100	010	Add with carry
00001000	011	Subtract with borrow
00010000	100	And
00100000	101	Or
01000000	110	Complement
10000000	111	Complement + 1

Figure 2.3-2. No encoding vs single level encoding for specifying an ALU operation in a microinstruction.

In single level (or direct) encoding, the microoperations that a particular hardware resource can perform are represented as a field rather than as individual bits (see Figure 2.3-1b). Since the microoperations that are combined into a field are mutually exclusive, no information is lost in this single level encoding scheme. As an example, consider an ALU that can perform eight different arithmetic and logic operations. As shown in Figure 2.3-2, eight bits are required to specify the operation when there is no encoding. In a single microinstruction, however, only one of the eight ALU operations can be performed. With single level encoding, the ALU operation can therefore be specified with three bits as shown in Figure 2.3-2.

In two level encoding, mutually exclusive microoperations may be combined to form fields as in single level encoding. The meaning of a field, however, depends not only on its value but

some other value as well. This other value may be contained in
another field of the microinstruction; this scheme is called
bit steering (see Figure 2.3-1c). The controlling value may
alternatively be contained in a machine register. In this
scheme, called format shifting, the interpretation of a
microinstruction depends on the machine state, e.g., I/O
processing or instruction processing.

While encoding reduces the length of microinstructions and
hence the size of control store, additional hardware (viz.,
decoding nets) and time (on the order of a few gate delays) are
required to decode microinstructions. Extensive encoding may
obfuscate machine operation, and as a result microprogramming
may become more difficult.

Because vertical microinstructions effect single
operations, they typically employ two level encoding. The
operation code (or some part thereof) in each microinstruction
indicates the proper interpretation of the remaining bits –
what bits are grouped into fields and what the fields
represent. As operations in vertical microinstructions range
from ALU function to memory I/O to conditional sequencing, the
remaining fields in the microinstructions may indicate register
operands, memory addresses, control store addresses, etc. Not
all vertical microinstruction utilize two level encoding,
however, and in several computers the microinstructions employ
a combination of encoding schemes.

2.3.4 Microinstruction Designs for the SMM

Let's consider two alternative microinstruction sets for
the SMM. Figure 2.3-3 illustrates a vertical microinstruction
repertoire that generally uses two level encoding. Figure 2.3-4
shows the format of a horizontal microinstruction for the
machine. These figures do not include sequencing
microoperations, which will be subsequently discussed.

Simple register transfers

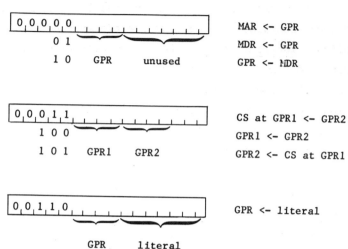

```
0 0 0 0 0                          MAR <- GPR
0 1                                MDR <- GPR
1 0    GPR    unused               GPR <- MDR
```

```
0 0 0 1 1                          CS at GPR1 <- GPR2
1 0 0                              GPR1 <- GPR2
1 0 1   GPR1    GPR2               GPR2 <- CS at GPR1
```

```
0 0 1 1 0                          GPR <- literal

       GPR     literal
```

Transformation Operations

```
0 1 0 0 0                          GPR1 <- GPR1 + GPR2
0 1 0 0 1                          GPR1 <- GPR1 - GPR2
0 1 0 1 0   GPR1    GPR2           GPR1 <- GPR1 + GPR2 + carry bit in
                                                   status register
0 1 0 1 1                          GPR1 <- GPR1 & GPR2
0 1 1 0 0                          GPR1 <- GPR1 v GPR2
0 1 1 0 1                          GPR1 <- not GPR1
```

```
1 0 0 0 0 V W X Y Y Y Y Z Z Z Z    GPR1 <- GPR1 shifted
                                     V - shift direction
                                         0 - left
                                         1 - right
                                     W - shift type
```

64

```
                              0 - arithmetic
                              1 - logical
                          X - shift out
                              0 - end off
                              1 - circular
                          YYYY - GPR1
                          ZZZZ - GPR2 contains shift amount


1 0 0 0 1 V W X Y Y Y Y Z Z Z Z     GPR1 <- GPR1 shifted
                                    V, W, X, Y as above
                                    ZZZZ - shift amount
```

Memory operations
_____

| 1 | 1 | 0 | 0 | 0 | 0 | 0 | 0 | 0 | 0 | 0 | 0 | 0 | 0 | 0 | 0 | Read

| 1 | 1 | 0 | 0 | 1 | 0 | 0 | 0 | 0 | 0 | 0 | 0 | 0 | 0 | 0 | 0 | Write

Figure 2.3-3. A vertical microinstruction repertoire for the SMM.

2.3.5 Microinstruction Sequencing

During the execution of a microinstruction it is necessary
to determine the address in control store of the next
microinstruction to be executed. There are basically two
techniques for accomplishing this microinstruction sequencing.
The first sequencing technique is like the one used in most
machine languages: the control store address of the next
microinstruction to be executed is one greater than the address

65

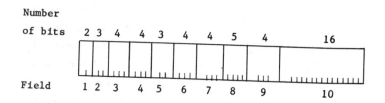

Field code points

1　Memory operation

　　0 - no operation

　　1 - read memory

　　2 - write memory

2　Register transfer

　　0 - No operation

　　1 - MAR <- GPR1

　　2 - MDR <- GPR2

　　3 - GPR1 <- MDR

　　4 - CS at GPR1 <- GPR2

　　5 - GPR1 <- GPR2

　　6 - GPR2 <- CS at GPR1

　　7 - GPR1 <- literal (field 10)

3　GPR1

4　GPR2

5　Transformation operator　GPR3 <- GPR3 operator GPR4

　　0 - No operation

　　1 - +

　　2 - -

　　3 - + with carry

66

4 - &

5 - v

6 - not

6   GPR3

7   GPR4

8   Shift operator

     Bits 1-2 Shift operation

       0 - No operation

       1 - Shift amount in GPR5

       2 - Shift amount is literal

     Bit 3 Shift direction

       0 - left

       1 - right

     Bit 4 Shift type

       0 - arithmetic

       1 - logical

     Bit 5 Shift out

       0 - end off

       1 - circular

9   GPR5 or shift literal

10 literal

Figure 2.3-4. A horizontal microinstruction format for the SMM.

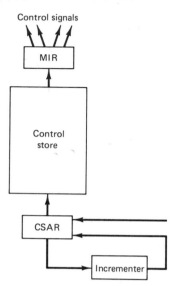

Figure 2.3-5. Control Store with a CSAR and Associated
Incrementer for Sequential Execution

of the microinstruction being executed. This technique is
usually implemented by associating an incrementing unit with
the CSAR. The incrementer adds one to the CSAR or the MIC
during the execution of each microinstruction (see Figure
2.3-5).* The sequential execution of microinstructions may be
altered by conditional or unconditional branch microoperations,
which insert new addresses into the MIC. These addresses may
originate from several sources:

1. The MIR. In this case the microinstruction in the MIR
contains a branch microoperation, and the address part of the
microinstruction is moved from the MIR to the MIC.

* Because this technique is so common, incrementers are seldom
  drawn in general architecture diagrams of machines.

68

...				
Other micro- instruction fields	Address if condition one is true	Address if condition two is true	Address if both conditions one and two are true	Address if neither condition one nor two is true

Figure 2.3-6. A microinstruction format with several possible next addresses.

2. A general purpose register. This facilitates general address calculation.

3. Some other memory location. Several machines use a hardware stack to save control store addresses temporarily; the SMM (Figure 1.3-1) is an example. In executing a microprogram subroutine or handling an interrupt, for example, the address of the next sequential microinstruction is pushed onto the stack. When the subroutine has been completed, the address in the top stack register is popped and assigned to the MIC, so that execution of microinstructions in the original sequence may resume.

Variations and combinations of these techniques have been used. Some computers have a skip microoperation in which the CSAR is incremented by two instead of one. A conditional skip microoperation facilitates efficient one microinstruction subroutines. Another common sequence microoperation combines sequential stepping and assigning an address to a register. This facility, along with a microoperation that conditionally transfers control to the control store address in the register, may be used to implement loops in microprograms.

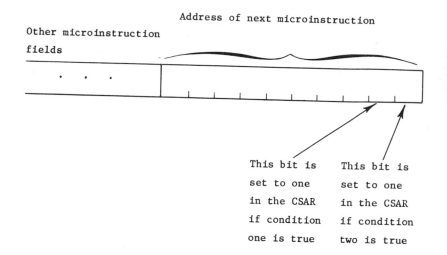

Figure 2.3-7. Modifying the address of the next microinstruction depending on possible conditions.

In another technique used for microinstruction sequencing, each microinstruction contains the address in control store of the next microinstruction to be executed. In this scheme the control store may be considered a chained list. Conditional branching with this technique may be accomplished in two ways. The first is to include several addresses in the microinstruction. The selection of a particular address then depends on certain conditions that arise during microinstruction execution (see Figure 2.3-6). While this scheme provides flexibility, its prodigal use of control store seldom merits its implementation. A second way in which conditional branching may be effected is to set certain bits in

Conditional Branch

| 1 | 1 | 1 | 0 | W | W | W | X | Y | Y | Y | Y | Z | Z | Z | Z | 0 |

WWW — condition
  0 — no condition
  1 — ALU result = 0
  2 — ALU result < 0
  3 — ALU carry out
  4 — Shift out bit
X — True (1) or false (0)
Sequence operation
  0 — Normal step
  1 — Push CSAR+1 to stack
  2 — Pop stack and assign
      to CSAR
  3 — Skip
  4 — CSAR <- GPR
ZZZZ — GPR

Unconditional branch to literal

| 1 | 1 | 1 | 1 | | | | | | | | | | | | | |

literal

Figure 2.3-8. Vertical microinstructions to perform sequencing
operations in the SMM.

71

Number
of bits   3 1 3   4

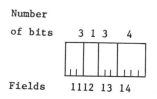

Fields   1112 13 14

Field code points

  11 Condition (see Figure 3.2-7)

  12 True (1) or false (0)

  13 Sequencing operation

       0 - Step

       1 - Push CSAR+1 to stack

       2 - Pop stack and assign to CSAR

       3 - Skip

       4 - CSAR <- GPR5

       5 - CSAR <- literal (field 10)

  14 GPR5

Figure 2.3-9. Continuation of the SMM horizontal microinstruction format to include sequencing operations.

the next microinstruction address field depending on the occurrence of unusual conditions (see Figure 2.3-7). In this scheme, sixteen-way branching could be provided with four conditions as in the SMM.

To the microinstructions in Figures 2.3-3 and 2.3-4 we now add the sequencing microinstructions in Figures 2.3-8 and 2.3-9 to complete the vertical and horizontal microinstruction repertoires for the SMM.

Residual microinstructions

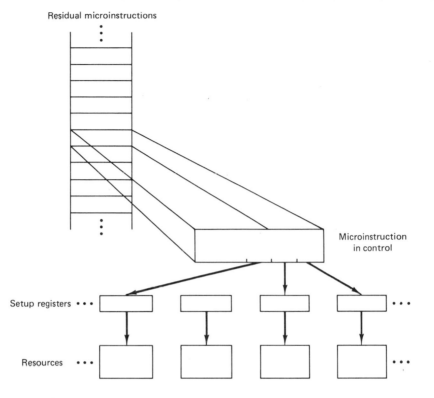

Figure 2.3-10a. Residual Control

2.3.6 Residual Control

All the microoperations and microinstructions described so far have illustrated immediate control - the microoperations are converted into control signals which directly and immediately control machine resources. An alternative method, called residual control, uses several setup registers to control hardware resources. In the residual control scheme, microoperations do not control resources directly, but rather

73

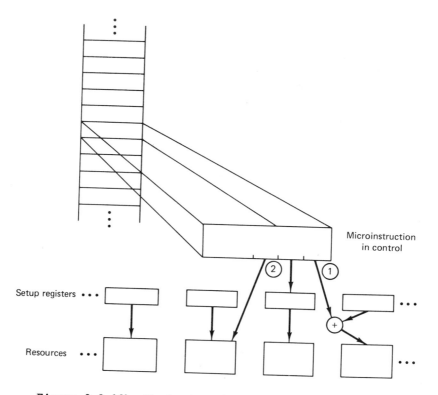

Figure 2.3-10b. Variations in a Residual Control Scheme
1) Combined immediate and residual control
2) Direct control to override setup register

each setup register controls a particular resource. The value of a setup register may indicate the microoperation a functional unit is to perform or the address of a register or memory word. Microinstructions may replace or alter the values in one or more setup registers as shown in Figure 2.3-10a. A simple variation of the residual control scheme is the combinational residual control scheme in which an immediate value in the microinstruction and the value in a setup register are combined (e.g., by addition) to control a hardware resource. Some computers use both immediate control and residual control in their microinstructions. These schemes are illustrated in Figure 2.3-10b.

In situations where some functional unit repeatedly performs the same operation or where the same memory unit is used repeatedly, the residual control scheme provides substantial control store saving. The setup registers may be manipulated with short vertical microinstructions, yet they simultaneously control several resources as do horizontal microinstructions.

2.3.7 Control Store Literals

It is often convenient for microinstructions to contain literal data. This data is a sequence of bits that represents a number or an address. It may be used for assignment to a register, to indicate a shift amount, or to indicate the address of the next microinstruction to be executed. Much like the immediate field used in some machine language instructions, this has been called a control store literal or an emit field.

2.4 Microinstruction Implementation

2.4.1 Introduction

Although the hardware control mechanisms employed to execute microinstructions are functionally similar to those which hardwired machines use to implement machine language instructions, the relative simplicity of microoperations facilitates microinstruction implementation. Unlike the implementation of machine language instructions, however, the effects of microinstruction implementation are usually not hidden from the microprogrammer. It is, unfortunately, often the case that the microprogrammer needs to be aware of the timing constraints involved in the execution of a microinstruction and in the execution of sequences of microinstructions.

2.4.2 The Serial-Parallel Characteristic

The serial-parallel characteristic measures the amount of overlap between the execution phase of the current microinstruction and the fetch and decode phases of the next microinstruction to be executed. The execution phase of a microinstruction involves performing the microoperations indicated by the microinstruction. Fetching the next microinstruction to be executed involves updating the CSAR, selecting the microinstruction at the indicated control store address, and reading the microinstruction into the MIR. Both of these processes may be fairly complex and time consuming in machines with sophisticated hardware units and control store address generation facilities, so it is difficult to assert the fact that one process takes more time than the other.

In a serial implementation (see Figure 2.4-1a), fetching the next microinstruction to be executed does not begin until the execution phase of the current microinstruction terminates. The advantage of this serial (sequential) implementation is simplicity of realization; the hardware need not control execution and fetch simultaneously. Furthermore, the MIC and CSAR are always set to the proper value before microinstruction fetch begins.

In a parallel implementation, the other extreme, fetching the next microinstruction to be executed is performed in parallel with the execution phase of the current microinstruction (see Figure 2.4-1b). The advantage of parallel

76

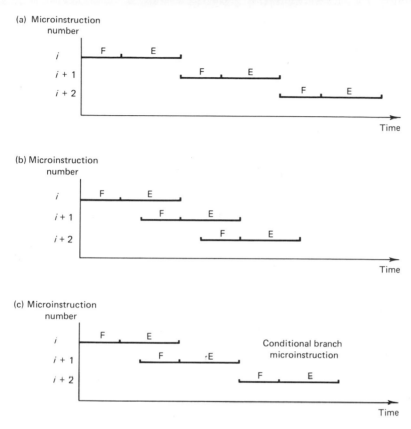

Figure 2.4-1. The Serial-Parallel Characteristic.

fetch is the time saving. If microinstruction fetch and execution require the same length of time then a parallel implementation runs twice as fast as a serial implementation.

The disadvantage of parallel implementation becomes evident in executing microinstructions containing conditional branch microoperations. In this case the control store address of the next microinstruction to be executed may depend on a condition arising in the execution of a microoperation in the current microinstruction. Thus the control store address of the

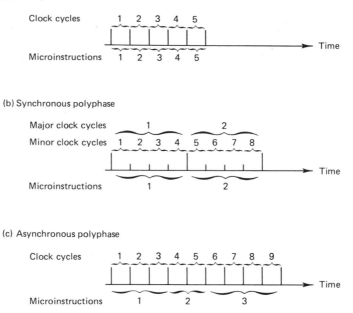

Figure 2.4-2 Monophase-polyphase characteristics

next microinstruction may not be known until the end of microinstruction execution.* When this is true, the fetching of the next microinstruction to be executed cannot be initiated until the execution of the current microinstruction is complete. A combined serial-parallel approach is useful in this case (see Figure 2.4-1c). In the combined approach, fetching the next microinstruction is performed in parallel with the execution phase of the current microinstruction unless the current microinstruction contains a conditional branch microoperation. The performance of the combined serial-parallel

---

* In some machines the control store address of the next microinstruction to be executed can be readily determined because the conditions tested are those set by the previous microinstruction.

method may be improved by guessing that the tested condition will be true and will fetch in parallel the microinstruction at the guessed address. Serial microinstruction fetch is then necessary only when the guess is incorrect.

2.4.3 The Monophase-Polyphase Characteristic

The monophase-polyphase characteristic refers to the number of phases (also called minor cycles or subcycles) required to execute a microinstruction (see figure 2.4-2).

In a monophase implementation there are no distinct subcycles of the major clock cycle; a microinstruction is effected by a single simultaneous issue of control signals. Such an implementation is useful when the microoperations are simple. For example, the transfer of information from one register to another requires just the opening of gates in a data path so this microoperation is amenable to monophase implementation. The advantage of monophase implementation is simplicity of realization.

In a polyphase implementation the execution of a microinstruction is broken into several distinct phases, and control signals may be issued at each phase. In one type of polyphase implementation, called synchronous polyphase, each microinstruction is executed in one major clock cycle which comprises several minor clock cycles; all microinstructions require the same amount of time for execution. In a second type of polyphase implementation, called asynchronous polyphase, the number of phases required to effect a microinstruction depends on the complexity of its microoperations. Complex microoperations may require several phases and simple microoperations may require only a few, so the execution of some microinstructions may take more time than the execution of others. Polyphase implementation allows interaction among resources in the same microinstruction, e.g., the selection of operands, operating on these operands, and the assignment of the result register. Polyphase implementation also facilitates parallel fetch and execution of microinstructions. The disadvantage of polyphase implementation is the need for more complex timing control. It should be noted that polyphase execution of microinstructions requires a sequential logic implementation much in the same way that hardwired sequential logic is required to implement machine instructions. The difference between such microinstructions and machine instructions lies in the complexity and specification of operations in the instructions.

As with the design of microinstructions, the implementation of microinstructions in contemporary machines varies considerably. Many machines employ variations or combinations of the implementation techniques that have been described.

Annotated Bibliography

1. J. Clapp, "The Application of Microprogramming Technology," SIGMICRO Newsletter, Volume 3 Number 1 (April 1972), pp. 8-47.

An extensive report on microprogramming that includes an introduction to the subject, comparisons of microprogramming to hardware and software, a survey of microprogrammed computers, a description of microprogramming applications, and a discussion of research and development tasks in microprogramming.

2. R. L. Davis, "Uniform Shift Networks," Computer, Volume 7 Number 9 (September 1974), pp. 60-71.

A discussion of combinational uniform shift networks that can shift a binary word a variable number of bit positions.

3. M. J. Flynn and R. F. Rosin, "Microprogramming: An Introduction and a Viewpoint," IEEE Transactions on Computers, Volume C-20 Number 7 (July 1971), pp. 727-731.

As guest editors for a special issue, Flynn and Rosin introduce microprogramming and discuss some basic concepts: dynamic microprogramming, emulation, horizontal microprogramming, and residual control. Provides interesting perspective on microprogramming applications and the role of microprogramming in computer systems.

4. G. Hoff, "Design of Microprogrammed Control for General Purpose Processors," International Advanced Summer Institute on Microprogramming, Hermann, Paris, 1972, pp. 202-230. (Reprinted in SIGMICRO Newsletter, Volume 3 Number 2 (July 1972), pp. 57-64.)

An excellent discussion of the various techniques for microinstruction design and implementation: the encoding characteristic, the serial-parallel characteristic, and related aspects.

5. S. S. Husson, Microprogramming Principles and Practices, see Chapter 1 entry.

Chapter 2 of ths book includes a detailed discussion of tradeoffs in the organization and control of microprogrammed computers. Later chapters give details on these aspects for some of the first commercial microprogrammed computers. The concepts and computers provide an interesting contrast with the microprogrammable computers of today.

6. L. H. Jones, "Microinstruction Sequencing and Structured Programming," Seventh Annual Workshop on Microprogramming Preprints, ACM, September 1974, pp. 277-289.

An exploration of the relation between the sequencing functions of microprogrammable computers and the implementation of control constructs of structured programs. Investigates the sequencing functions of several computers.

7. R. M. McClure, "Parallelism in Microprogrammed Controls," International Advanced Summer Institute on Microprogramming, Hermann, Paris, 1972, pp. 307-327.

An interesting discussion of "long word" versus "short word" microprogramming and the serial-parallel characteristic of microinstruction implementation.

8. S. R. Redfield, "A Study in Microprogrammed Processors: A Medium Sized Microprogrammed Processor," IEEE Transactions on Computers, Volume C-20 Number 7 (July 1971), pp. 743-750.

An early but thorough description of the tradeoffs involved in microinstruction design and implementation and an analysis of these implications in a particular medium sized computer, the Univac C/SP.

9. A. D. Robbi, "Microcache: A Buffer Memory for Microprograms," COMPCON 72 Digest of Papers, IEEE, September 1972, pp. 123-125.

A discussion of the organization and tradeoffs of a computer in which microprograms reside in main memory but are buffered by a special purpose cache memory.

10. R. F. Rosin, "Contemporary Concepts of Microprogramming and Emulation," see Chapter 1 entry.

Includes a discussion of basic microprogrammed architecture and early definitions of vertical and horizontal microprogramming.

11. B. P. Shay, "A Microprogrammed Implementation of Parallel Program Schemata," Ph. D. Dissertation, Department of Electrical Engineering, University of Maryland, College Park, Maryland, 1975.

Presents a model of a horizontal microprogram approach for controlling concurrently executable resources and describes the design of a prototype of such a machine.

12. H. D. Toong, "Microprocessor Control Store Technology," Fifth Annual IEEE International Computer Society Conference, 1971, page 89.

An overview of modern developments in the area of memory technology that could be used for control store in dynamically microprogrammable computers.

13. M. Tsuchiya and C. V. Ramamoorthy, "Design of a Multilevel Microprogrammable Computer and a High-Level Micropogramming Lanugage," Technical Report No. 135, Information Systems Research Laboratory, Electronics Research Center, The University of Texas at Austin, Austin, Texas, August 15, 1972.

The proposed multilevel computer has, in addition to main memory, a memory buffer for temporarily holding microinstructions and a control store cache from which microprograms are executed.

CHAPTER 3

MICROPROGRAMMING LANGUAGES AND SUPPORT SOFTWARE

3.1 Introduction

Even with the wide variety of designs and implementations, microinstructions are strings of binary digits, and microprograms are sequences of these strings. The development of microprograms therefore involves the generation of sequences of binary strings, which when interpreted by a machine to produce some result. This development process may be broken into two parts – representing microprograms and checking the effects of their execution. Accordingly, there are two main types of support software that have been developed to facilitate the process of microprogramming.

The first type of support is microprogramming languages, which enable microprograms to be represented in a form that is easier to write and understand than the actual binary microprograms themselves. Associated with a microprogramming language is a translator to convert the higher level representation into actual microinstructions. Since a higher level representation and the binary representation of microprograms have essentially the same meanings we refer to both as microprograms. The second type of support software is simulators, which perform the operations of microprograms. Microprogram simulators usually permit user interaction with the simulated microprogram to facilitate microprogram debugging.

	High level (Machine independent)			Low level (Machine dependent)		
Language level	Natural	Problem oriented	Procedure oriented	Macro Assembler	Assembler	Machine
Examples	English	COGO ECAP	PL/I Fortran COBOL	S/360 OS assembler language		

Figure 3.2-1. Spectrum of programming languages.

3.2 Microprogramming Languages and Their Translators

Historically, the development of microprogramming languages has followed the development of programming languages, and microprogramming languages demonstrate the influence of various levels of programming languages. To provide background for a discussion of microprogramming languages let us briefly review some programming language terminology.

Today there exists a wide variety of programming languages. Programming languages may be classified using various criteria, however, making specific classifications may be inappropriate due to the the variations in features among similar languages. The general classification shown in Figure 3.2-1 provides a useful frame of reference. A machine language is the actual set of symbols (sequences of bits) which the computer interprets as its basic instruction set. The implementation of the interpreting function may be hardwired or microprogrammed. Assembler languages are mnemonic and symbolic representations of machine languages. In assembler languages mnemonics represent instruction codes and relative symbolic addresses represent the absolute machine addresses. Macro assembler languages extend assembler languages by providing facilities for defining statements which are translated, with paramteric substitution, into several assembler language statements. With extensive macro libraries, programmers may not need detailed knowledge of the assembler or machine language. Procedure oriented languages allow definition of nontrivial data and program structures, provide complex operators for manipulating these structures, and permit specification of operations in a fairly natural format. Problem oriented languages offer users the capability to interact with the computer via nonprocedural statements which employ terminology indigenous to their specific discipline. Ideally, problems and solutions would be expressed in natural languages with computers providing the transformation. Because natural languages are imprecise and ambigous, this approach to computer assisted problem solving has seen limited success.

Since microprograms often interpret machine language instructions, it is natural to classify a micro language, i.e., the actual microinstruction repertoire of a computer, at a level lower than machine languages. Just as the programs written in languages at levels higher than machine language are representative of and are translated into machine language programs, so programs written in languages at levels higher than micro languages are representative of and are translated into micro language programs. The languages that represent micro languages are called microprogramming languages (see

	High level			Low level		
Language level	Procedure oriented machine independent	Procedure oriented machine dependent	Macro register transfer	Register transfer	Assembler and flowchart	Micro

Figure 3.2-2. Spectrum of microprogramming languages.

Programming language Levels	Natural	Problem oriented	Procedure oriented		Macro Assembler		Assembler machine
Micro programming language levels		Problem oriented	Procedure oriented machine independent	Procedure oriented machine dependent	Macro register transfer	Register transfer	Assembler and flowchart	Micro

Figure 3.2-3. Relation between spectra of programming languages and microprogramming languages.

Figure 3.2-2). The spectra of programming languages and microprogramming languages are not independent; Figure 3.2-3 shows some of the relationships.

The lowest level of microprogramming languages, micro languages, corresponds to the lowest level of programming languages, machine languages. Like machine language programs, micro language programs are sequences of instructions each represented as series of bits. The formats of micro language instructions are determined by design decisions concerning the architecture and microinstruction characteristics discussed in Chapter 2. With several different types of characteristics and a large variability within the characteristics, the variation in micro languages is probably greater than in machine languages. The availability of higher level languages for microprogramming considerably simplifies the task of microprogramming. Some tasks, however, still require knowledge of micro languages. For example, in some computers the microinstructions in control store can be changed only by physically setting bits. This may be done by punching (or not punching) holes in a card to indicate a bit value of one (or zero), or by setting bits into a writable control store from the control panel of a computer.

Assembler microprogramming languages give users the capability to express microinstructions in a mnemonic and symbolic form similar to that of traditional assembler languages. These languages are usually card oriented, and card images comprise several fields. Most fields correspond to microinstruction fields – operators, operands, modifiers, etc. Additional fields facilitate symbolic addressing (label field) and comments. Microinstructions may be written in a fairly free format like

LABEL   OPERATION CODE   OPERANDS   COMMENTS

```
*  META 4 MICROPROGRAM TO PERFORM A BLOCK MOVE INSTRUCTION
*  MOVE N WORDS OF MEMORY FROM ONE LOCATION TO ANOTHER.
*    OVERLAPPING FIELDS CAUSE UNDEFINED RESULT.
*    REGISTER USAGE:
*        SP REGISTER - ADDRESS OF SOURCE FIELD, UPDATED AS WE GO ALONG.
*        DP REGISTER - ADDRESS OF DESTINATION FIELD, ALSO UPDATED.
*        L REGISTER - LENGTH OF SOURCE & DESTINATION FIELDS, = 0 ON RETURN
*
MOVE BRZ  L          RET    W      IF L IS ZERO, JUST RETURN.
LOOP MOVE SP MA             MR     READ A WORD FROM SOURCE FIELD,
     ADDI SP SP   1                AND INCREMENT SP
     MOVE DP MA                    SELECT CORRESPONDING WORD IN DESTINATION
     ADDI DP DP   1                FIELD, AND INCREMENT DP.
     MOVE MD MD           PZ,MW    WRITE SOURCE WORD INTO DESTINATION
     SUBI L  L    1                DECREMENT LENGTH,
     BNZ  L          LOOP   W      AND DO ANOTHER IF NOT EXHAUSTED.
RET  RETURN
```

Figure 3.2-4. Example of an assembler language microprogram.

that is characteristic of computers with vertical microinstructions where there are typically five or fewer fields. Such languages are very similar to traditional assembler languages which represent machine languages similar to vertical micro languages. A fixed-field format in which certain card columns are reserved for each microinstruction field characterizes assembler language formats for computers with horizontal microinstructions. The fixed-column-field definitions simplify translation, which can be a formidable task when the number of fields in a microinstruction is large.

90

In writing microinstructions in these assembler languages, fields are generally coded as mnemonic representations of machine registers or operation codes, symbolic representations of addresses or constants, or numeric constants. The flavor of such languages is illustrated by the example in Figure 3.2-4, which shows a microprogram for the Digital Scientific META 4 computer. Assembler microprogramming languages are used for most of the computers described in Chapters 4 through 6.

In flowchart microprogramming languages, networks of boxes represent microprograms. As illustrated in Figure 3.2-5, each box represents one microinstruction. Flow lines connecting boxes indicate possible subsequent microinstructions. An example of this is illustrated in Figure 3.2-6. Principally used for the various models of the IBM System/360, flowchart languages often represent horizontal microinstructions. There are typically several subcommands, which represent microoperations, in each box. These subcommands appear on separate lines in a microinstruction box, and a single character on the left edge of the box may indicate the type of subcommand on that line. Within subcommands, registers and other machine facilities may be represented mnemonically. In terms of capabilities, flowchart languages are similar to assembler languages.

Some of the constructs of higher level programming languages are available in register transfer microprogramming languages. Move operations may use the format of assignment statements*, unary and binary operations may be written in algebraic notation, and conditional execution may be represented by simple IF statements. The subcommands which constitute the microinstructions in a register transfer language often represent several microoperations or fields in the actual microinstruction. For example, the subcommand,

---

*These operations specify transfers of information among registers, hence the name register transfer languages.

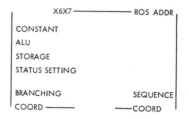

Format of Symbolic Representation

```
         01 ───────────── 115D
1101
R + KH → DC
WRITE
HZ → S4,   LZ → S5

G4, G5                    C4
C4 ───────         ───── CD
```

Figure 3.2-5 Symbolic representation of a System/360 model 30 microprogram word.

$$A = RSH\ (B + C)$$

would indicate that registers B and C are the ALU inputs, the ALU operation is addition, the shift operation is a right shift of the ALU result, and the destination of the ALU/shifter result is register A. Often machine registers and other resources may be given mnemonic names to facilitate microprogramming. Although these languages provide "syntactic sugar," they display many of the characteristics of assembler languages.

1. Programming requires familiarity with the hardware configuration and characteristics.

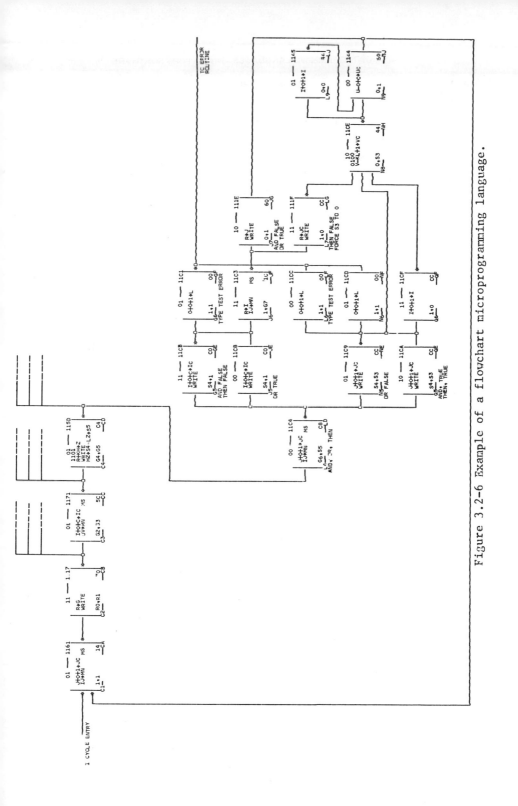

Figure 3.2-6 Example of a flowchart microprogramming language.

ADDRESS	MICROINSTRUCTION

```
0   "SPAU MICROPROGRAM EXAMPLE - ADD COMPLEX NUMBERS
0        ASSUME BSM 0 CONTAINS N PAIRS OF COMPLEX NUMBERS,
0        EACH COMPLEX NUMBER IS STORED IN ONE 32 BIT BSM WORD.
0        SUM SUCCESSIVE PAIRS OF NUMBERS AND STORE THEM IN BSM 1.
0        ASSUME SUMS DO NOT OVERFLOW."
0
0
0   "INITIALIZE"
0
0        A5: BARA=W(1); $  "BUFFER ADDRESS REGISTER A POINTS TO INPUT
1                            DATA, WHOSE ADDRESS IS STORED IN W(1)"
1        A6: BARB=W(2); $  "BUFFER ADDRESS REGISTER B POINTS TO OUTPUT
2                            DATA, WHOSE ADDRESS IS STORED IN W(2)"
2        A5: INCA=W(3);  A6: INCB=W(3); $
3            "SET ADDRESS INCREMENT REGISTERS TO 1, WHICH IS IN W(3)"
3        CTRI = W(4); $ "SET CTRI TO THE NUMBER OF PAIRS
4                            OF COMPLEX NUMBERS TO BE ADDED,
4                            WHICH IS STORED IN W(4)"
4
4
4   "FILL UP PIPE"
4
4        X(1)=BUFA;  A5: BARA=BARA+INCA;  $
5            "READ THE FIRST COMPLEX NUMBER INTO X(1)
5            INCREMENT THE POINTER TO THE INPUT DATA"
5
5        Y(1)=BUFA;  A5: BARA=BARA+INCA;  DECI;  $
6            "READ THE SECOND COMPLEX NUMBER INTO Y(1)
6            INCREMENT THE POINTER TO THE INPUT DATA
6            DECREMENT COUNTER AS HAVE JUST READ ONE PAIR OF NUMBERS"
6
```

```
6
6  "LOOP TO SUM NUMBERS AND PRINT THEM OUT"
6
6  LOOP# A1: R1=X1(1)+Y1(1);   A2: R2=X2(1)+Y2(1);
6        X(1)=BUFA;  A5: BARA=BARA+INCA;  $
7            "ADD REAL AND IMAGINARY PARTS OF THE TWO COMPLEX NUMBERS
7             READ THE FIRST NUMBER OF PAIR INTO X(1)
7             INCREMENT POINTER TO INPUT DATA"
7
7        BUFB=R1R2;  A6: BARB=BARB+INCB;  Y(1)=BUFA;
7            A5: BARA=BARA+INCA;
7        DECI; IF NOT CTRI THEN GO TO LOOP; $
8            "WRITE COMPLEX SUM INTO BUFFER 1
8             INCREMENT POINTER TO OUTPUT DATA
8             READ SECOND NUMBER OF PAIR INTO Y(1)
8             INCREMENT POINTER TO INPUT DATA
8             DECREMENT COUNTER I AND IF ALL DATA HAS NOT BEEN READ
8                 THEN CONTINUE LOOPING"
8
8
8  "FLUSH PIPE"
8
8     A1: R1=X1(1)+Y1(1); A2: R2=X2(1)+Y2(1); $
9            "ADD REAL AND IMAGINARY PARTS OF THE TWO COMPLEX NUMBERS"
9
9
9      BUFB=R1R2; $$  "WRITE THE LAST SUM INTO BUFFER 1"
```

Figure 3.2-7. ANIMIL microprogram- An example of a register transfer microprogramming language.

2. There is a one-to-one correspondence between statements in the language and machine instructions.

3. There are but a few simple data types.

Register transfer languages are often used for computers with very wide microinstructions, where assembler and flowchart languages are awkward due to the large number of fields in a microinstruction word. Macro register transfer microprogramming languages additionally contain general equivalence and macro facilities, which permit mnemonic representations of registers, subcommands, microinstructions, etc., and alteration by parametric substitution. An example of a register transfer language is the ANIMIL microprogramming language illustrated in Figure 3.2-7. The ANIMIL language was developed for the Naval Research Laboratory's Signal Processing Arithmetic Unit.

In the domain of procedure oriented machine-dependent microprogramming languages, the basic one-to-one relationship between language statements and microinstructions no longer holds. In the simplest type of machine-dependent microprogramming languages, microprograms are sequences of simple subcommands; the sequences are composed by the compiler (rather than by the microprogrammer) into a series of horizontal microinstructions. In more advanced machine-dependent microprogramming languages the subcommands and statements are more complex and may be translated into several microoperations or microinstructions. They often effect higher level language constructs such as flow of control primitives (IF...THEN...ELSE..., DO loops, BEGIN...END blocks, etc.), compound arithmetic and logical expressions, and data structures (such as arrays). In general, the use of machine registers, operations, and other facilities must be specified explicitly, however, some constructs may represent a set of machine capabilities, e.g., a variable may represent the

```
PROC PARSERX(RX);
          DCL 1 RX DWORD, "32 BIT RX INSTRUCTION"
               2 OPCODE BIT(8), "OPERATION CODE"
               2 REG1 BIT (4), "SOURCE/TARGET REGISTER"
               2 STORAGE_ADDRESS BIT (20),
                    3 INDEX BIT(4), "INDEX REG"
                    3 BASE BIT (4), "BASE REG"
                    3 DISPLACEMENT BIT(12);

          DCL PARSED_OPCODE WORD IN LSB(8); "LOCAL STORE B, LOC 8"
          DCL REGNO WORD IN LSB (9);
          DCL EFFEC_ADDRH WORD IN LSB(10);
          DCL EFFEC_ADDRL WORD IN LSB(11);

          "SIMULATED GENERAL PURPOSE REGISTERS"
          DCL 1 GPR (0:15) DWORD IN BSM1(100), "BUFFER STORE"
               2 HIGH WORD,
               2 LOW WORD;
```

"THIS ROUTINE IS PASSED A /360 RX TYPE INSTRUCTION AS A
PARAMETER, STORES THE OPCODE AND REGISTER OPERAND IN LOCAL STORE, AND
CALCULATES THE EFFECTIVE ADDRESS OF THE STORAGE OPERAND (BASE REGISTER
+ INDEX REGISTER + 12 BIT DISPLACEMENT). IT THEN CALLS EXECRX TO
EXECUTE THE INSTRUCTION."

```
          PARSED_OPCODE <- OPCODE;  "SET OPCODE IN LSB"
          REGNO <- REG1; "SET REG # IN LSB"
          EFFEC_ADDRH <- 0; "ZERO HIGH 16 BITS OF EA"
```

"CARRYOUT RETURNS THE VALUE OF THE ADDER CARRY WHEN EVALUATING THE
EXPRESSION USED AS AN ARGUMENT. AS A SIDE EFFECT, THE 16 BIT RESULT
MAY BE ASSIGNED WITHIN THE FUNCTION."

```
          EFFEC_ADDRH <- CARRYOUT(EFFEC_ADDRL <-
               DISPLACEMENT+LOW(BASE)) + HIGH(BASE);
          IF INDEX -=0 THEN
```

```
        IF CARRYOUT(EFFEC_ADDRL <- EFFEC_ADDRL+LOW(INDEX))
            THEN EFFEC_ADDRH <- EFFEC_ADDRH+1;

        "ZERO HIGH BYTE OF SUM (24 BIT ADDRESSING)"
        EFFEC_ADDRH <- (EFFEC_ADDRH+HIGH(INDEX)) & X'00FF';

        CALL EXECRX;  "EXECUTE THE RX INSTRUCTION"

END PARSERX;                              "C. BERGMAN, AUG 73"
```

Figure 3.2-8. PUMPKIN microprogram- an example of a higher level machine dependent microprogramming language.

concatenation of two machine registers, and an operation may represent a sequence of machine operations. Machine-dependent microprogramming languages resemble the form of and provide capabilities similar to those of PL360 [Wirth 1968], a machine-dependent programming language for the IBM System/360. Figure 3.2-8 illustrates a sample microprogram in PUMPKIN, a machine-dependent language (presently unimplemented) for the Naval Research Laboratory's Microprogrammed Control Unit.

Over the years the development and use of machine-dependent microprogramminglanguages has been restricted for two main reasons. The first is the possible inefficiency of compiled microprograms. This is the same problem that was encountered by proponents of higher level programming languages decades ago. A trend similar to the use of higher level languages for programming is likely to be seen for microprogramming. Another reason for restricted use of higher level machine-dependent microprogramming languages has been the paucity of user microprogrammable computers. Within the last few years, several manufacturers have introduced user microprogrammable computers. As their use becomes more popular, there should be an increase in the use of higher level languages for microprogramming.

The use of procedure oriented machine independent languages, like Fortran and PL/I, as microprogramming languages has been given some attention. With their declaration facilities these languages may also provide the description capabilities of computer description languages. While there are problems involved in developing compilers to translate such higher level languages into relatively efficient microprograms for contemporary microprogrammable computers, some research work has been done in this area.* A factor of major importance in the use of higher level machine independent microprogramming languages is that they mitigate conversion problems involved in moving microprograms from one computer to another.

The implementation of assembler and flowchart microprogramming languages is straightforward; translation of these languages is generally one-to-one into micro languages. Owing to their functional similarity to assembler languages, register transfer languages are also implemented by translation to micro language. The translation of these low level languages is often performed by software cross translators, i.e., microprograms are translated on a separate computer and the resulting microcode is loaded into the machine that executes the microcode. This cross translation method is used for practical reasons – to allow concurrent development of microprogrammable computers and microprograms for them and to facilitate use of computers not well equipped to perform the

* For a discussion of work on higher level microprogramming languages see Chapter 7.

99

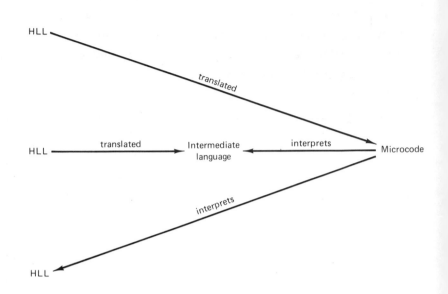

Figure 3.2-9 Microprogrammed implementation of higher level languages.

translation function. Figure 3.2-9 illustrates the variety of implementations of higher level languages. When higher level languages are translated into some intermediate language and then interpreted, or interpreted directly, the application becomes microprogrammed execution of higher level languages rather than higher level languages for microprogramming.* While the translation of higher level representation of microprograms

* The microprogrammed execution of higher level languages is discussed in Chapter 8.

100

is generally accomplished by software programs, it may also be performed by firmware routines.

3.3 Simulators and Their Implementation

As mentioned earlier a simulator is an interpreter of a program expressed in some machine or micro language. As such a simulator repetitively fetches the instructions of the interpreted program and performs the operations they indicate, and so may be considered to have a main routine that fetches and decodes instructions and several subroutines that perform the various instructions. The design of microprogram simulators may, however, be much more complex than machine language simulators for several reasons.

1. The first reason is the more complex instruction format. Machine language instructions generally have but a few fields while microinstructions may have several.

2. Microinstructions with several fields may indicate several operations that are to be performed in parallel; simulating parallel operations may be difficult on a system that allows neither parallel processing nor multitasking.

3. In some microinstruction formats, field interpretation depends on the value of some register.

4. Some microprogrammed computers use complex schemes for selecting the address of the next microinstruction to be executed.

5. Various microoperations may require different times for execution. For example, a main memory read or write operation typically takes several machine cycles while most move and transformation operations require only one or two cycles.

1. SET facility-name = data;

2. PRINT facility-name;

3. SAVE facility-name ON file-name;

4. ADD facility-name TO LIST;

5. DELETE facility-name FROM LIST;

6. SET BREAKPOINT AT control-store-address;
   SET TRACEPOINT AT control-store-address;

7. REMOVE BREAKPOINT AT control-store-address;
   REMOVE TRACEPOINT AT control-store-address;

8. BREAK INTERVAL IS integer;
   TRACE INTERVAL IS integer;

9. START;

10. STOP;

Figure 3.3-1. Sample simulator commands.

Notes

facility-name is the name of a local store register,
the address of a word or field in control store, or the
address of a word or byte in main memory.
file-name is the name of an external file on which to

store data for later retrieval.

When the execution of a simulated microprogram reaches a breakpoint address or when the number of simulated microinstructions since the last breakpoint is the break interval, the simulator returns control to the user.

Trace works like break except that at tracepoints, the values of the facilities on the LIST are printed and control is not returned to the user.

To facilitate microprogram checkout it is important that a simulator permit user interaction with the execution of the simulated microprogram. This user interface generally takes the form of commands that allow the user to stop the simulated microprogram at desired locations, inspect and change machine and microprogram status, and continue execution. A general command repertoire might include commands such as those listed in Figure 3.3-1. In a typical session with the simulator, a user might load a microprogram into the simulated control store, initialize various registers and memory locations, set up break and trace points, and initiate execution to observe the performance of his microprogram. At any time a user may change the microprogram, observe the effects of different initial data, or terminate execution. Figure 3.3-2 shows a short session with the simulator developed for the Naval Research Laboratory's Signal Processing Arithmetic Unit. To let the user utilize the simulator's capabilities quickly and easily, human factors are very important in the design of an interactive simulator.

1. The command language should be not only comprehensive but also mnemonic and free format so that it is easy to learn and use.

```
SPAU COMMAND PROCESSOR
? LOAD SPACMX "LOAD SIMULATED CONTROL STORE WITH MICROPROGRAM"
CONTROL STORE FILE SPACMX LOADED
READY
? SET BUF 0(0-11)=1,2,3,4,5,6,7,8,9,10,11,12; "INITIALIZE MEMORY"
SET COMMAND
READY
? SET W(1)=0, W(2)=4096, W(3)=1, W(4)=3;  "SET PARAMETERS"
SET COMMAND
READY
? TRACERANGE 4-10; ADD R1,R2, BARA, CTRI; "SET UP TRACE POINTS"
TRACE AND OR BREAKPOINT MODIFICATION COMMAND
ADD COMMAND
READY
? BREAK 10; "SET UP BREAK POINT"  GO; "INITIALIZE EXECUTION"
TRACE AND OR BREAKPOINT MODIFICATION COMMAND
GO COMMAND     SIMULATION BEGINS AT ADDRESS  0
```

CLOCK	ADDR	R1	R2	BARA	CTRI
4	4	0	0	0	3
5	5	0	0	1	3
6	6	0	0	2	2
7	7	4	6	3	2
8	6	4	6	4	1
9	7	12	14	5	1
10	6	12	14	6	0
11	7	20	22	7	0
12	8	20	22	8	65535
13	9	0	0	8	65535
14	10	0	0	8	65535

```
-----BREAKPOINT----- CLOCK  14  NEXT ADDRESS  10  LAST ADDRESS   9
```

```
SPAU COMMAND PROCESSOR
? PRINT BUF1(0-5); "PRINT RESULTS"
PRINT COMMAND
            4          6         12         14         20         22
      BUF1(0)    BUF1(1)    BUF1(2)    BUF1(3)    BUF1(4)    BUF1(5)
READY
? END; "END OF SIMULATOR RUN"
END COMMAND
      STOP
```

Figure 3.3-2. Sample simulator session for the Naval Research Laboratory signal processing arithmetic unit. The simulated microprogram appears in Figure 3.2-7.

2. The user should have access to all the resources of the simulated computer.

3. Error messages should be explicit yet brief.

4. Other desirable features include the abilities to define new commands in terms of old ones and to symbolically reference variables.

Microprogram simulators are generally implemented by conventional software programs. With the complexity of microinstructions in several contemporary computers, such implementations may be very slow. The ratio of execution speed for the simulated computer to the actual computer may range to more than 1000:1. Simulators are often used to simulate computers that are under development; it is sometimes the case that simulation results effect a redesign of the machine. When the microprogrammed computer has been built, one way to improve this situation is to let the computer execute the microcode directly while maintaining a user interface to control microprogram execution. Such an implementation is called a debugger. In this implementation the user interface should handle untoward conditions such as invalid memory addresses, illegal microinstructions, external interrupts, etc. Debuggers are often used to check for timing and machine environment problems that may be difficult to find in software simulation. While debuggers improve execution speed of simulated microprograms, they may hinder machine utilization when only one microprogram may be debugged at a time. The slow human who continually stops the running program to ascertain its status may idle the machine thus preventing it from performing other tasks. Simulators, on the other hand, can generally be run on a time sharing system with little difficulty.

3.4 Computer Description Languages

Computer description languages provide facilities for describing a machine in terms of its

1. hardware components,
2. microinstruction design, and
3. microinstruction implementation.

A standard translator and simulator interface with the computer design language so that when the design of a proposed machine is changed a new translator and simulator need not be developed. Computer design languages have been used to reduce the cost of changing translators and simulators in large projects where a number of machines were being designed.

Annotated Bibliography

1. J. L. Brame and C. V. Ramamoorthy, "An Interactive Simulator
   Generating System for Small Computers," 1971 Spring Joint
   Computer Conference Proceedings, AFIPS Press, Montvale, New
   Jersey, pp. 425-449.

   Describes and gives an example of an interactive program
   for designing and simulating a small computer.

2. Y. Chu, editor, Computer, Volume 7 Number 12 (December 1974).

   An issue devoted to hardware description languages that
   surveys many of the developments in this area.

3. M. Gasser, "An Interactive Debugger for Software and
   Firmware," Sixth Annual Workshop on Microprogramming
   Preprints, ACM, September 1973, pp. 113-119.

   In a dual processor system, the microprogram controlled
   debugger runs in one processor, and the firmware and software
   to be debugged run in the other.

4. S. S. Husson, Microprogramming Principles and Practices, see
   Chapter 1 entry.

   Detailed descriptions of early microprogramming support
   packages for several models of the IBM System/360, the RCA
   Spectra 70/Model 45, and the Honeywell H4200. Support included
   flowchart and assembler languages, computer description
   languages, and simulators.

5. W. Kent, "Assembler-Language Macroprogramming: A Tutorial
   Oriented Toward the IBM 360," Computing Surveys, Volume 1
   Number 4 (December 1969), pp. 183-196.

An introduction to the basic concepts of macros and how they are used in assembler language programming. Good background for assembler and macro assembler microprogramming languages.

6. G. R. Lloyd and A. vanDam, "Design Considerations for Microprogramming Languages," 1974 National Computer Conference Proceedings, AFIPS Press, Montvale, New Jersey, pp. 537-543.

An introduction to the PUMPKIN language, a machine dependent microprogramming language, follows a general discussion of microprogramming languages that is interesting but does not always distinguish between design and implementation.

7. P. W. Mallett and T. G. Lewis, "Approaches to Design of High Level Languages for Microprogramming," Seventh Annual Workshop on Microprogramming Preprints, ACM, September 1974, pp. 66-73.

This excellent discussion of the design and implementation of higher level languages for microprogramming is broken into five areas: the syntax of the higher level language, the design of intermediate languages, microinstruction formts, the translation of the higher level syntax into the intermediate language, and the translation of the intermediate language into actual microinstructions. Timing and concurrency are also discussed, and a tool for research in microcompiler development is proposed.

8. A. J. Nichols III, "A Microprogramming Framework for Experimental Machine Design," SIGMICRO Newsletter, Volume 2 Number 2 (July 1971), pp. 17-26.

Description of a computer program which permits a designer to simulate the operation of a machine he wishes to create.

9. T. G. Rauscher, "Towards a Specification of Syntax and Semantics for Languages for Horizontally Microprogrammed Machines," Proceedings of ACM SIGPLAN-SIGMICRO Interface Meeting, May 1973, pp. 98-111.

Reviews past languages for microprogramming computers with horizontal microinstructions and introduces the ANIMIL register transfer micrprogramming language.

10. T. G. Rauscher et al, "AN/UYK-17 (XB-1) (V) Signal Processing Element Microprogramming Support Software," Naval Research Laboratory Report 7777, Washington, D. C., 1975.

Includes descriptions of two register transfer microprogramming languages and a simulator used for two microprogrammable machines.

11. J. E. Sammet, Programming Languages History and Fundamentals, Prentice-Hall, Englewood Cliffs, New Jersey, 1969.

A monumental work on programming languages. The fundamentals and characterstics of languages described provide interesting comparisons with microprogramming languages.

12. N. Wirth, "PL360, A Programming Language for the 360 Computers," Journal of the ACM, Volume 15 Number 1 (January 1968), pp. 37-74.

Describes a machine dependent programming language for the IBM System/360. A prototype for machine dependent microprogramming languages.

13. S. Young, "A Microprogram Simulator," SIGMICRO Newsletter, Volume 2 Number 3 (October 1971), pp. 43-56.

Description of a simulator and computer description language for assisting in the development of a microprogrammed machine.

CHAPTER 4

COMPUTERS WITH VERTICAL MICROINSTRUCTIONS

4.1 Introduction

Since its use in some computer systems in the mid 1960's,
microprogramming has   been   used   in   developing   several
commercially available computers.   As microprogramming offers
the   computer   designer tremendous flexibility in   creating
systems, users   now   can choose from not only a variety of
manufacturers but   also from different architectures.   In   an
effort   to   study   different   architectures   that   use
microprogramming we examine the characteristics of a number of
systems in this and the next two chapters.

This chapter describes two machines that utilize vertical
microinstructions - the Standard Logic CASH-8 and the Burroughs
B1700.   While both machines have sixteen bit microinstructions,
their purpose, design,   and   cost are considerably different.
This difference emphasizes both the variety of machine designs
that can be implemented via microprogramming and the variety of
microprogram architectures.

4.2 The Standard Logic CASH-8

4.2.1 CASH-8 Background

The CASH-8 is manufactured by Standard Logic Inc. as an
inexpensive microprogrammable computer/controller   that bridges

111

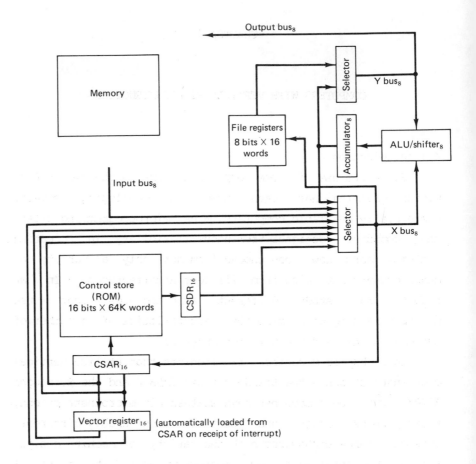

Figure 4.2-1. Organization of the Standard Logic CASH-8.

the gap between special purpose hardwired controllers and general purpose minicomputers. In its simplest use, the CASH-8 provides a flexible substitute for hardwired controllers in applications such as process control. In the hybrid mode, the CASH-8 controls the flow of data between a read/write memory and system peripherals. Applications of this mode include acting as a buffer between a computer and its peripherals and formatting the display on a CRT terminal. In the computer mode, the CASH-8 functions like a general purpose microprogrammed minicomputer; the microinstructions interpret machine instructions stored in a read/write memory.

4.2.2 CASH-8 Architecture

4.2.2.1 CASH-8 Functional Units

Simplicity is the key to the CASH-8 architecture (see Figure 4.2-1). There is no main memory built into the system, however, a variety of memories can easily be attached as I/O devices.

The control store is a simple memory array of up to 65,536 sixteen bit words. A variety of memory types (from ROM to read/write) are available for control store implementation; this is the determining factor in processor speed. With ROM and bipolar random access memory (RAM), the processor clock cycle is 200 n sec. Associated with the control store are the standard CSAR (called the P register) and the CSDR (called the I register). Associated with the CSAR is a vector (V) register. Upon receipt of an external interrupt, the CASH-8 stores the CSAR in the vector register and sets the CSAR to zero, the address of the interrupt service routine.

The ALU has the capability to perform a large number of arithmetic, logic, and shift operations on eight bit operands.

113

These are described in detail with the microinstruction repertoire. Almost all of the CASH-8 registers may be selected as ALU inputs; the accumulator always receives the ALU result. Associated with the ALU are two one bit registers, the carry flag and the shift flag, which are set and used by certain ALU operations.

Local store comprises 16 eight bit working storage registers organized as a file, i.e., a sixteen word memory. Each CASH-8 microinstruction may reference at most one of these file registers.

All data paths in the machine are eight bits wide. Busses are used for inputs to the ALU, the file registers, and the CSAR. The input and output busses provide external interfaces.

4.2.2.2 CASH-8 Microinstruction Repertoire

CASH-8 microinstructions, which are sixteen bits long, may be divided into four classes: arithmetic/logic, branch, register file, and shift (see Figure 4.2-2). The microinstructions generally specify a single operation and hence may be classified as vertical. Two level encoding is used, with field definition depending on the operation code in bits four and five. Microinstruction implementation is parallel (fetching the next microinstruction to be executed is overlapped with the execution phase of the present microinstruction). While most microinstructions are executed in one clock cycle (200 n sec with the fast control store), some microinstructions require multiple cycles. Moving the CSAR to two file registers and two file registers to the CSAR, for example, requires four cycles.

Figure 4.2-2. CASH-8 Microinstructions.

a. Arithmetic/logic microinstructions

Bit

number 0 1 2 3 4 5 6 7 8 9 10 11 12 13 14 15 16

```
┌───────────┬─────┬─────────┬──────────────────┐
│  │  │  │  │ 0 │ 0 │  │  │  │  │  │  │  │  │  │  │
└───────────┴─────┴─────────┴──────────────────┘
```

Field   Register   Opera- Y   X bus   Function
                    tion   bus select
                    code   select

Register - address of the file register to be
           manipulated
Operation code - 00 denotes an ALU microinstruction;
                 perform the operations and put the
                 result in the accumulator
Y bus select
     0 - register from regiter file
     1 - accumulator
X bus select
     000 - input bus
     001 - registèr from register file
     010 - CSAR (upper 8 bits)
     011 - vector register (upper 8 bits)
     100 - accumulator
     101 - CSDR (lower 8 bits)
     110 - CSAR (lower 8 bits)
     111 - vector register (lower 8 bits)

115

Function

Bits 10–11 Bits 12–15	00	11
0000	X	not X
0001	X v Y	not X & not Y
0010	X v not Y	not X & Y
0011	-1	0
0100	X + (X & not Y)	not X v not Y
0101	(X v Y) + (X & not Y)	not Y
0110	X - Y - 1	X * Y
0111	X & not Y - 1	X & not Y
1000	X + (X & Y)	not X v Y
1001	X + Y	not (X * Y)
1010	(X v not Y) + (X & Y)	Y
1011	(X & Y) - 1	X & Y
1100	X + X	1
1101	(X v Y) + X	X v not Y
1110	(X v not Y) + X	X v Y
1111	X - 1	X

Notation: & and, v or, * exclusive or

When bits 10 and 11 are 0 and 1 the functions are
like those in column 00 except that a carry
bit of one is added.

When bits 10 and 11 are 1 and 0 the functions are
like those in column 00 except that the carry
bit is added or subtracted.

b. <u>Branch microinstructions</u>

116

Bit
number   0   1   2   3   4   5   6   7   8   9 10 11 12 13 14 15 16

```
┌───┬───┬───┬───┬─┬─┬───┬───┬───┬───┬───────────┐
│   │   │   │   │0│1│   │   │   │   │           │
└───┴───┴───┴───┴─┴─┴───┴───┴───┴───┴───────────┘
```

Field   Register   Opera- True Subop- Unused Condition
                      tion   False eration
                      code

Register - address of the file register containing the
            branch address
Operation code - 01 denotes branch microinstruction;
                      test the condition, and if satisfied
                      perform the indicated suboperation
True/False - Test to see of the condition is true or
            false
Condition -
        0 - accumulator <= 0
        1 - accumulator not = 0
        2 - carry flag = 1
        3-6 - external lines 0-3 = 1
        7 - (always true)
        8-15 - accumulator bits 0-7 set
Suboperation -
        100 - move file register to CSAR (lower 8 bits)
        110 - move address of next microinstruction to two
            adjacent file registers (the first is the
            one designated in bits 0-3), move the next
            two file registers to the CSAR
        101 - move register file and the next higher file
            register to the CSAR
        111 - move vector register to CSAR

If the first bit of the suboperation is 0, then the
       condition is indicated by bits 0-3, and bits

117

8-15 contain a literal that is moved to the CSAR
(lower 8 bits)

c. Register file microinstructions

Bit
number 0 1 2 3 4 5 6 7 8 9 10 11 12 13 14 15 16

		1 0		

Field   Register Opera-   Subopera-   I/O device address
                   tion   tion code
                   code

Register - address of the file register to be
            manipulated
Operation code - 10 indicates a register file,
                   accumulator, or I/O bus transfer
Suboperation code
    0100 - move input bus contents to file register
    0111 - move accumulator to file register
    0000 - move file register to output bus
    1000 - move accumulator to output bus

If the first two bits of the suboperation code are
    11, then bits 8-15 contain a literal that is
    moved to the file register

d. Shift microinstructions

118

```
Bit
number    0  1  2  3  4  5  6  7  8  9 10 11 12 13 14 15 16
```

```
        ┌──────────────┬──────┬────────────┬─────────────────┐
        │              │ 1  1 │            │                 │
        └──────────────┴──────┴────────────┴─────────────────┘
```

Field   Unused   Opera- Un- Subopera-   Unused
                    tion used tion code
                    code

Operation code – 11 indicates an accumulator shift
                 operation. All shifts are 1 bit
                 shifts. For logical shifts, the
                 shifted out bit is stored in the shift
                 flag and a zero is inserted. For
                 circular shifts, the shifted bit is
                 stored in the shift flag. For
                 arithmetic shifts the shift flag is
                 inserted.

Suboperation code
     1000 – logical left shift
     0100 – logical right shift
     1001 – circular left shift
     0101 – circular right shift
     1010 – arithmetic left shift
     0110 – arithmetic right shift

4.2.3 CASH-8 Microprogrammability

A variety of memory types may be used for the control
store in the CASH-8. When writable, these memories can be
loaded from an extenal device, but this is seldom done because
the CASH-8 is intended to be used as a dedicated processor and
the control store is usually changed only during development.

119

The CASH-8 was, however, designed to be microprogrammed for or by the user. Standard Logic does prepare application microprograms and provide an assembler for users.

4.3 The Burroughs B1700

4.3.1 Burroughs B1700 Overview

The Burroughs B1700 line of computers is being marketed as small to medium scale data processing system. While most of the machines that have been installed are turn key systems using Burroughs developed applications software, the B1700 was designed to be a powerful general purpose computer capable of supporting a variety of applications. The design goals of the machine were

(1) to allow any language at all to be used for computing;
(2) to interpret programming languages faster than hard-wired systems can execute them; and
(3) to optimize throughput in a small-scale, general-purpose, commercial system.*

To achieve these design goals, the Burroughs B1700 utilizes several unusual architectural features.

Several models in the B1700 line have been announced. We will concentrate our attention on the B1726 which differs from the B1714 and B1712 in that

1. it has a faster processor clock (six megahertz as opposed to four and two for the B1714 and B1712),

2. it has a separate control store of up to 2,048 words (the B1714 and B1712 always fetch microinstructions from main memory), and

3. it can accomodate more main memory and I/O devices.

* [Wilner 1972a], page 103.

4.3.2 B1726 Architecture

4.3.2.1 B1726 Functional Units

The most unusual feature of the B1726 is the architecture and use of main memory. Although it is <u>physically</u> organized into nine bit words (eight data bits and one parity bit), the main memory is logically bit addressable, i.e., data addresses in main memory need not be aligned on a byte, half-word, or word address. Furthermore, there is no fixed word size of data items in main memory; data may have a length varying from 1 to 65,535 bits. This <u>defined-field</u> concept is implemented in hardware with the aid of the F register (whose two parts – FA and FL – contain the bit address of the data item and its length). The defined-field scheme is thus available at the microprogram level and can significantly improve memory utilization on the B1726 [Wilner 1972c]. In combination with the defined-field concept, main memory is used to meet the stated design goals. Main memory does not hold traditional machine language instructions, indeed no machine language is built into the hardware. The main memory contains so called "S-language" instructions. An S-language* is an intermediate language that efficiently represents the constructs of a higher level language. Thus for each higher level language there is a unique S-language. Burroughs has developed S-languages for COBOL, RPG, Fortran, BASIC, and SDL (a Burroughs software development language). The level of S-language instructions is generally much higher than that of traditional machine language instructions. It is often the case that a statement in a higher level language is translated into one S-language instruction. To execute a higher level language program on this machine, the program is translated into an S-language program which is then

---

* The S connotes soft, system, specialized, simulated, or source.

121

interpreted by microprograms. The first design goal of the B1700 may thus be reformulated to be the efficient interpretation of arbitrary S-languages.

As with the main memory, the architecture of the control store of the B1726 differs significantly from its implementation. The physical implementation includes

1. a control store of 1024 or 2048 sixteen bit words,

2. the main memory,

3. the twenty-four bit microinstruction base register (MBR) which contains the lowest bit address in main memory at which microinstructions can be stored,

4. the four bit top of control memory register (TOPM) which contains a number that when multiplied by 512 indicates the number of words in the physical control store,

5. the twenty-four bit MAXS register that indicates the size of main memory in bits,

6. an address stack (the A stack) which contains 32 twenty-four bit words, and

7. the fourteen bit CSAR (called the A register) and the sixteen bit CSDR (called the M register).

The fetch and execution of microinstructions proceeds as illustrated in Figure 4.3-1. Note that microinstructions are automatically fetched from main memory when the address in the CSAR is higher than the highest physical control store address. Since the read access time of main memory (666 2/3 n sec) is four times slower than control store (166 2/3 n sec), it is advantageous to have the most frequently executed microinstructions in the physical control store. The control store is writable under microprogram control. The B1726 utilizes the address stack associated with the control store to implement subroutines at the microprogram level. The subroutine

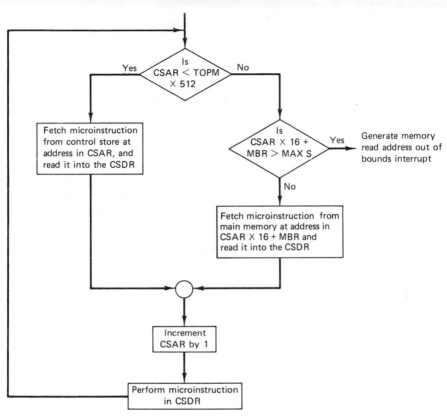

Figure 4.3-1. Fetching and executing B1700
microinstructions.

call microinstructions push the next microinstruction address
onto the top of the stack. The stack is twenty-four bits wide,
so it may also be used for operand storage. By referencing the
TAS (top of address stack pseudo register) data may be pushed
into or popped from the A stack. Moving an address from the top
stack word to the CSAR effects a subroutine return. An
interesting capability of the B1726 microinstruction
fetch-execute scheme is that the execution of a

123

Name	Size in bits	Usage*	Functions	
General purpose registers				
X	24	S,D	ALU input, main memory input and output	may be shifted separately or
Y	24	S,D	ALU input, main memory input and output	together as a 48 bit register
T	24	S,D	Addressable in 4 bit units, may be shifted and extracted, main memory input & output	
L	24	S,D	Addressable in 4 bit units, main memory input and output	
Registers associated with control store				
A	14	S,D	Control store address register	
M	16	S,D	Control store data register	
TAS	24	S,D	Top of stack pseudo register, stack is 32 elements deep	
TOPM	4	S,D	Contains number of words in control store divided by 512	
MBR	24	S,D	Lowest bit address in main memory at which microinstructions may be stored	
Registers associated with main memory				
F	48	S,D	Contains several subregisters	
FA	24	S,D	Bit address in main memory of data item	
FL	16	S,D	Length of main memory data item	
FU	4	S,D	Used to set CPU and CPL registers	
FT	4	S,D	Describes field size in memory	
Scratchpad	48	S,D	Sixteen registers that hold operand descriptors, i.e., a backup for F register	
BR	24	S,D	Base register for memory protection	
LR	24	S,D	Limit register for memory protection	

MAXS	24	S	Size of main memory in bits

Special purpose registers

C	24	S,D	A collection of independent subregisters
CA	4	S,D	General purpose source and destination
CB	4	S,D	General purpose source and destination
CC	4	S,D	Four one bit interrupt flags dealing with processor state
CD	4	S,D	Four one bit interrupt flags dealing with memory protection
CP	8	S,D	A collection of 3 subregisters
CYF	1	S,D	Carry flip-flop
CPU	2	D	Indicates ALU data type (0-binary, 1-4 bit binary, 3-8 bit numeric)
CPL	5	S,D	Length of ALU operands
FLCN	4	S	Indicates comparison between F register and first scratchpad register
BICN	4	S	Indicates special ALU conditions
XYCN	4	S	Indicates relative values of X and Y
XYST	4	S	Indicates values of X and Y
INCN	4	S,D	Indicates I/O interrupts
NULL	24	S	Contains 0
U	16	S	Input microinstruction from cassette
DATA	24	S,D	I/O data
CMND	24	D	I/O command

Figure 4.3-2. B1726 local store registers.

* S : source, D : destination.

microinstruction can modify the contents of the CSDR, which (due to the parallel implementation) contains the next microinstruction to be executed. Thus a microinstruction can be modified after it is fetched from control store and before it is executed.

The B1726 contains a large variety of local store registers as described in Figure 4.3-2. The registers associated with main memory and control store are also shown in this figure. The large number of registers and connecting data paths among them characterizes an unusually complex architecture.

The B1726 contains two ALUs for the transformation of data. The inputs to the twenty-four bit ALU are the X register, the Y register, and the carry flip-flop (CYF). The CPU and CPL registers (see Figure 4.3-2) specify the representation of the input data for the twenty-four bit ALU. The transfer of data to the X or Y register (e.g., via a register move or read memory microinstruction) or an alteration of the CYF, CPU, or CPL registers activates the ALU. Microinstructions following the one which activates the ALU may use the result of any ALU operation (addition, subtraction, complement, and, or, exclusive or, and mask) or condition register set by the ALU. The two inputs to the four bit ALU are a four bit control store literal from the Manipulate microinstruction (the only microinstruction that references the four bit ALU) and one of several four bit registers or subregisters. The four bit ALU performs the following operations: assignment, and, or, exclusive or, addition, and subtraction. This independent ALU for the four bit registers provides a general facility for setting and testing condition registers without interrupting the use of the twenty-four bit ALU performing general data processing operations.

Name	Format	Comments
Register move	`0 0 0 1` | Source Register | Destination Register	This microinstruction is used for arithmetic operations by moving the result from a pseudo operation register
Scratchpad move	`0 0 1 0` | Source or Destination Register | D | Scratchpad Address	D indicates direction 0 – to scratchpad 1 – from scratchpad Scratchpad address indicates the left or rightmost 24 bits of a scratch pad register
Four bit manipulate	`0 0 1 1` | Register to be manipulated | Operation | Literal	Operations include skip the next microinstruction if there is a carry or borrow in addition or subtraction
Relative branch if bit test false	`0 1 0 0` | Register to be tested | B | S | Literal	B specifies the bit in the register to be tested If the S bit is one go to the next microinstruction Literal is the number to be added to the CSAR if the tested bit meets the condition
Relative branch if bit test true	`0 1 0 1` | Register to be tested | B | S | Literal	
Skip when	`0 1 1 0` | Register to be tested | Variant | Mask	Variant specifies condition to be tested for skip to occur The mask field masks the four bit register selected
Read or Write Memory	`0 1 1 1` | R W | Variant | Register | FD | Memory field length	RW indicates read or write Variant specifies incrementing or decrementing FA and FL Register is X, Y, T, or L FD – field direction forward or backward

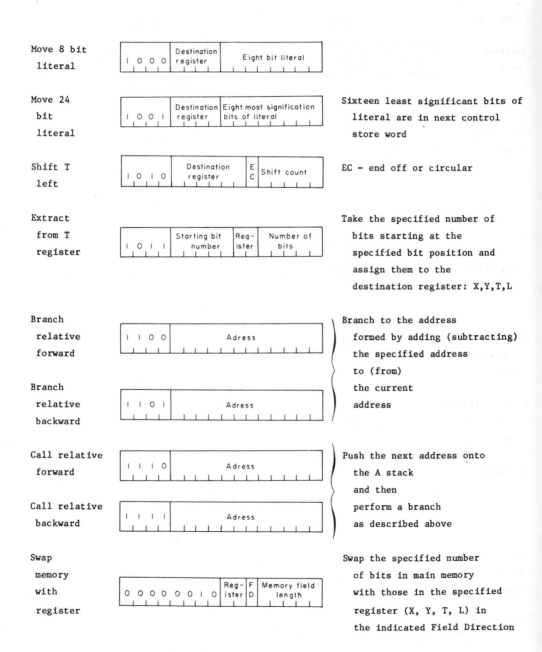

Move 8 bit literal

| I O O O | Destination register | Eight bit literal |

Move 24 bit literal

| I O O I | Destination register | Eight most signification bits of literal |

Sixteen least significant bits of literal are in next control store word

Shift T left

| I O I O | Destination register | E C | Shift count |

EC – end off or circular

Extract from T register

| I O I I | Starting bit number | Reg-ister | Number of bits |

Take the specified number of bits starting at the specified bit position and assign them to the destination register: X,Y,T,L

Branch relative forward

| I I O O | Adress |

Branch relative backward

| I I O I | Adress |

Branch to the address formed by adding (subtracting) the specified address to (from) the current address

Call relative forward

| I I I O | Adress |

Call relative backward

| I I I I | Adress |

Push the next address onto the A stack and then perform a branch as described above

Swap memory with register

| O O O O O O I O | Reg-ister | F D | Memory field length |

Swap the specified number of bits in main memory with those in the specified register (X, Y, T, L) in the indicated Field Direction

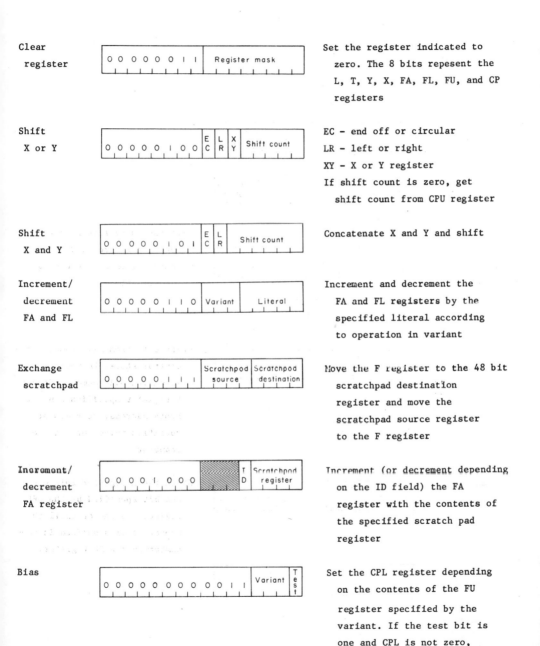

Clear
register

`0 0 0 0 0 0 1 1 | Register mask`

Set the register indicated to
zero. The 8 bits repesent the
L, T, Y, X, FA, FL, FU, and CP
registers

Shift
X or Y

`0 0 0 0 0 1 0 0 | E C | L R | X Y | Shift count`

EC - end off or circular
LR - left or right
XY - X or Y register
If shift count is zero, get
shift count from CPU register

Shift
X and Y

`0 0 0 0 0 1 0 1 | E C | L R | Shift count`

Concatenate X and Y and shift

Increment/
decrement
FA and FL

`0 0 0 0 0 1 1 0 | Variant | Literal`

Increment and decrement the
FA and FL registers by the
specified literal according
to operation in variant

Exchange
scratchpad

`0 0 0 0 0 1 1 1 | Scratchpad source | Scratchpad destination`

Move the F register to the 48 bit
scratchpad destination
register and move the
scratchpad source register
to the F register

Increment/
decrement
FA register

`0 0 0 0 1 0 0 0 | | T D | Scratchpad register`

Increment (or decrement depending
on the ID field) the FA
register with the contents of
the specified scratch pad
register

Bias

`0 0 0 0 0 0 0 0 0 0 1 1 | Variant | T e s t`

Set the CPL register depending
on the contents of the FU
register specified by the
variant. If the test bit is
one and CPL is not zero,
skip the next microinstruction

129

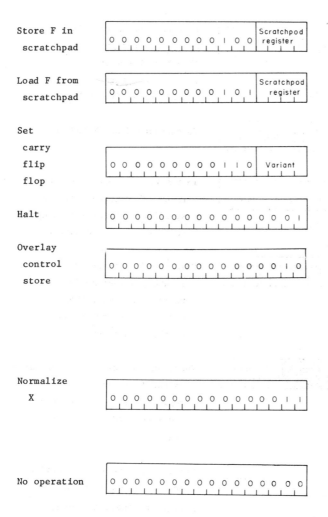

Store F in scratchpad

`0 0 0 0 0 0 0 0 0 1 0 0` | Scratchpad register

Load F from scratchpad

`0 0 0 0 0 0 0 0 0 1 0 1` | Scratchpad register

Set carry flip flop

`0 0 0 0 0 0 0 0 0 1 1 0` | Variant

Set the carry flip flop to zero, one, carry from ALU, or borrow from ALU depending on variant

Halt

`0 0 0 0 0 0 0 0 0 0 0 0 0 0 0 1`

Overlay control store

`0 0 0 0 0 0 0 0 0 0 0 0 0 0 1 0`

Write data from main memory into control store. FA register specifies main memory address. L register specifies control store address. FL register specifies number of bits to transfer.

Normalize X

`0 0 0 0 0 0 0 0 0 0 0 0 0 0 1 1`

Shift the X register left until the bit specified by the CPL register is one or until the number of bits shifted is the number in the FL register.

No operation

`0 0 0 0 0 0 0 0 0 0 0 0 0 0 0 0`

Figure 4.3-3. B1726 microinstruction repertoire summary.

130

Microinstruction | 0 | 0 | 0 | 1 | 1 | 0 | 1 | 1 | 1 | 0 | 1 | 0 | 0 | 1 | 0 | 0 |

```
                  Operation   Source    Source  Dest-  Destination
                             Register  Register ination  Register
                               Row       Column Register   Row
                                                 Column
```

Move top of stack to CSAR

Figure 4.3-4. Example of register referencing in a B1726 microinstruction.

4.3.2.2 B1726 Microinstruction Design

The B1726 microinstruction repertoire is summarized in Figure 4.3-3. The microinstructions are sixteen bits long. Each microinstruction performs one microoperation so the microinstructions may be classified as vertical. Two level encoding is used and field definitions are predicated on the operation code, which may be four, eight, twelve, or sixteen bits long. The technique used for referencing registers is somewhat unusual. Burroughs has defined a matrix with sixteen rows and four columns. Each entry in the matrix is the name of a register. A register is referenced by its row (requiring four address bits) and column (requiring two address bits) so that normally six bits are required to reference a register. An example appears in Figure 4.3-4. For some microinstructions the register must be in one of the first two columns (requiring one address bit) so that only five bits may be needed to reference a register.

131

4.3.2.3 B1726 Microinstruction Implementation

As illustrated in Figure 4.3-1 the B1726 microinstruction fetch and execute phases are distinct. The B1726 takes advantage of this by performing microinstruction fetch in parallel with the execution of the previous microinstruction. In fact, the CSDR receives the next microinstruction to be executed before the execution of the present microinstruction terminates. This implementation provides the following capability. When the CSDR is the destination in a register move microinstruction, the operation is changed from assignment to logical or. Thus all or part of the microinstruction to be executed can be changed. An example of such a modification is inserting a computed relative branch address into a branch forward microinstruction; this technique may be used in decoding S-language instructions.

Most B1726 microinstructions require a single cycle for execution; there are no distinct subcycles of the basic clock cycle. Some microinstructions (like read or write main memory and overlay control store) require several cycles for completion.

4.3.3 B1726 Microprogrammability

The B1726 control store is writable under microprogram control via the Overlay Control Store microinstruction. This microinstruction reads data from main memory and into control store; any number of locations may be written. The FA register supplies the main memory address of the microinstructions, the L register supplies the control store address, and the FL register supplies the number of bits that are to be read from main memory and written into control store. As described

132

previously, microinstructions may also be fetched and executed from main memory.

Support software for the B1726 includes a microprogramming language and a master control program. The higher-level-like language is not typical of microprogramming languages for commercially available machines and so is described in some detail in the Section 4.3.4. The purpose of the master control program (MCP) is to provide efficient system utilization by administrating control store, multiprogramming microprograms, and providing other support facilities. The MCP allows microprograms to reside in the File System, just like ordinary source and object files. In this case microcode does not have special status so that S-language programs and their interpreters may be associated together as late as run time. Thus a user may choose a different interpreter for a compiled program each time he runs it.

To assist in the design of S-languages, Burroughs has developed and made extensive use of monitoring techniques to investigate microinstruction usage. There is a hardware monitor microinstruction which provides bit patterns that may be picked up by an external monitor. The effect of such monitoring has been to improve main memory utilization through the use of frequency based encoding of data and instructions [Wilner 1972c]. From this discussion it should be evident that the B1700 is highly microprogrammable.

4.3.4 B1726 Microprogramming Language

Burroughs has developed a fairly sophisticated language, called MIL (Micro Implementation Language), for microprogramming the B1726. While MIL is like an assembler language in that each statement generally represents one microinstruction, it provides several features to facilitate microprogramming. MIL provides a block structure - declarations

133

No.	Code	Source image	Comments
1	0040	MULTIPLY STORE F INTO S0	% SAVE F REG. IN THIS SUBROUTINE
2	11A3	MOVE Y TO L	% HOLD MULTIPLICAND IN L, TO BE
			% ITERATIVELY ADDED TO PRODUCT
3	8A18	MOVE 24 TO FL	% FIND MOST SIGNIFICANT BIT OF
4	8100	MOVE 0 TO Y	% MULTIPLIER, BY NORMALIZING IT
5	0003	NORMALIZE	% AND AVOID UNNECESSARY SHIFTS
6	10A2	MOVE X TO T	% PUT M'ER WHERE IT CAN BE SHIFTD
7	8000	MOVE 0 TO X	% XY WILL BE PRODUCT, INITIALIZE
8	0061	MULT CARRY 0	% INITIALIZE CARRY INTO LSB
9	4067	IF T(0) THEN	% EACH '1' BIT IN MULTIPLIER
		BEGIN	% MEANS ADD MULTIPLICAND
10	10AB	MOVE X TO FA	% SAVE HIGH-ORDER BITS
11	13A0	MOVE L TO X	% DO LOW-ORDER BITS FIRST
12	10EB	MOVE SUM TO TAS	% HOLD NEW LOW BITS; FREE XY
13	18A0	MOVE FA TO X	% POSSIBLE CARRY INTO HIGH-ORDER
14	8100	MOVE 0 TO Y	% BITS, SO ADD INTO THEM
15	10E0	MOVE SUM TO X	% HIGH-ORDER BITS OF NEW PRODUCT
16	1BA1	MOVE TAS TO Y	% BRING BACK LOW-ORDER BITS
		END	%
17	06C1	COUNT FL DOWN BY 1	% ITERATE ONCE FOR EACH MM'ER BIT
18	5782	IF FL=0 THEN	% IF ALL MULTIPLIER BITS HAVE
		BEGIN	% BEEN CONSIDERED, THEN XY IS
19	0050	LOAD F FROM S0	% COMPLETE PRODUCT
20	1BA4	EXIT	% RETURN TO FETCH NEXT S-INSTRUC.
		END	
21	A281	SHIFT T LEFT BY 1 BIT	% EXAMINE NEXT MULTIPLIER BIT
22	0501	SHIFT XY LEFT BY 1 BIT	% ALIGN PRODUCT FOR NEXT ADDITION
23	D010	GO TO MULT	%

Figure 4.3-5. B1726 Microprogram to form unsigned product of 2 twenty-fou
bit integers. (While this microprogram and the one in Figure 4.3-6 use
Burroughs' MIL language, they are not instances of Burroughs software or

firmware but merely illustrative examples prepared especially for this book. Burroughs software and firmware is better documented than the microprograms shown here.)

Comments: General - Multiplier in X register, multiplicand in Y, result in X and Y.

1. Save F register in scratchpad register zero, so that it can be used in this routine.

2. Move Y, the multiplicand, to L.

3. Use move eight bit literal microinstruction to set FL, to count number of times through loop.

4. Set Y to zero. The move eight bit literal microinstruction moves the eight bit literal (zero in this case) right justified into iCe destination and left fills the destination with zeros.

5. Shift X, the multiplier, left until the leftmost bit is one. For each bit shifted, decrement FL by one.

6. Move X, the normalized multiplier to T.

7. Set X to zero.

8. Set the carry flip flop to zero.

9. Test the leftmost bit of the T register. If it is not one, then go to step 17.

10. Here the leftmost bit of the shifted multiplier is one, so we'll add the multiplicand to the accumulated partial product. Save X, the high order bits of the accumulated partial product, in the FA register.

11. Move L, the multiplicand, to X.

135

12. Move the sum of the X register (the multiplicand), the Y register (the rightmost bits of the accumulated partial product), and the carry flip flop (zero) to the top of the address stack (TAS).

13. Move FA, the high order bits of the accumulated product, to X.

14. Set Y to zero.

15. Move the sum of the X register (the high order bits of the accumulated product), the Y register (which contains zero), and the carry flip flop (which may have been set by the addition in step 12) to the X register.

16. Move the top of the address stack (the low order bits of the accumulated product) to the Y register. At this point the multiplicand has been added to the accumulated partial product in the X and Y regs.

17. Decrement FL, which counts the number of times through the loop, by one.

18. If FL is not equal to zero go to step 21.

19. Here FL is zero so we have computed the product in X and Y. Restore the F register from scratchpad register 0.

20. Exit, i.e., move the address from the top of the address stack (the address of the microroutine to fetch the next machine language instruction) to the control store address register.

21. Shift the T register (which contains the multiplier) left one bit.

22. Shift the X and Y registers (which contain the accumulated partial product) left one bit.

23. Go back to step 8.

No.	Code	Source image	Comments
1	28A1	BUBBLE	MOVE S1A TO FA	% BEGIN BY EXAMINING TOP ELEMENT
2	8A00		MOVE 0 TO FL	% INITIALIZE ADDRESS OF LAST SWAP
3	7110	AGAIN	READ 16 BITS TO X INC FA	% FETCH I-TH ARRAY ELEMENT
4	7050		READ 16 BITS TO Y	% FETCH (I+1)-TH ARRAY ELEMENT
5	4C83		IF X>Y THEN	% ARRAY IS ORDERED IF ITH<(I+1)TH
			BEGIN	
6	7870		WRITE 16 BITS REVERSE FROM Y	% PUT (I+1)TH INTO ITH SLOT
7	7810		WRITE 16 BITS FROM X	% PUT I-TH INTO (I+1)-TH SLOT
8	18AA		MOVE FA TO FL	% RECORD ADDRESS OF THIS SWAP
			END	
9	18A1		MOVE FA TO Y	% COMPARE CURRENT ADDRESS
10	20B1		MOVE S1B TO X	% WITH BOTTOM OF UNORDERED PART
11	5C99		IF X>Y THEN GO TO AGAIN	% IF NOT AT BOTTOM, REPEAT
12	2A91		MOVE FL TO S1B	% SAVE ADDRESS OF BOTTOM OF UNORD
13	579D		IF FL_0 THEN GO TO BUBBLE	% IF ANY SWAPS WERE DONE REPEAT
14	1BA4		EXIT	% NO SWAPS MEANS ARRAY IS ORDERED

Figure 4.3-6. B1726 microprogram to sort an array of integers in main memory.

Comments

General: Scratchpad register one contains the main memory address of the first
word in the array (in the A part of the scratchpad register) and the
main memory address of the last word in the array (in the B part).

1. Move the address of the start of the array into the FA register.

2. Set the FL register to zero. The FL register will be assigned the address of
the last pair of interchanged words.

3. Read a word from memory addressed by the FA register into the X register and

increment the FA register.

4. Read a word from memory addressed by the FA register into the Y register.

5. If X is not greater than Y (the words are in proper order) then go to step 9.

6. Here the pair of words in memory are not in proper order and need to be interchanged. Write Y into memory at the location where X was. Note that the REVERSE option obviates changing the FA register which addresses memory.

7. Write X into memory at the location where Y was to complete the interchange.

8. Move the FA register to the FL register to save the address of this interchange.

9. Set Y to FA, the address of the current word in memory being considered.

10. Set X to scratchpad register one part B, the memory address of the last word in the array.

11. If X > Y, i.e., if the current word is not the last one to be tested, go back to step 3 to compare the next pair of words.

12. At this point we have compared successive pairs of words in the memory array. If no interchanges were made then the arrray is in order and the microprogram is complete. Move FL, the address of the last interchanged word, to scratchpad register one part B.

13. If FL is not zero, i.e., an interchange was performed, then go back to step 1 to make another pass.

14. Exit from this microprogram.

have limited scope and statements may be grouped for conditional execution. There is a segmentation facility and an IF...THEN...ELSE... statement. Machine components may be given symbolic names. There are general compile time facilities – text substitution, macro definition and invocation, conditional compilation, and library inclusion. Statements use imperative English verbs (giving the language a COBOL flavor), symbolically named objects, prepositional phrases, and a few subordinate clauses. Unfortunately, Burroughs restricts the distribution of the details of MIL and its translator.

4.3.5 Sample B1726 Microprograms

Figures 4.3-5 and 4.3-6 illustrate some simple microprograms for the B1726 written in MIL.

Bibliography

A. CASH-8

1. "CASH-8 Computer Controller."

2. "CASH-8 Reference Manual," June 15, 1973.
            Available from
                    Standard Logic Inc.
                    3841 South Main
                    Santa Ana, California 92707

B. B1700

1. W. T. Wilner, "Microprogramming Environment on the Burroughs B1700," COMPCON 72 Digest of Papers, IEEE, September 1972, pages 103-106.

2. W. T. Wilner, "Design of the Burroughs B1700," 1972 Fall Joint Computer Conference Proceedings, AFIPS Press, Montvale, New Jersey, pages 489-497.

3. W. T. Wilner, "Burroughs B1700 Memory Utilization," 1972 Fall Joint Computer Conference Proceedings, AFIPS Press, Montvale, New Jersey, pages 579-586.

4. "Burroughs B1700 Systems Reference Manual Preliminary Edition," Burroughs Corporation, Detroit, Michigan, 1972.

CHAPTER 5

COMPUTERS WITH DIAGONAL MICROINSTRUCTIONS

5.1 Introduction

A number of currently available computers have microinstructions with the capability to perform one basic microoperation and one or more special purpose microoperations like memory input/output and conditional branching. Owing to the limited parallelism such microinstructions cannot be classified as vertical or horizontal; we call them diagonal. Owing to the large variety of capabilities of microinstructions on different machines, however, it is difficult to categorize most microinstructions as uniquely vertical, diagonal, or horizontal. The classification in our discussion is based to some extent on comparisons among machines.

In this chapter we examine in some detail the characteristics of four machines which have diagonal microinstructions. Of the four computers, one has twenty-four bit microinstructions and three have thirty-two bit microinstructions, but the uses, architectures, and supported machine languages of the different computers vary considerably. The chapter concludes with brief discussions of a few other computers that employ diagonal microinstructions.

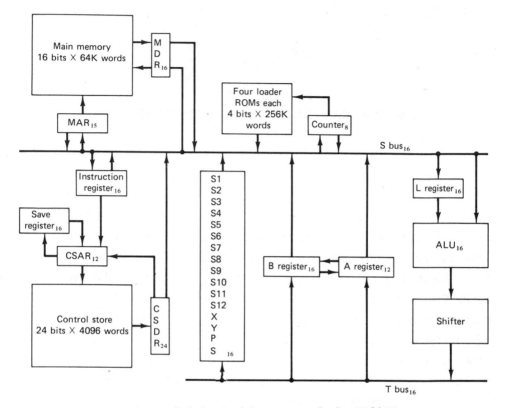

Figure 5.2-1. Architecture of the HP21MX.

5.2 The Hewlett-Packard HP21MX

5.2.1 HP21MX Background

The Hewlett-Packard HP21MX Series is a family of general purpose minicomputers featuring user microprogramming and a choice of semiconductor memory systems. The first two computers in the series are the HP2105A and the HP2108A, announced around May 1974. These computers have a machine instruction repertoire of 128 instructions, eighty of which are identical to the instructions of the earlier Hewlett-Packard HP2100, which was also user microprogrammable. The forty—eight new instructions perform indexing, byte and bit manipulation, byte and word moves, byte string scanning, and single precision floating point instructions. The main difference between the HP2105A and the HP2108A is size (the HP2108A supports more main memory and I/O channels). Even though most processor characteristics of the two machines are identical, here we concentrate on the HP2108A.

5.2.2 HP21MX Architecture

5.2.2.1 HP21MX Functional Characteristics

Although it resembles its predecessor, the HP2100, in many ways, the HP21MX provides additional and more general facilities to the microprogrammer. The architecture of the HP21MX, illustrated in Figure 5.2-1, is based on a simple bus structure that connects the various functional units.

The control store is a simple array that is physically realized as sixteen 256 word sections. Sections 0 and 1, implemented in ROM, contain the microinstructions that interpret the basic instruction set. Sections 14 and 15, also implemented in ROM, contain the microinstructions that interpret the floating point instructions and the instructions in the extended instruction group. Sections 2 through 11 may be used for additional Hewlett—Packard developed microprograms (such as those to perform Fortran functions and decimal arithmetic operations) or user developed microprograms, and sections 12 and 13 are reserved for user microprograms. These sections may be implemented as writable or read only memories. Both the writable and read only control store sections have a read access time of 60 n sec. The twenty—four bit microinstructions are basically vertical but do allow some special operations to be performed in parallel with the basic operation, which is usually an ALU operation. In addition to the usual control store address register and control store data register, the HP21MX has a twelve bit save register that may store control store addresses.

The HP21MX ALU/shifter uses the typical two input - one output structure. The shifter is serially connected to the ALU output so that an ALU result may be shifted during the execution of the same microinstruction that computed it. Inputs to the ALU are the sixteen bit Latch (L) register and the S bus, which is the primary vehicle for communication among the various functional units. Results are put on the T bus for assignment to local store registers. ALU operations include

1. add   6. exclusive or
2. subtract   7. nand
3. multiply step   8. nor
4. divide step   9. increment by one
5. not(complement)   10. decrement by one.

The ALU can perform several additional operations such as adding the S bus value, the complement of the L register, and one. A wide variety of shift operations can be performed - arithmetic and logical, circular and end off, single and double word, and right and left. To assist in double word shift operations, the HP21MX utilizes a pair of registers, the A and B registers, and a one bit extend register to connect them. The extend register may also indicate a carry from the most significant bit of the A or B register in operations like add, subtract, or multiply step. The extend register may be selectively assigned a value or tested under microprogram control. Another register associated with the ALU is the one bit overflow register which, when set, indicates that an ALU result contains too many bits to represent in a machine register. Six other flags are associated with the ALU to indicate special conditions.

In addition to the A, B, L, and other registers which serve special purposes in their association with the ALU/shifter, there are several local store registers that serve a variety of purposes. There is a sixteen word array of sixteen bit registers that contains twelve scratch pad registers for general use and four registers that serve special purposes:

1. the X and Y registers serve as index registers for machine language instructions,

2. the P register serves as the machine language program (location) counter, and

3. the S register serves as a general purpose register for machine instructions and for storage of the front panel switch register.

The eight bit counter register, which can be incremented while the ALU performs another operation, is used in repeat microinstructions and as a loop index in microprograms. The instruction register holds a sixteen bit machine language instruction. Associated with the instruction register are tables which determine the control store address of the microprogram to interpret the machine instruction. To further facilitate machine instruction decoding, parts of the instruction register may be assigned to the S bus. Each of the four loader ROMs contains 256 four bit bytes which can be assigned to the S bus. The two most significant bits in the instruction register select one of the four ROMs, and the eight bit counter register indicates which byte in the selected ROM is to be assigned to the S bus.

23   Type 1 — Common   0

Operation	ALU	S bus	Store	Special

Type 2 — Immediate

Immediate operation	Modifier	Operand	Store	Special

Type 3 — Conditional jump

Jump operation	Condition	T F	Operand	CNDX special code

Type 4 — Unconditional jump

Jump operation		Operand	Jump modifier

Figure 5.2-2. HP21MX microinstruction formats.

The main memory in the HP21MX is entirely solid state
semiconductor. The memory cycle time is 650 n sec, which is
twice the microinstruction execution time, and the word length
is sixteen bits. Associated with the main memory are a memory
address register and a sixteen bit memory data register. Memory
may be expanded to 64K words with a memory management unit.

5.2.2.2 HP21MX Microinstruction Repertoire

The HP21MX microinstructions may be classified into the
four types shown in Figure 5.2-2. Type-1 microinstructions
indicate data transfers and ALU functions. The twelve
operations (microorders in Hewlett-Packard terminology)
indicated by the operation field include shifts, multiply step,
divide step, read memory, and write memory. The operations
indicated by the ALU field were mentioned earlier. When data is
to be moved from one register to another without
transformation, e.g., the B register to the S register, the ALU

may not perform any operation but simply pass the input data through. The S bus field indicates the register whose contents are to be placed on the S bus, and the store field indicates the register into which data on the T bus (as a result of an ALU/shift operation) or on the S bus is to be stored. The special field indicates special operations such as manipulating the condition registers, incrementing the counter, enabling and disabling interrupts, transferring control to a microprogram based on the instruction in the instruction register, performing shifts on ALU results, checking for main memory protection, repeating the next microinstruction the number of times indicated in the counter register, and moving the save register to the CSAR.

Type—2 microinstructions specify the movement of immediate data to a register. The immediate operation field indicates that the eight bit operand in bits 10 – 17 of the microinstruction are to be placed on the S bus; the other eight bits are all ones. The modifier field indicates whether the eight bits that constitute the operand are to be the most or least significant bits on the S bus. The modifier also specifies whether or not the data on the S bus is to be complemented as it passes through the ALU/shifter to the T bus. The store and special fields are the same as for type-1 microinstructions.

Type—3 microinstructions are indicated by a specific value in each of the jump operation and the CNDX special code fields. The condition field specifies the condition that is to be tested. The conditions include

1. bit 0 of the ALU result equals one,
2. bit 15 of the ALU result equals one,

    3. the four least significant bits of the counter register are all 1's,

    4. the ALU operation generated a carry out,

    5. the extend register equals one,

    6. an interrupt is pending,

    7. bit 2 of the instruction register equals 1,

    8. all sixteen bits of the ALU result were 1's,

    9. the last ALU operation generated an overflow, and

    10. the last shift result was 0.

The TF field indicates whether the tested condition should be true or false for the branch to occur. Note that the operand, which is moved to the CSAR if the appropriate conditions hold, has only nine bits, so that the branch range for the conditional jump microinstruction is 512 words.

    The type-4 microinstructions, which indicate unconditional branches, specify a twelve bit address – a branch range of 4096 words. The two unconditional branch operations are branch and subroutine call (which saves the address of the next microinstruction in the save register and then branches). The jump modifier may indicate one of the following: disable normal interrupts, jump to the address of the microprogram routine to execute the instruction in the instruction register, replace the four least significant bits (bits 0-3) of the operand with bits 0-3 of the instruction register, replace the four least significant bits of the operand with bits 4-7 of the instruction register, and jump to the address in the save register.

    While the format of the HP21MX microinstructions is basically vertical, the capability of some microinstructions to perform additional operations, such as those indicated in the special field, indicate a horizontal influence. The two level encoding is generally based on the operation indicated in bits 23-20 of each microinstruction. Microinstruction execution time

148

is 325 n sec, and the fetch and execute phases are overlapped.

5.2.3 HP21MX Microprogrammability

A significant portion of the control store in the HP21MX may be implemented as a writable memory for user written microprograms. Microprograms can be loaded into writable control store under program control by calling a utility program that treats writable control store as an I/O device and loads it from main memory. Alternatively, microprograms may be "burned" into a programmable read only memory and physically inserted into the machine. The machine instructions 105XXX and 101XXX (base 8), where X indicates one of the digits zero through seven, indicate that a user microprogram is to be executed. The number XXX determines the control store location of the user microprogram.

The support software for developing HP21MX microprograms runs on the HP21MX computers and includes a microprogram assembler, a microprogram debugger (called the Micro Debug Editor or MDE), and a writable control store I/O utility subroutine. The microprogram assembler accepts an assembler language representation of microinstructions and produces an object file on disk or tape. The assembler language is a fixed column language with seven fields per microinstruction:

1. label (columns 1 - 9),

2. operation (columns 10 - 14),

3. special, CNDX special code, or jump modifier (columns 15 -19),

4. ALU, modifier, or condition (columns 20 - 24),

5. store or TF (columns 25 -29),

6. operand or S bus (columns 30 -39),

149

Command	Meaning
LOAD	Load the object microprogram into main memory
WRITE	Write the object microprogram in main memory into the writable control store (WCS)
READ	Read the microprogram from WCS into main memory
DUMP	Dump the microprogram in main memory onto an external device
PREPARE	Prepare a set of tapes for burning PROMs
VERIFY	Compare the contents of the PROM tapes to the microprogram in main memory
SHOW	Display specified WCS contents
MODIFY	Change specified parts of the microprogram in main memory and in WCS
BREAK	Set a breakpoint at the specified microprogram address
CHANGE	Change the contents of specified registers
EXECUTE	Begin execution at the specified address and continue until control reaches the breakpoint address or until the microprogram completes
MOVE	Move the microprogram to another location
FINISH	Terminate debugger execution

Figure 5.2-3. HP21MX debugger commands.

7. comments (columns 40 - 80).

Mnemonics represent the various operations or operands for the different fields. The debugger reads the object program into main memory, writes it into the writable control store, and allows the user to run the microprogram and monitor its execution. Figure 5.2-3 describes the debugger commands. The writable control store I/O utility subroutine provides the capability to write a microprogram into writable control store

Label	Op Code	Spec-ial	ALU	Store	S bus	Comments

```
* HP21MX MICROPROGRAM TO SWAP MEMORY LOCATIONS
* POINTED TO BY THE A & B REGISTERS
SWAP    READ       INC  M    A        ASSIGN THE A REGISTER TO THE MAR VIA THE
*                                      S BUS. INITIATE MEMORY READ. INC SETS
*                                      UP LOGIC FROM THE T BUS WHICH
*                                      ALLOWS THE A AND B REGISTERS TO BE
*                                      ADDRESSED WHEN TAB MICROORDERS
*                                      ARE USED
        MPCK PASS       M        WHILE MAIN MEMORY IS BEING READ, CHECK
*                                      THE MAR FOR PROTECTION.
             PASS S1    TAB      ASSIGN DATA TO SCRATCH PAD
*                                      REGISTER 1 (S1) VIA THE S BUS, ALU
*                                      (WHICH PASSES DATA UNCHANGED), & T BUS
        READ       INC  M    B        SIMILARLY, STORE THE MEMORY WORD POINTED
        MPCK PASS       M                 TO BY THE B REGISTER INTO SCRATCH
             PASS S2    TAB              PAD REGISTER 2
        WRTE       PASS TAB  S1       ASSIGN SCRATCH PAD REGISTER 1 TO MDR
*                                      (VIA THE S BUS) AND INITIATE MEMORY
*                                      WRITE. NOTE THAT MAR STILL CONTAINS
*                                      ADDRESS OF SECOND OPERAND.
                   INC  M    A        ASSIGN THE A REGISTER TO THE MAR VIA THE
*                                      S BUS. INCREMENT S BUS VALUE TO TEST
*                                      FOR MEMORY PROTECT
        WRTE RTN   PASS TAB  S2       ASSIGN SCRATCH PAD REGISTER 2 TO MDR
*                                      AND INITIATE MEMORY WRITE. RETURN TO
*                                      FETCH NEXT MACHINE INSTRUCTION.
```

Figure 5.2-4. HP21MX microprogram to swap memory locations.

151

```
          Op   Spec-
Label     Code ial  ALU Store S bus          Comments

* HP21MX MICROPROGRAM TO MOVE A GROUP OF WORDS FROM ONE MEMORY LOCATION TO
*   ANOTHER.  ÁSSUME THAT THE A REGISTER CONTAINS THE NEGATIVE VALUE OF THE
*   NUMBER OF WORDS TO BE MOVED, THE FROM ADDRESS IS IN THE B REGISTER, AND
*   THE TO ADDRESS IS IN THE MEMORY LOCATION POINTED TO BY THE P REGISTER.
MOVE               PASS S1   A      ASSIGN SCRATCH PAD REGISTER 1 THE VALUE
*                                     IN THE A REGISTER VIA THE S BUS,
*                                     ALU (WHICH PASSES DATA UNCHANGED),
*                                     AND THE T BUS
          JMP  CNDX TBZ      OUT    IF ALU RESULT WAS ZERO (A REG CONTAINED
*                                     WHICH MEANS MOVE ZERO WORDS) GO TO OU
          READ      INC M    P      ASSIGN THE P REGISTER TO THE MAR VIA THE
*                                     S BUS.  INITIATE MEMORY READ.
                    PASS S2  TAB    ASSIGN DATA, THE TO ADDRESS, TO SCRATCH
*                                     PAD REGISTER 2 VIA THE S BUS, ALU,
*                                     AND T BUS.
LOOP      READ      INC M    B      ASSIGN THE B REGISTER TO THE MAR VIA THE
*                                     S BUS.  INITIATE MEMORY READ.
                    PASS S3  TAB    ASSIGN THE DATA, A MEMORY
*                                     WORD IN THE FROM FIELD, TO SCRATCH
*                                     PAD REGISTER 3
                    INC  M   S2     ASSIGN SCRATCH PAD REGISTER 2 TO MAR, SO
*                                     MAR CONTAINS TO ADDRESS
                    INC  S2  S2     INCREMENT THE TO ADDRESS IN SCRATCH PAD
          WRTE      PASS T   S3     MOVE SCRATCH PAD 3 (WORD IN FROM FIELD)
*                                     TO MDR AND INITIATE MEMORY WRITE
                    INC  B   B      INCREMENT B REGISTER (THE FROM ADDRESS)
                    INC  S1  S1     INCREMENT S1 REGISTER (THE WORD COUNT)
          JMP  CNDX TBZ      RJS LOOP  IF THE LAST ALU RESULT WAS NOT ZERO
*                                     (S1 WAS NOT ZERO, SO NOT ALL WORDS
*                                     HAVE BEEN MOVED), JUMP TO LOOP
OUT            RTN INC  P    P      INCREMENT THE P (PROGRAM COUNTER) TO ONE
```

MORE THAN THE TO ADDRESS AND RETURN
TO FETCH NEXT MACHINE INSTRUCTION

Figure 5.2-5. HP21MX microprogram to move a block of data.

in an assembler, Fortran, or ALGOL program. This routine
obviates the running of the debugger to load a debugged
microprogram into writable control store.

5.2.4 HP21MX Microprogram Examples

Figures 5.2-4 and 5.2-5 illustrate simple HP21MX
microprograms to swap memory locations and to move a block of
data from one memory location to another.

5.2.5 Additional HP21MX Features

In addition to the features already described, the HP21MX
provides facilities for performing I/O and handling interrupts
through microprogramming. The IOG special field operation
specifies that at the beginning of the next I/O cycle (I/O
cycles last 1.625 microseconds) control signals indicated by
bits 6 through 11 of the instruction register are to be sent to
the device indicated by bits 0 through 5 of the instruction
register. One of the store operations assigns data on the S bus
to the I/O bus which is connected to various peripheral
devices. One of the S bus operations assigns data on the I/O
bus to the S bus. Another S bus operation assigns the contents
of an I/O interrupt register to the S bus and generates an
acknowledge interrupt. Pending interrupts may · be detected by
conditional jump microinstructions in which the tested

condition is pending interrupts. If there is a pending interrupt when a jump or return from subroutine microoperation indicates a next address of control store location zero (the location of the routine to fetch and decode machine language instructions), the CSAR is set to four, the location of the interrupt handling microprogram.

5.3 The Digital Scientific META 4*

5.3.1 META 4 Background

The Digital Scientific META 4 is a fast general purpose minicomputer designed for emulation and user microprogramming. Digital Scientific supplies emulators for the IBM 1130 and 1800 as standard products. With a basic microinstruction execution speed of 90 n sec, the META 4 also finds applications in real time processing. User microprogramming, which may enhance the performance of the 1130 and 1800 emulators or be used for special application programs or emulators, is facilitated by a large support software package.

5.3.2 META 4 Architecture

5.3.2.1 META 4 Functional Components

The architecture of the META 4, summarized in Figure 5.3-1, illustrates some common features of microprogrammable minicomputers. Except for the control store and its associated registers, the machine generally uses a sixteen bit word length. Main memory has a capacity of 65,536 sixteen bit words. The cycle time of main memory is 900 n sec, ten times slower than control store. The sixteen bit ALU/shifter performs the operations

* META 4 is a registered trademark.

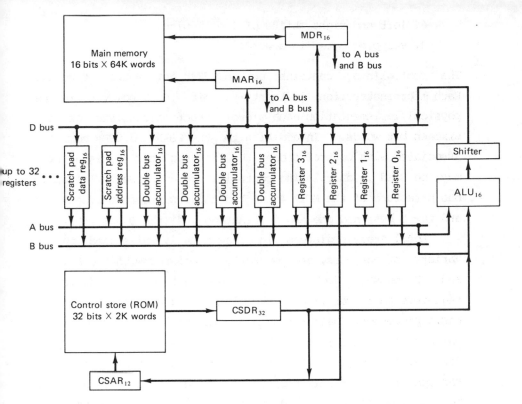

Figure 5.3-1. Organization of the DSC META4.

1. and,

2. or,

3. exclusive or,

4. add,

5. one step of a multiply or divide operation (essentially an add and a shift),

6. left and right shifts of 1 or 8 bits,

8. swapping bytes in a word.

The control store contains up to 2048 thirty-two bit words. Each microinstruction is thirty-two bits long, however, in the physical implementation each microinstruction consists of two sixteen bit words. In addition to the CSAR and CSDR normally associated with control store, the link register (register two) may be used in calculating control store addresses. The basic bus structure of the META 4 has two ALU input busses (the A bus and the B bus) and one ALU destination bus (the D bus).

Local store registers in the META 4, while used for a variety of purposes, are generally associated with the A, B, and D busses. Registers zero through three are dedicated registers that constitute the minimal register set for the basic processor. Register zero always has the value zero and may not be changed; it can be used as a source or as a dummy destination. Register one serves two functions. Bits eight through fifteen of this register constitute a counter which may be set, decremented, and tested under microprogram control. Bits zero through three of register one are condition bits specifying carry, overflow, shift out, and arithmetic sign. Register two (the link register) serves as a source in control store address calculations and hence is used in microprogram sequencing. Register three is a general purpose double bus accumulator, i.e., it may serve as a destination for the ALU result and its value may be transferred to the ALU via the A bus or the B bus. Additional registers are optional and may be included in a particular machine to enhance the performance of certain microprograms. The additional registers constitute four groups:

1. double bus accumulators,
2. memory registers,
3. scratch pad and control registers, and
4. I/O registers.

The double bus accumulators serve the same purpose as register three. The memory registers are pairs of registers associated with the main memory; in each pair of registers one register serves as a memory address register and the other serves as a memory data register. Sixty-four registers constitute a scratch pad memory that is controlled by an address register and a data register. The I/O registers control I/O communication by transferring I/O commands and data.

5.3.2.2 META 4 Microinstruction Repertoire

META 4 microinstructions may be grouped into the four types shown in Figure 5.3-2:

Register-to-register

```
External        Loop   Shift   Shift   Arithmetic
device         Control carry control   carry
control                control         control
```

Register-immediate

```
External
device
control
```

157

Register load

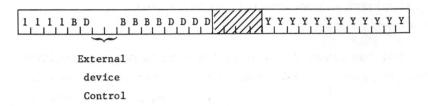

External
device
Control

Branch

External   Test   Bit   Branch   Bit,
Device   for   byte   con-   byte,
Control   Zero   or   trol   or
              or   word   word
              Nonzero test   test

Figure 5.3-2. META 4 microinstruction formats.

Legend: X - bit is part of operation code;
A, B, D - bit is part of A, B, or D bus specification;
I - bit is part of an immediate field;
Y - bit is part of a control store address field.

1. register-to-register,
2. register-immediate,
3. register load, and
4. branch.

The register-to-register microinstructions perform data transformations and moving operations by transferring data from registers via the A bus and B bus to the ALU/shifter, transforming it, and transferring the result to another register via the D bus. The basic operations are and, or, exclusive or, add, multiply step, and divide step. The register-immediate microinstructions are like the register-to-register microinstructions except that a sixteen bit control store literal serves as an ALU input instead of an A bus register. There are four microinstruction in this class. They perform the operations and, or, exclusive or, and add. The register load microinstruction loads a specified destination register with a value resulting from the exclusive or of a register on the B bus and a sixteen bit value from control store. The address of the control store data is the result of the or operation on the control address specified in the microinstruction and the link register. This calculated control store address is the address of a sixteen bit word. While control store words are logically thirty-two bits long, they are physically sixteen bits long so that sixteen bits of data can be easily referenced even though the microinstructions are thirty-two bits long. Although this scheme allows data to reside in control store, microinstructions must be aligned on thirty-two bit word boundaries, i.e., the control store address of a microinstruction must be an even address. The branch microinstruction permits microprogram sequencing by testing all or part of a register for zero or nonzero. If the specified condition is true, the address of the next microinstruction is taken from the literal in the microinstruction.

External device control

        Initiate memory read

        Initiate memory write

        Initiate I/O timing cycle

        Wait for memory or I/O completion

Loop control

        Decrement counter (register 1, bits 8–15) by 1

        Jump to address specified in the link register (register 2)

        Decrement counter and if it is nonzero jump to the address specified

Shift carry control

        Fill the position created by shifting with the shifted out bit

        Fill the position created by shifting with the shift bit from the
            condition register (register 1, bit 2)

Shift control

        Shift ALU result right one bit

        Shift ALU result left one bit

        Shift ALU result right eight bits

        Shift ALU result left eight bits

        Shift ALU result right one bit and introduce appropriate sign

        Replace the leftmost eight bits of the ALU result with the sign bit (the
            leftmost) of the rightmost eight bits of the ALU result

        Exchange the leftmost eight bits of the ALU result with the rightmost
            eight bits of the ALU result

Arithmetic carry control

        Add the carry bit from the condition register (register 1, bit 0) to the
            ALU result

        Add one to the ALU result

Branch control

        Form the branch address by the or of the link register (register 2) with
            the literal address specified in the microinstruction

For a successful branch execute one microinstruction at the branch
location, then return to the microinstruction following the branch
microinstruction (i.e., perform a one microinstruction subroutine)

Bit, byte, or word test
Test entire register
Test rightmost eight bits of register
Test leftmost eight bits of register
Test rightmost eight bits of register and if these do not satisfy the
condition test the leftmost eight bits
Test any bit in register

Figure 5.3-3. Summary of META 4 modifiers.

From this discussion and Figure 5.3-2, it is evident that
META 4 microinstructions are basically vertical
microinstructions. Bits zero through three specify an operation
code, and two level encoding is used. The META 4
microinstructions, however, have the capability of specifying
modifiers to provide more power. These modifiers, indicated by
bracketed descriptions in Figure 5.3-2, give the
microinstructions some parallel execution facilities, so the
microinstructions are classified as diagonal. Figure 5.3-3
summarizes the operations indicated by the modifiers.

5.3.3 META 4 Microprogrammability
The META 4 control store is a ROM that can be simply
prepared by users. The control store is implemented on 16 or
more logic boards, each of which contains 32 thirty-two bit

```
              Op   B  D  A
Label Code Registers Operand Modifiers Comments


   * META 4 MICROPROGRAM TO PERFORM A BLOCK MOVE INSTRUCTION
   *  MOVE N WORDS OF MEMORY FROM ONE LOCATION TO ANOTHER.
   *   OVERLAPPING FIELDS CAUSE UNDEFINED RESULT.
   *   REGISTER USAGE:
   *       SP REGISTER - ADDRESS OF SOURCE FIELD, UPDATED AS WE GO
   *                       ALONG.
   *       DP REGISTER - ADDRESS OF DESTINATION FIELD, ALSO UPDATED.
   *       L REGISTER - LENGTH OF SOURCE & DESTINATION FIELDS, = 0 ON
   *                       RETURN
   *
1 MOVE BRZ  L          RET   W       IF L IS ZERO, JUST RETURN.
2 LOOP MOVE SP MA            MR      READ A WORD FROM SOURCE FIELD,
3       ADDI SP SP   1               AND INCREMENT SP
4       MOVE DP MA                   SELECT CORRESPONDING WORD IN
   *                     DESTINATION
5       ADDI DP DP   1               FIELD, AND INCREMENT DP.
6       MOVE MD MD          PZ,MW    WRITE SOURCE WORD INTO DESTINATION
7       SUBI L  L    1               DECREMENT LENGTH,
8       BNZ  L        LOOP  W         AND DO ANOTHER IF NOT EXHAUSTED.
   RET  RETURN
```

Figure 5.3-4. META 4 microprogram to perform a block move instruction.

Comments:

1. If L (the W modifier specifies test the entire L register) is zero, branch to RET

2. Move SP to MAR (memory address register) and initiate memory read (MR modifier)

3. Increment SP by adding the one in the immediate field.

4. Move DP to MAR (and wait for previous read to complete)

5. Increment DP

6. Wait for memory read to complete (PZ modifier), move the MDR (memory data register) to itself, and write the data from the MDR (that was just read) into memory at the destination address

7. Subtract one from the L register

8. If the L register is not zero branch to LOOP to move next word

words. The bits in each ROM board are initially set to one and may be changed to zero by manually removing metallic spots.

To aid the user in writing microprograms for the META 4, Digital Scientific provides a software utility package. This package includes a microprogram assembler, simulator, and ROM board image lister. The microprogram assembler language uses a fixed column format with fields for label, operation, B bus register, D bus register, operand (e.g., an immediate operand or address), modifiers and comments, and an eight character identifier. The assembler is a two pass assembler that runs on the META 4 with the IBM 1130 emulator or on the 1130 itself. It produces an object file on disk. Once a microprogram has been assembled it can be simulated with the "ROM Debug Package." This simulator, which also runs on the 1130 or the META 4 1130 emulator, performs the actions of the META 4 microinstructions and provides facilities for defining a particular META 4

```
           Op   B  D  A
Label  Code  Registers  Operand  Modifiers  Comments

  * META 4 MICROPROGRAM TO PERFORM A TABLE SEARCH
  *    SEARCH A TABLE OF WORDS FOR ONE MATCHING THE SUPPLIED KEY.
  *    REGISTER USAGE:
  *         TP - THIS REGISTER POINTS TO THE FIRST TABLE ENTRY UPON
  *              STARTING.
  *              IT WILL BE UPDATED TO POINT TO THE MATCHING ENTRY.
  *         TL - THIS REGISTER CONTAINS THE LENGTH OF THE TABLE.  IT WILL
  *              BE DECREMENTED AS WE SEARCH.  IF IT EQUALS ZERO UPON
  *              RETURN, THEN THERE WAS NO MATCHING ENTRY.
  *         KY - THIS REGISTER CONTAINS THE KEY FOR WHICH WE ARE LOOKING.
  *
1 SRCH BRZ  TL        RET     W       IF TL IS ZERO, JUST RETURN.
2 LOOP MOVE TP MA             MR      FETCH A TABLE ENTRY VIA TP.
3      XOR  MD R3 KY           PZ      IS THE ENTRY EQUAL TO THE KEY
4      BRZ  R3        RET     W       IF YES, WE ARE ALL DONE
5      ADDI TP TP     1               IF NO INCREMENT TP TO NEXT ENTRY
6      SUBI TL TL     1               DECREMENT TL,
7      BNZ  TL        LOOP    W       AND SEARCH IF TL NOT EXHAUSTED.
  RET   RETURN
```

Figure 5.3-5. META 4 microprogram to perform a table search.

Comments:

1. If TL (the W modifier specifies test the entire TL register) is zero branch to RET

2. Move TP to MAR (memory address register) and initiate memory read (MR modifier)

3. Wait for the memory read to complete (PZ modifier), set register R3 to the exclusive or of the MDR (memory data register) and the KY register

4. If register R3 is zero (the key matches the word read from memory) branch to RET

5. Increment TP by adding the one in the immediate field

6. Subtract one from TL

7. If the TL register is not zero branch to LOOP to check next word in table

configuration, loading an assembled microprogram into a simulated control store, loading programs and data into simulated main memory, changing the contents of a register, a control store word, or a main memory word, setting and clearing trace points, step-by-step simulation, and saving the contents of simulated control store. The ROM board image lister reads an assembled object microprogram and prints a table from which ROM boards are easily peeled.

5.3.4 META 4 Examples

Figures 5.3-4 through 5.3-6 illustrate some sample META 4 microprograms. Figures 5.3-4 and 5.3-5 show how the META 4 performs the simple operations of moving several words in main memory from one location to another and sequentially searching a table of main memory words for a specified key. Figure 5.3-6 illustrates the more complex operation of multiplying two

165

```
        Op   B  D  A
Label  Code  Registers  Operand  Modifiers  Comments

   * META 4 MICROPROGRAM TO PERFORM A MULTIPLY INSTRUCTION
   *    MULTIPLY TWO SIGNED NUMBERS IN TWOS COMPLEMENT NOTATION,
   *    PRODUCING A DOUBLE PRECISION SIGNED PRODUCT.
   *    REGISTER USAGE:
   *         MC - MULTIPLICAND REGISTER
   *         MR - MULTIPLIER REGISTER UPON ENTRY, THEN USED TO CONTAIN
   *              HIGH ORDER WORD OF PRODUCT.
   *         WK - REGISTER THAT HOLDS MULTIPLIER DURING LOOP, AND CONTAINS
   *              LOW ORDER WORD OF PRODUCT WHEN DONE.
   *         CT - COUNTER REGISTER
   *         LK - LINK REGISTER
   *
 1 MULT COPY MR WK        R1,SO   SHIFT MULTIPLIER TO WK, SAVING LOW
   *                              ORDER BIT
 2      MOVE 0  MR                CLEAR HIGH ORDER PRODUCT WORD
 3      LDI     CT   15           COUNTER WILL COUNT 15 TIMES,
 4      LDI     LK   LOOP         WHILE LINK IS USED FOR LOOPING.
 5 LOOP MULT MC MR MR     SK,SO   ADD MULTIPLICAND TO RESULT IF
   *                              MULTIPLIER BIT IS ON, SHIFT RESULT.
 6      COPY WK WK        R1,SI,SO,D,J  SAVE NEXT BIT OF MULTIPLIER,
   *                              SHIFT IN LOW ORDER RESULT
   *                              BIT, AND LOOP 15 TIMES.
 7      BS           MRNG        JUMP IF MULTIPLIER IS LESS THAN
   *                              ZERO.
 8      COPY MR MR        SK,SO   ADJUST HIGH ORDER RESULT,
 9      JMP          AJLO        AND GO ADJUST LOW ORDER.
10 MRNG XORI MC MC   FFFF$       MULTIPLIER IS LESS THAN ZERO SO ADD
11      MULT MC MR MR     +1,SK,SO  MULTIPLICAND TO HIGH ORDER RESULT
   *                              AND ADJUST
```

166

```
12 AJLO COPY WK WK              R1,SI   ADJUST LOW ORDER RESULT.
        RETURN
```

Figure 5.3-6 META 4 microprogram to perform a multiply instruction.

Additional Comments

1. Shift MR register right one bit (R1 modifier), save the shifted out bit (SO modifier), and move the shifted result to WK

2. Set MR to zero

3. Set counter to fifteen

4. Set link register (register 2) to address of microinstruction labelled LOOP

5. Add MR to MC if shifted out bit was one, shift the result right one bit, save the shifted out bit (SO modifier), and store the final result in MR

6. Shift WK right one bit (R1 modifier), fill the vacated position with previous shifted out bit (SI modifier), save the shifted out bit (SO modifier), decrement the counter (D modifier), and jump to LOOP if the counter is not zero

7. Branch to MRNG if the shifted out bit is one, i.e., if the multiplier was less than zero

8. Shift MR right one bit and adjust the sign of MR (SK modifier), and save the shifted out bit (SO modifier)

9. Jump to AJLO

10. Here the multiplier is less than zero, so complement the MC regis

11. Same as step 5 but add one to the ALU result (the +1 modifier)

12. Adjust the low order word of the product by shifting WK right one
    bit (R1 modifier), filling the vacated position with the previous
    shifted out bit (SI modifier), and storing the result in WK

signed numbers (in twos complement representation) and
generating a double precision signed product. Note the
extensive use of modifiers in this example, especially in the
two microinstruction loop that forms the partial product.

5.4 The INTERDATA Model 85

5.4.1 INTERDATA Model 85 Background

The INTERDATA Model 85 is a fast, low-cost minicomputer
designed to perform a wide range of industrial control, data
processing, and scientific computations. With an architecture
much like that of the IBM System/360 (except that the word
length is sixteen bits), the INTERDATA Model 85 is upward
compatible with several minicomputers in the INTERDATA family -
Models 3, 4, 5, 70, 74, and 80. Indeed the Model 85 is
essentially a Model 80 with the addition of a 1024 word
writable control store (called "Dynamic Control Store" - DCS)
for user microprograms, and instructions to reference it.

168

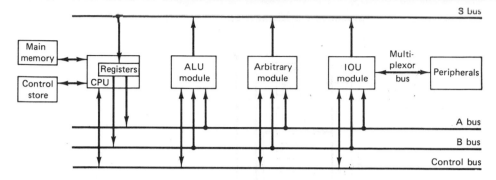

Figure 5.4-1. INTERDATA Model 85 system level architecture.

5.4.2 INTERDATA Model 85 Architecture

5.4.2.1 INTERDATA Model 85 Functional Components

Viewed from the system level, the architecture of the INTERDATA 85 consists of a set of basic modules which communicate with one another over a common bussing structure (see Figure 5.4-1). Microinstructions direct the flow of information among the modules (over the A, B, and S busses) and specify operations the modules are to perform (over the C bus). The basic machine has three modules - the CPU (which contains the processor registers and controls main memory, control store, microinstruction sequencing, and other functions), the ALU, and the Input/Output Unit. Five additional modules, such as floating point, Boolean manipulators, or special purpose modules, may be added to the machine.

The control store of the INTERDATA 85 is a simple array (see Figure 5.4-2) of thirty-two bit words. Microinstructions are also thirty-two bits long, and the control store may store data as well as microinstructions. In the standard control store there are 2048 words, the first 1024 interpret the machine language instruction set and are implemented in a ROM which has a 60-n sec access time. The remaining 1024 words are writable under program control and have an access time of 150

169

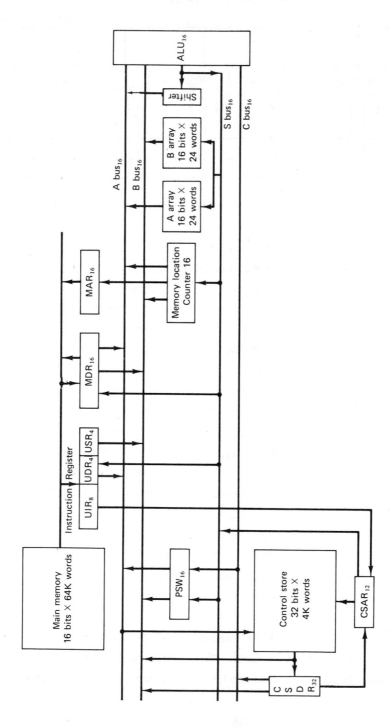

Figure 5.4-2. Architecture of the INTERDATA Model 85.

n sec. With a 100-n sec processor clock, the INTERDATA 85 fetches and executes simple microinstructions from ROM in 200 n sec and from writable control store in 300 n sec. The usual control store address register and control store data register are associated with the control store. The INTERDATA 85 does not have dedicated registers associated with the CSAR for storing microprogram addresses, but rather the CSAR is connected to the S bus so that data in the CSAR may be stored in registers connected to the S bus.

The INTERDATA 85 arithmetic and logic unit is one of the standard machine modules shown in Figure 5.4-1. Communication with the ALU is asynchronous. While the ALU can perform most operations in 100 n sec (so that microinstruction execution time from ROM is around 200 n sec), for operations that require additional time (such as shifts, multiplies, and divides), the ALU does not respond with a completion cycle until it has computed the result. ALU inputs are taken from the A and B busses. The ALU results are output to the S bus, and special conditions (such as carry) are put on the C bus. The ALU operations reflect the machine language operations:

1. add,
2. add with carry,
3. subtract,
4. subtract with carry,
5. and,
6. exclusive or,
7. or,
8. single and double shifts (logical left and right, arithmetic left and right, and circular left and right),
9. multiply (signed and unsigned), and
10. divide.

The multiply, divide, and double-shift operations can only be performed on the twenty-four general registers in the A and B arrays. The hardware multiply and divide operations are somewhat unusual for a minicomputer. Their execution time of 2.1 microseconds is significantly faster than the time that would be required to execute a microprogrammed sequence of shift and add or subtract operations.

The local store of the INTERDATA 85 has several registers, some of which are used for special purposes (see Figure 5.4-2). The general purpose registers are in the A and B arrays, each of which contains 24 sixteen bit words. The A and B arrays are logically identical (i.e., corresponding registers in the two arrays contain the same value), however, they are physically separate so that different values may be read onto the A and B busses simultaneously. The first sixteen registers in each array represent the sixteen general purpose registers seen by the machine language programmer. The remaining eight registers in each array are for general purpose use by the microprogrammer. The remaining three registers have special purposes in implementing the machine instruction set. The memory location counter (MLC) is a sixteen bit register that contains the address of the next machine instruction to be executed. The MLC can, under microprogram control, be incremented by two, incremented by four, and stored in the memory address register. The instruction register, which has three parts, contains the first sixteen bits of the machine language instruction being executed. The first part of the instruction register is the UIR, which contains the eight bit machine operation code. It is transformed to the control store address of the microprogram that interprets the represented operation. The UDR and USR are four bit subregisters that contain the numbers of the destination and source registers for

172

various operations. The bits in the Program Status Register contain the Program Status Word (PSW) and are used to control hardware interrupts and indicate the condition code of the machine (e.g., overflow bit, shift out bit, and sign of arithmetic operation bit).

In keeping with the philosophy of asynchronous external communications, main memory operates only on request by a microinstruction. Associated with main memory are the normal memory address register and memory data register. The main memory is partially overlapped so that a thirty-two bit machine language instruction may be fetched in 480 n sec. The first sixteen bits of a fetched thirty-two bit instruction are assigned to the instruction register and the last sixteen bits are assigned to the memory data register.

5.4.2.2 INTERDATA 85 Microinstruction Repertoire

Figure 5.4-3 illustrates the basic microinstruction formats for the INTERDATA 85. In keeping with the modular system architecture, the first three bits of a microinstruction select the module which is to perform the microinstruction.

Module zero is the control (CPU) module. Its microinstructions have a different format than those for other modules. In executing the address link microinstruction the address of the next microinstruction is stored into the register specified in the link register field. Then if the condition indicated in the F field (see Figure 5.4-4) is true, a branch to the address in the control store address field is performed. The register link microinstruction is executed similarly except that the branch address is contained in bits three through fourteen (the least significant twelve bits) of the register indicated by the B field, and the bits in the address mask field are used to mask the low order six bits of

173

Control Module Microinstructions

Address link

0 0 0 1	X	E	D	MC	Link register	F	Control store address	*

Register link

0 0 0 0	X	E	D	MC	Link register	F	B	Address mask	////

Microinstructons for other modules

Register-to-register and transfer

M	0 0	I	S	A	F	B	Address	C

Register-to-register control

M	0 1	I	S	A	F	B	K	E	D	MC

Register immediate

M	1 0	I	S	A	F	Immediate

Control store write

Figure 5.4-3. INTERDATA model 85 microinstruction formats.

Legend: A - addresses first operand register (A bus);

B - addresses second operand register (B bus);

C - indicates conditional transfer if set;

D - decodes next machine instruction;

E - enables setting of condition code;

F - selects function of addresses module (see Figure 5.4-4 for
      control module microinstructions);

I - indicates that second operand (B) is an immediate address;

K - extends F field;

M - indicates module address;

MC - indicates memory operation;

S - addresses result register (S bus);

X - indicates an execute rather than a branch.

this address. In addition to storing an address in a register
and performing a conditional branch operation, the control
module microinstructions can perform a memory operation and
decode the next user machine instruction. The MC field controls
the memory operations, details of which are illustrated in
Figure 5.4-5. The D field controls decoding the next user
microinstruction which involves determining the control store
address of the appropriate microprogram and transferring
control to it. The E field enables setting the condition code
(bits twelve through fifteen of the PSW). The X field, when

175

F Field	Condition
0000	ALU result = 0
0001	ALU result < 0
0010	ALU result > 0
0011	(User M1 field & Condition code) = 0
0100	ALU result not = 0
0101	ALU result >= 0
0110	ALU result <= 0
0111	(User M1 field & Condition code) not = 0
1000	ALU carry
1001	ALU overflow
1010	Unconditional
1011	Unconditional (and enable interrupts)
1100	No ALU carry
1101	No ALU overflow
1110	Unconditional (mask console interrupt)
1111	Unconditional (and disable interrupts)

Figure 5.4-4. Test conditions indicated by F field for control module microinstructions on the INTERDATA model 85.

set, indicates that instead of branching to the indicated control store address, only one microinstruction at the branch address should be performed, i.e., a one microinstruction subroutine is performed.

There are four types of microinstructions for other modules. Bits three and four of these microinstructions determine the format of the microinstruction. The register-to-register and transfer microinstruction is effectively a four address instruction in that it indicates the

First two

bits of

MC field	Memory operation
00	No operation
01	Initiate instruction read
10	Initiate data read
11	Initiate data write

Last two

bits of

MC field	Register operation
00	No operation
01	Increment MAR by 2*
10	Increment MAR by 4 and increment MLC by 4
11	Set MAR to MLC

Figure 5.4-5. Memory operations indicated by the MC field in INTERDATA model 85 microinstructions.

* if this is done with the initiation of an instruction read, then also increment the MLC by 2.

register addresses of two operands (the A and B fields), the function to be performed (the F field, which represents the ALU and shift operations described earlier), the register address of the result (the S field), and the address of the next microinstruction (the address field). The address field determines the six low-order bits of the next control store address (the high-order bits remain unchanged) if the conditional (C) field is set and the addressed module returns a special signal (for the ALU the signal is the carry condition). The I field, when set, indicates that the B field register is an indirect address. The register-to-register control microinstruction is like the register-to-register and transfer microinstruction except for the addressing. Like the address link microinstruction, the register-to-register control microinstruction provides the capability to perform memory operations, decode the machine language instruction, and enable condition code setting. In addition, it can indicate, via the K field, additional control for the addressed module. When the K field is set, for example, the ALU performs double shifts rather than single shifts. The register immediate microinstruction format is also like that of the register-to-register and transfer microinstruction except that the B and address fields are replaced by a twelve bit immediate field (control store literal) that is sign extended to sixteen bits and substituted for the B operand. The control store write microinstruction specifies that the data in the register addressed by the A field is to be written into control store at the address in the register indicated by the B field. The E, D, and MC fields control condition code setting, instruction decoding, and main memory operations as before.

Although the basic format of several microinstructions emphasizes a single operation, the capability to perform such operations as memory I/O, instruction decoding, and branching in parallel with the primary operation gives the microinstructions a horizontal flavor. Encoding is two level, based on the first five bits of the microinstruction. Microinstruction fetch and execution involves two distinct phases, and the execution of some long microinstructions, e.g., multiply and divide, require several machine clock cycles for completion. The design of microinstructions in the INTERDATA 85 can be seen to depend on the System/360-like machine language instruction repertoire. Register-register (RR) and register-storage (RS) machine instructions often require only one microinstruction for execution. The register-index (RX) instruction involves three or four microinstructions plus a wait for an operand to be read from memory.

5.4.3 INTERDATA 85 Microprogrammability

As mentioned earlier, part of the control store of the INTERDATA 85 is writable under program control. There are four machine language instructions that support access to the writable conrol store. The Branch to Control Store instruction causes an unconditional microprogram branch to an address in control store specified in the instruction. The Write Control Store instruction transfers one or more data words from main memory into control store. The Read Control Store instruction reads one or more data words from control store into main memory. The Enter Control Store instruction transfers microprogram control to one of the first sixteen locations in the writable control store.

To assist the user in preparing microprograms, INTERDATA provides an assembler and a debugger. The assembler language has fields for label, operation, operands and modifiers, and comments as illustrated by the example in the next section. The facilities of the debugging program include entering breakpoints in the microprogram after it has been loaded into control store. This permits full speed testing of selected portions, or all, of the microprogram in writable control store.

179

Flowchart

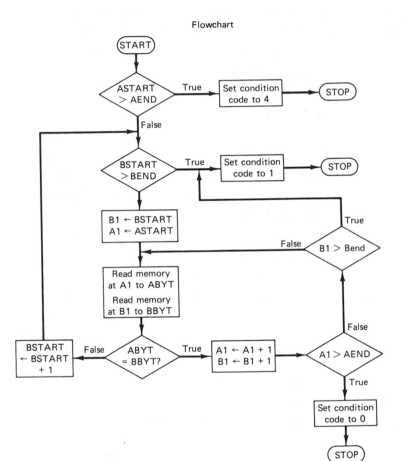

Instruction format

Operation code	R2

Register usage

Register	Contents
R 2	Address of first character in string A
R 2 + 1	Address of last character in string A
R 2 + 2	Address of first character in string B
R 2 + 3	Address of last character in string B

Algorithm

Legend

ASTRT	Starting address of A string
AEND	Ending address of A string
BSTRT	Starting address of B string
BEND	Ending address of B string
B1	Temporary address in B string
A1	Temporary address in A string
ABYT	Character in A string
BBYT	Character in B string
MRi	Memory register i

Figure 5.4-6. Index machine instruction for the INTERDATA Model 85.

5.4.4 INTERDATA 85 Microprogram Example

To illustrate the use of INTERDATA 85 microprogramming capabilities, consider the index machine instruction described in Figure 5.4-6. The index instruction takes as operands two character strings and determines the index of the first string in the second string, i.e., the location in the second string at which the first string starts. Figure 5.4-7 shows an INTERDATA 85 microprogram which implements the index instruction.

181

```
* INTERDATA 85 MICROPROGRAM TO INTERPRET INDEX INSTRUCTION
*
* DEFINE REGISTER USAGE
ASTRT EQU    '10'            ASTRT IS IN REGISTER 10
AEND  EQU    '11'            AEND IS IN REGISTER 11
BEND  EQU    '12'            BEND IS IN REGISTER 12
A1    EQU    '13'            A1 IS IN REGISTER 13
A2    EQU    '14'            A2 IS IN REGISTER 14
ONE   EQU    '15'            ONE IS A REGISTER TO HOLD THE CONSTANT 1
*
* SET UP REGISTERS
INDEX A      YDI,NULL,YSI    UDR (YDI FIELD) <-- USR (YSI FIELD) + 0
      A      ASTRT,YD,NULL   ASTRT <-- CONTENTS OF UDR (YD FIELD) + 0
      AI     YDI,YDI,1       UDR <-- UDR + 1
      A      AEND,YD,NULL    AEND <-- CONTENTS OF UDR + 0
      AI     YDI,YDI,2       UDR <-- UDR + 2
      A      BEND,YD,NULL    BEND <-- CONTENTS OF UDR + 0
      SI     YDI,YDI,1       UDR <-- UDR - 1 (SO UDR CONTAINS BSTRT)
      LI     ONE,1           ONE <-- 1
* TEST TO SEE IF ASTRT > AEND
      SX     MR7,ASTRT,AEND,LOOP1,C   MR7 <-- ASTRT - AEND
*                                     IF RESULT < ZERO BRANCH TO LOOP1
      BALD   ERROR(MR7),IR2  BRANCH TO ERROR AND ENABLE INTERRUPTS
*                            READ NEXT MACHINE INSTRUCTION AND
*                            INCREMENT MAR AND MLC BY 2 BYTES
* TEST TO SEE IF BSTRT > BEND
LOOP1 SX     MR7,YD,BEND,LOOP11,C   MR7 <-- BSTRT - BEND
*                                   IF RESULT < 0 BRANCH TO LOOP11
      BALD   ENDB(MR7),IR2   BRANCH TO ENDB AND ENABLE INTERRUPTS
*                            READ NEXT MACHINE INSTRUCTION AND
*                            INCREMENT MAR AND MLC BY 2 BYTES
* SET A1 AND B1
LOOP11 L     A1,ASTRT        A1 <-- ASTRT
      A      B1,YD,NULL      B1 <-- BSTRT (STORED IN UDR) + 0
* CHECK THAT BYTES AT A1 AND B1 ARE IDENTICAL
```

```
LOOP2 L      MAR,A1,DR        MAR <-- A1, READ MAIN MEMORY INTO MDR
      AI     A1,A1,1          A1 <-- A1 + 1 (DURING WAIT FOR MEMORY READ)
      LB     MR7,NULL,MDR     MR7 <-- FIRST BYTE IN MDR (NEXT BYTE IN A
*                                      STRING)
      L      MAR,B1,DR        MAR <-- B1, READ MAIN MEMORY INTO MDR
      LB     MR6,NULL,MDR     MR6 <-- FIRST BYTE IN MDR (NEXT BYTE IN B
*                                      STRING)
      S      MR6,MR6,MR7      MR6 <-- MR6 - MR7 (COMPARE MR6 AND MR7)
      BALZ   MATCH(MR7)       IF RESULT = 0 (MR6 = MR7) BRANCH TO MATCH
      AX     YD,YD,ONE,LOOP1  BSTRT <-- BSTRT + 1, BRANCH TO LOOP1
* HERE BYTES EQUAL, SEE IF ENTIRE A STRING HAS BEEN EXAMINED
MATCH AI     B1,B1,1          B1 <-- B1 + 1
      SX     MR7,A1,AEND,M1,C    MR7 <-- A1 - AEND, IF RESULT < 0 BRANCH TO
*                                                                        M1
      BALD   ENDA(MR7),IR2    ROUTINE COMPLETE; INDEX IS IN BSTRT,
*                             BRANCH TO ENDA AND ENABLE INTERRUPTS,
*                             READ NEXT MACHINE INSTRUCTION AND INCREMENT
*                             MAR AND MLC BY 2 BYTES
M1    SX     MR7,B1,BEND,LOOP2,C    MR7 <-- B1 - BEND,
*                                IF RESULT < 0 BRANCH TO LOOP2
      BALD   ENDB(MR7),IR2    BRANCH TO ENDB AND ENABLE INTERRUPTS,
*                             READ NEXT MACHINE INSTRUCTION AND
*                             INCREMENT MAR AND MLC BY 2 BYTES
* SET CONDITION CODE AND PREPARE FOR NEXT MACHINE INSTRUCTION
ENDB  NI     PSW,PSW,'FF0'    CLEAR CONDITION CODE (LAST FOUR BITS OF
*                                      PSW)
      O      PSW,PSW,ONE,IRJ,D   SET CONDITION CODE TO ONE, DECODE THE
*                                NEXT USER INSTRUCTION, & READ THE NEXT
*                                INSTRUCTION AND SET MAR <-- MLC
ENDA  NI     PSW,PSW,'FF0'    CLEAR CONDITION CODE
      L      NULL,NULL,IRJ,D  DECODE NEXT USER INSTRUCTION, AND READ THE
*                             NEXT INSTRUCTION AND SET MAR <-- MLC
ERROR NI     PSW,PSW,'FF0'    CLEAR CONDITION CODE
      OI     PSW,PSW,4        SET CONDITION CODE TO 4
      L      NULL,NULL,IRJ,D  DECODE NEXT USER INSTRUCTION, AND READ THE
*                             NEXT INSTRUCTION AND SET MAR <-- MLC
```

Figure 5.4-7. INTERDATA model 85 microprogram to interpret the index instruction.

183

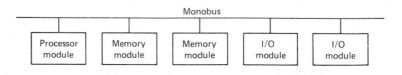

Figure 5.5-1. Microdata 3200 system organization.

5.5 The Microdata 3200

5.5.1 Microdata 3200 Background

The Microdata 3200 is   a modular sixteen bit minicomputer which may be used to emulate a wide range of computer systems. As   the first computer in a family, the Microdata 3200 with specific microprograms is   marketed as   separate Microdata products. The Microdata 3230, for example, is a Microdata 3200 microprogrammed to emulate the Microdata 830 and 1630 series of computers. The Microdata 32/S is a stack-oriented machine that utilizes special features of the 3200 architecture to perform stack operations efficiently. The architecture of the Microdata 32/S was   designed in conjunction with   MPL   (Microdata Programming   Language),   a machine-dependent higher   level programming language based on PL/I. The purpose of MPL is to provide efficient control of the 32/S machine at a level that corresponds to assembler language on most other computers, and furthermore to provide the advantages of   a higher level language to simplify applications such as systems programming and real time programming.

5.5.2 Microdata 3200 Architecture

5.5.2.1 Microdata 3200 Functional Units

The system architecture of the Microdata 3200 (see Figure 5.5-1) consists of a set of independent modules connected to an asynchronous high-speed bus, called the Monobus. Any number of processor, memory, and I/O modules may be attached to the Monobus to a limit of 256K bytes of address space. Figure 5.5-2 illustrates the architecture of the Microdata 3200 CPU. The local store registers and various functional units are connected by a series of busses that are described in subsequent paragraphs.

The Microdata 3200 control store is an array of up to 4,096 thirty-two bit words. As many as 2,048 control store words may contain the microprograms to emulate the Microdata 3230 or 32/S. Additional control store modules may be implemented as read only, programmable read only, or writable memory. The control store cycle time matches the microinstruction execution time of 135 n sec. Associated with control store are the twelve bit control store address bus and the thirty-two bit control store data bus. The control store address bus provides the address of the next microinstruction, which may be in one of several physical control store modules. The control store data bus receives the microinstruction to be executed from a thirty-two bit C register associated with one of the control store modules and may assign data to other processor locations. To assist in the formation of the next control store address, the Microdata 3200 uses a twelve bit L register, which holds the address of the last microinstruction executed, and a twelve bit S register, which is used to save control store addresses. The scheme for microinstruction sequencing on the Microdata 3200 is quite unusual and is described in detail in Section 5.5.2.2.

The Microdata 3200 arithmetic and logic unit performs the following operations:

1. add,
2. add with carry,
3. subtract,
4. subtract with borrow,
5. decrement,
6. and,
7. or,
8. exclusive or, and
9. complement.

Shift logic applies only to three registers and is not a general ALU function. The ALU receives inputs from the sixteen bit A and B busses, and the result is assigned to the sixteen bit F bus. The sources for the A and B busses are the X, Y, and Z registers (or certain parts of them); a four or eight bit control store literal from the microinstruction; and the sixteen bit I bus. The X, Y, and Z registers may be shifted left or right independently in one bit shifts, and the Z and Y registers may be shifted together to effect double word shifts. The status register records four conditions based on the ALU result - zero result, negative result, carry or borrow, and overflow.

Local store in the Microdata 3200 comprises a variety of registers, busses, and special purpose functional units. A sixteen bit scratch pad memory with thirty-two file registers serves as the principal storage unit. The two bit T register is a counter that points to one of the file registers and is used in microprogramming stack operations. The stack consists of the Y register and four local store registers. The Y register represents the top stack item, and the T register points to the

file register that represents the second item on the stack. The
four bit G register and the low-order four bits of the Z
register also address the file registers. The four bit W
register is a counter that may be used to control microprogram
looping. Testing the W register for zero value causes it to be
decremented by one. The sixteen bit F bus is the primary route
for transfer of data among local store registers. The F bus may
receive data from the ALU, the file registers, the bit
generators, and the Monobus data line. As illustrated in Figure
5.5-2, it may assign data to a variety of registers. The single
bit generator places a word on the F bus that contains zeros in
fifteen bit positions and a single one bit. The location of the
one bit is determined in the same manner that a file register
is addressed. The four bit generator places a word on the S bus
whose high-order twelve bits are zero and whose low-order four
bits are four bit sequences from the Z register (bits 0-3, 4-7,
8-11, or 12-15), four bits from the Y register (bits 4-7), or
selected conditions.

Transfers of data and control information over the Monobus
are asynchronous, so memories of different types and speeds may
be attached to the system. The standard memory module contains
16,384 bytes of storage and has a write cycle time and read
access time of 300 n sec. Loading the M register, which
specifies an address in memory or some other I/O device,
initiates a Monobus operation with the M register serving as a
source for the Monobus address line. Data to be written into
main memory or an I/O device resides in the sixteen bit D
register, which is connected to the Monobus data line, and data
received from memory or an I/O device via the Monobus data line
is usually assigned to the F bus. If the received data is a
machine language instruction, which was requested by assigning

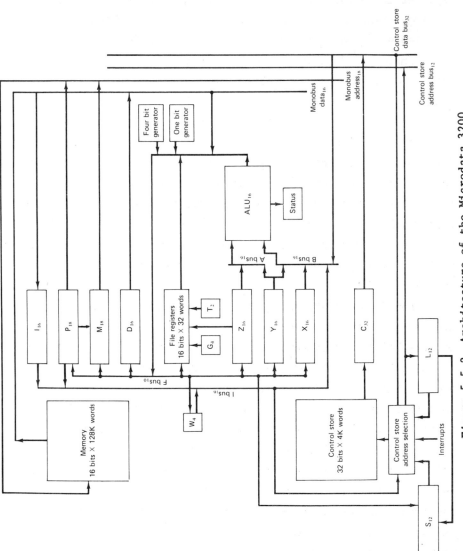

Figure 5.5-2. Architecture of the Microdata 3200.

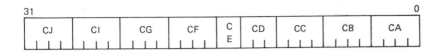

Figure 5.5-3. Microdata 3200 microinstruction format.

a new address to the P (program counter) register, then the instruction is assigned to the I (instruction) register. The sixteen bit I bus transfers information from the I, P, and W registers to the B bus for input to the ALU, and also transfers the operation code in the instruction register to the control store address selection unit so that it may be translated into the control store address of the microprogram that executes the instruction.

5.5.2.2 Microdata 3200 Microinstruction Repertoire

The thirty-two bit microinstructions in the Microdata 3200 comprise nine fields as illustrated in Figure 5.5-3. Before describing the entire microinstruction format in detail, let's examine the control store addressing scheme. This scheme differs from those described previously and impacts the description of several fields in the microinstruction.

The control store in the Microdata 3200 may be considered to be organized into eight pages, each of which contains sixteen blocks. Each block contains sixteen locations, and each location contains two microinstructions called the "- microinstruction" and the "+ microinstruction." Microinstruction addresses thus have four fields as illustrated in Figure 5.5-4. The significance of these four fields is that each microinstruction specifies the address of the next microinstruction to be executed by indicating the fields in the

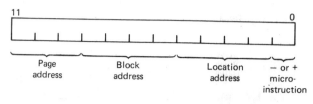

Figure 5.5-4. Microdata 3200 microinstruction address format.

current microinstruction address that are to be changed and the values for these fields. Selection of the – or + microinstruction depends on the condition specified by the CA field of the microinstruction which is extended in some cases by the CB field to increase the number of test conditions. If the specified condition is true, the + microinstruction is selected, if false the – microinstruction is selected. Conditions include carry, overflow, shift bits, W register equal zero, and many others. In addition, the – or + microinstruction may be selected unconditionally, and optionally the L register, which contains the address of the current microinstruction, may be stored in the S register (except that the least significant bit which specifies – or + microinstruction is complemented) to facilitate subroutine return. The condition tested cannot be a condition generated by the current microinstruction because the Microdata 3200 overlaps fetching the next microinstruction with executing the current microinstruction. The CD field in the microinstruction specifies the sources for the remaining three fields in the next microinstruction address as indicated in Figure 5.5-5. The procedure code used in the procedure code or first digit branch (see Figure 5.5-5) is a priority encoding of sixteen external and internal conditions which require the execution of a microprogram. If one or more of these conditions are true, then

Block branch

11	10	9	8	7	6	5	4	3	2	1
L_{11}	L_{10}	L_9	L_8	L_7	L_6	L_5	CC_3	CC_2	CC_1	CC_0

Modulo 16 branch

11	10	9	8	7	6	5	4	3	2	1
L_{11}	L_{10}	L_9	CC_3	CC_2	CC_1	CC_0	L_4	L_3	L_2	L_1

Full page branch

11	10	9	8	7	6	5	4	3	2	1
L_{11}	L_{10}	L_9	CC_3	CC_2	CC_1	CC_0	CB_3	CB_2	CB_1	CB_0

Page entry

11	10	9	8	7	6	5	4	3	2	1
CC_2	CC_1	CC_0	CC_3	0	0	0	CB_3	CB_2	CB_1	CB_0

Data branch

11	10	9	8	7	6	5	4	3	2	1
L_{11}	L_{10}	L_9	CC_3	CC_2	CC_1	CC_0	S_4	S_3	S_2	S_1

S register branch

11	10	9	8	7	6	5	4	3	2	1
S_{15}	S_{14}	S_{13}	S_{12}	S_{11}	S_{10}	S_9	S_8	S_7	S_6	S_5

Second digit branch

11	10	9	8	7	6	5	4	3	2	1
L_{11}	L_{10}	L_9	CC_3	CC_2	CC_1	CC_0	I_3	I_2	I_1	I_0

Procedure code or first digit branch

11	10	9	8	7	6	5	4	3	2	1
CC_2	CC_1	CC_0	CC_3	0	0	0	PC_3	PC_2	PC_1	PC_0

11	10	9	8	7	6	5	4	3	2	1
CC_2	CC_1	CC_0	CC_3	0	0	1	I_7	I_6	I_5	I_4

Legend

L_i — i^{th} bit in the L register (current microinstruction address)
CC_i — i^{th} bit in microinstruction field CC
CB_i — i^{th} bit in microinstruction field CB
S_i — i^{th} bit in the S register
I_i — i^{th} bit in the I register (instruction register)
PC_i — i^{th} bit in the procedure code

Figure 5.5-5. Specification of bits 1-11 of the next control store address in the Microdata 3200.

the branch is based on the condition of highest priority, otherwise, the branch is based on the first four bits of the operation code in the instruction register. Note that this scheme provides for a one of thirty-two way branch.

We have seen that the CA field in the microinstruction specifies a condition for selecting the - or + microinstruction at the next control store address location and that the CB field may be used to extend the number of conditions. The CB field is generally a four bit literal that is used in conjunction with other fields, e.g., with the CD field in forming the next microinstruction address. The CC field forms part of the next control store address as shown in Figure 5.5-5. The three bit CD field specifies which of the eight addressing modes shown in Figure 5.5-5 is to be used in determining the next control store address. The CE field serves as a modifier for the CF field which selects one or more registers (or parts thereof) that are to receive data from the F bus. The CG field may specify the source address for reading the file registers and manipulation of the source (e.g., use the G register to address the file registers and after the data in the register has been assigned to the F bus, increment the G register), the source address for the one bit generator and manipulation of the source, or the source address for writing the file registers and manipulation of the source. The CI field may specify the data sources for the F bus, the left or right shift inputs for the X, Y, and Z registers, or the ALU inputs. The CJ field selects the ALU function or the shift operation.

With a significant portion of each microinstruction word devoted to the specification of an ALU or shift operation and its associated source and result operands, the microinstructions of the Microdata 3200 have a vertical basis, however, the concurrent sophisticated next address determination procedure and the capability to initiate a Macrobus operation and perform other operations, like decrementing the counter and changing the address source for the file registers, gives the microinstructions a definite horizontal inclination. While single level encoding is evidenced by the single microinstruction format, the interpretation of a field sometimes depends on the contents of another, so two level encoding is used.

5.5.3 Microdata 3200 Microprogrammability

Control store in the Microdata 3200 may be implemented as combinations of ROM, PROM, and writable memory. Writable control store is treated as a memory module on the Monobus whose addresses lie in the range 38000 (base 16) to 3C000 (base 16). Thus the writable control store may be written via the Monobus like any other memory module, and thereafter it interfaces with the computer via the control store address and data busses.

To facilitate microprogramming, Microdata provides a cross microprogram assembler. The CAP32 cross assembler for the microinstruction set is written in PL/I, and may be run on any system supporting the IBM System/360 PL/I Level F compiler. The assembler language uses a free-field format with the label, operation, operands, and comments fields separated by one or more blanks. The operand field is a compound field that specifies the F bus destination (CF field), the next address (which may be omitted to imply sequential addressing), and miscellaneous information such as the CG microinstruction field and a control store literal. As described previously each microinstruction in the Microdata 3200 specifies the address of the next microinstruction to be executed. Owing to the variety of addressing modes, the assignment of addresses is a difficult

193

```
      *                      EXAMPLES
      *
      *   GROUP 3 - NEEDS 1 OPERAND IN STACK REGISTERS
      *
1     G3V      BRSET   INC,DEC,NEG,NOT,ABS,LLO,COER,CAA,
                       EQL,SL,SLB,ALB,AL,ANDL,ORL,XORL
2     G3VCTR VECTOR   SDB,G3V
      *
3     G3XA     Y        .,G3VCTR       NOP,DECODE SECOND DIGIT
4     G3XB     LM(SP,LG) MR:Z          MEM ADDR OF TOS TO MEM, SAVE PLACE
5              Z-2      LM(G)           DECR MEM TOS POINTER
6              D        Y,G3VCTR,IT     DATA TO Y, BUMP STK COUNT,
      *                                    DECODE SECOND DIGIT
7     INC      Y+1      Y,N1(SCHED)     ADD 1, EXIT
8     DEC      Y-1      Y,N1(SCHED)     SUB 1, EXIT
9     NEG      Y'       Y,INC           1'S COMP, GO ADD 1
10    NOT      Y'       Y,N1(SCHED)     1'S COMP, EXIT
11    ABS      Y        .,Y15(NEG)      NEGATE IF NEGATIVE
12             Y        .,N1(SCHED)     EXIT
13    LLO      0'       Z               -1 TO Z
14    LLO1     Y        F               TEST Y
15             SR(0)    Y,ZERO(LLO5)    SHIFT Y RIGHT AND SKIP IF IT WAS 0
16             Z+1      Z,LLO1          INCREMENT BIT NO, LOOP
17    LLO5     Z        Y,N1(SCHED)     BIT NO TO Y, EXIT
18    EQL      I        XU              GET TOP HALF
19             I        XL              GET BOTTOM HALF
20             Y-X      F               COMPARE
21             F(ZERO)  Y,N1(SCHED)     COMPARE RESULT TO Y, EXIT
22    SL       I        XU              GET UPPER
23             I        XL              GET LOWER
24    SL9      Y-X      Y,N1(SCHED)     SUBTRACT, EXIT
25    SLB      I        X,SL9           GET BYTE, GO TO SUBTRACT
26    ALB      I        X,AL9           GET BYTE, GO TO ADD
27    AL       I        XU              GET UPPER
28             I        XL              GET LOWER
29    AL9      X+Y      Y,N1(SCHED)     ADD, EXIT
```

194

30	ANDL	I	XU	GET UPPER
31		I	XL	GET LOWER
32		Y&X	Y,N1(SCHED)	AND, EXIT
33	ORL	I	XU	GET UPPER
34		I	XL	GET LOWER
35		Y|X	Y,N1(SCHED)	OR, EXIT
36	XORL	I	XU	GET UPPER
37		I	XL	GET LOWER
38		Y*X	Y,N1(SCHED)	XOR, EXIT

Figure 5.5-6. Microdata 3200 microprogram example.

Detailed Statement Comments

1. The BRSET pseudooperation defines a list of identifiers (machine instruction identifiers in this case) that are to serve as labels of a branch microinstruction.

2. This VECTOR pseudooperation indicates that branching to one of the labels listed in the previous statement depends on the value of the second hexadecimal digit (SDB) in the instruction (I) register.

3. Pass the Y register through the ALU (the Y operation) and assign it to no register (the . operand), i.e., perform a nooperation. Decode the second hexadecimal digit in the instruction register.

4. Put file register (abbreviated LM for Local Memory) pointed to by the stack pointer (SP) on the F bus and load the G register with the address (LG). Assign the register to the Z register and the M register and initiate a Microbus operation to read the data at the address in the M register.

5. Decrement the Z register by 2 in the ALU and assign the result to the

195

file register pointed to by G.

6. Assign the data read from memory to the Y register, increment the T register (IT), and decode the second hexadecimal digit in the instruction register.

Note: Microinstructions 4 through 6 have read the word on the top of the simulated stack into the Y register.

7. Increment the Y register (ALU performs increment with Y register as source and destination), and exit to get next machine instruction.

8. Decrement Y register and exit.

9. Perform the one's complement on the Y register and go to the microinstruction labelled INC.

10. Complement the Y register and exit.

11. Pass the Y register through the ALU and branch to the NEG microinstruction if it is negative.

12. Pass the Y register through the ALU (no operation) and exit.

13. Assign -1 to the Z register.

14. Pass Y through the ALU to set conditions in the status (F for flags) register.

15. Shift the Y register right one place and branch to microinstruction LL05 if it was zero.

16. Increment the Z register and branch to label LL01.

17. Set Y to Z and exit.

196

Note: Microinstructions 14 through 17 have counted the number of zeros
to the right of a one in the Y register.

18. Move the upper byte of the instruction to the B bus, through the
ALU, and into the upper byte of the X register.

19. Similarly for the lower byte.

20. Subtract X from Y and set the status register.

21. Compare the result to Y and exit.

22. Like 18.

23. Like 19.

24. Subtract X from Y, store the result in the Y register, and exit.

25. Assign one byte from the instruction register to the X register and
go to the subtract microinstruction.

26. Similarly for add.

27. Like 18.

28. Like 19.

29. Add the X and Y registers, assign the result to the Y register, and
exit.

30-32. Like 27-29 for and.

33-35. Like 27-29 for inclusive or.

36-38. Like 27-29 for exclusive or.

197

task for the microprogrammer. The microprogram assembler facilitates this task by performing the address allocation in conjunction with some pseudooperations specified by the microprogrammer.

5.5.4 Microdata 3200 Microprogram Example

Figure 5.5-6 illustrates a sample Microdata 3200 microprogram to perform several simple machine instructions. This microprogram is written in CAP32 assembler language.

5.6 Other Computers with Diagonal Microinstructions

5.6.1 The Datasaab FCPU

The Datasaab FCPU (Flexible Central Processing Unit) consists of several units which operate concurrently and asynchronously:

1. the arithmetic unit,

2. the field access unit which intefaces with main memory, and

3. the control unit which contains the control store.

Each of these units has eight "to-and-from" registers which are used to send and receive data in communicatons with other units. Data paths are sixty-four bits wide. The thirty-two bit encoded microinstructions are read two at a time from the writable control store which may contain up to 16K microinstructions. Microinstructions indicate operations in different units, and execution may depend on the status of the addressed unit (busy or idle), the state of a referenced to-and-from register, etc. Hardware Variable Logic Sets may be added to the FCPU to assist in performing special functions like instruction decoding for an emulated machine. The microprogramming language for the Datasaab FCPU is a higher level machine—dependent language and is described in Section 7.3.

5.6.2 The MLP-900

The MLP-900 is a dynamically microprogrammable computer that was manufactured by Standard Computer Corporation. The Programmable Research Instrument (PRIM) project at the University of Southern California Information Sciences Institute has an MLP-900 connected to a PDP-10, which in turn is connected to the ARPANET. The MLP-900 has two hardware units that operate concurrently. The Operating Engine contains 32 thirty-six bit general purpose registers and functional units to perform arithmetic and logical operations on data in the registers. The Control Engine controls microprogram execution and contains a sixteen-word subroutine return stack. The first bit in the thirty-two bit microinstructions determines whether the microinstruction will be executed by the Operating Engine or the Control Engine. As the microinstruction formats for the two units are different, this is an example of two level encoding. The control store may contain up to 4096 microinstructions. To enhance the capability of the MLP-900 in emulating a wide variety of systems, it is possible to use up to four special language boards on the machine. These language boards are hardware components that were designed to perform special operations, such as instruction decoding and address control for a particular emulated machine, in a very efficient manner. GPM, a higher level machine—dependent microprogramming language for the MLP-900, is discussed in Section 7.3.

5.6.3 The CONTROL DATA 5600*

The Control Data 5600 series of microprogrammable processors (MPPs) was developed mainly for military applicatons but can be used in a variety of data processing applicatons including emulation and device controlling. The machine does not have a fixed word size, but can be configured in sizes from eight bits to thirty-two bits in four bit increments. In addition to several standard local store registers, register files of 32 and 256 words may be included in a machine. The microinstruction execution time is 168 n sec, so the five or six microinstructions that constitute typical machine language instructions can be executed in about one microsecond, the normal memory cycle time. Control store, which can be writable or read only, may contain up to 8192 microinstructions in increments of 512. The thirty-two bit microinstructions consist of eight fields which provide some parallel operation. An assembler facilitates microprogram prepration for the MPP.

The recently announced Control Data Advanced Microprogrammable Processor (AMPP) is a faster and more powerful computer. Designed to be able to emulate any existing military computer, the AMPP has sixty-four bit microinstructions. Although more characteristic of a horizontal design than the MPP, the AMPP apparently is not intended as an MPP replacement, and the two machines are being marketed simultanously.

5.6.4 The Data General ECLIPSE**

The Data General ECLIPSE system is upward compatible with previous Data General computers. To achieve high performance, the ECLIPSE features a 200-n sec cache memory and interleaved main memory modules. The microprogrammed instruction set

* CONTROL DATA is a registered trademark.
** ECLIPSE is a trademark of Data General Corporation.

includes hardware stack instructions, an interrupt servicing instruction, and bit, byte, word, and block manipulation instructions. The writable control store, which may contain 256 fifty-six bit microinstructions, provides users the capability to write microprograms for special applications. Previous Data General machines were generally hardwired. Their use of microprogramming in the new ECLIPSE system represents an interesting trend.

Bibliography

A. HP21MX

1. J. Stedman, "Microprogramability Lets User Tailor New Minicomputer to His Reqirements," Electronics, May 2, 1974, pages 87-93.

2. W. G. Matheson, "User Microprogrammability in the HP-21MX Minicomputer," Seventh Annual Workshop on Microprogramming Preprints, ACM, September 1974, pages 168-177.

3. "21MX Computer Series Reference Manual," Manual Part No. 02108-90002, May 1974.

4. "Microprogamming 21MX Computers Operating and Reference Manual," Manual Part No. 02108-90008, August 1974.

      Available from

           Hewlett-Packard Company

           11000 Wolfe Road

           Cupertino, California 95014

B. META 4

1. B. J. Swain, "Emulation – the Key to Computer Power," Canadian Consulting Engineer, December 1973, pages 28-29.

2. J. G. Zornig and J. F. McDonald, "A High Speed Microprogrammed System for Generation and Acquistion of Signals," Rev. Sci. Instrum., Volume 44 Number 9 (September 1973), pages 1217-1222.

3. "META 4 Computer System Microprogramming Reference Manual," Publication No. 7043MO, 1972.

   Available from

      Digital Scientific Corporation
      11455 Sorrento Valley Road
      San Diego,California 92121

C. INTERDATA 85

1. "Model 85 Processor."

2. "INTERDATA Model 85 Dynamic Control Store Application Guide," August 1972.

3. "Model 80 Maintenance Manual," Publication Number 29-280R01, April 1973.

4. "Model 85 Dynamic Control Store Users Guide," Publication Number 29-281R01, December 1973.

5. "Dynamic Control Store Instruction Manual," Publication Number 29-308R02.

> Available from
>> INTERDATA, Inc.
>> 2 Crescent Place
>> Oceanport, New Jersey 07757

D. Microdata 3200

1. R. Burns and D. Savitt, "Microprogramming, Stack Architecture Ease Minicomputer Programer's Burden," Electronics, February 15, 1973, pages 95-101.

2. D. L. House, "Micro Level Architecture in Minicomputer Design," Computer Design, Volume 12 Number 10 (October 1973), pages 75-80.

3. "Microdata 3200 Computer."
4. "Microdata 3230 Computer."
5. "Microdata 32/S Computer."
6. "Microdata 3200 Microprogramming Manual (Preliminary)," Revision 2, June 21, 1973.
7. "Microdata 32/S Programming Language Reference Manual (MPL)," November 1973.
8. "Micro 32/S Computer Reference Manual," May 1974.

> Available from
>> Microdata Corporation
>> 17481 Red Hill Avenue
>> Irvine, California 92705

E. Datasaab FCPU

1. H. W. Lawson, Jr. and B. Magnhagen, "Advantages of Structured Hardware," Second Annual Symposium on Computer Architecture, IEEE, January 1975, pages 152-158.

F. MLP-900

1. H. W. Lawson, Jr. and B. K. Smith, "Functional Characteristics of a Multilingual Processor," IEEE Transactions on Computers, Volume C-20 Number 7 (July 1971), pages 732-742.

2. L. C. Richardson, "PRIM Overview," ISI/RR-76-19, February 1974.

3. D. R. Oestreicher and J. Goldberg, "MLP-900 Reference Manual Preliminary Version," March 1974.

        Available from

                University of Southern California
                Information Sciences Institute
                4676 Admiralty Way
                Marina del Rey, California

G. CDC 5600

1. "Control Data 5600 Series of Microprogrammable Processors Reference Manual," Publication No. 14232000, August 25, 1972.

2. "MICRO-71 Assembler Manual," GO2903, March 1973.

3. "Control Data Advanced Microprogrammable Processor," May 1974.

> Available from
>> Control Data Corporation
>> Aerospace Division
>> 3101 East 80th Street
>> Minneapolis, Minnesota

H. Eclipse

1. "Minicomputers Offer High Speed Cache Memory," Computer Design, Volume 13, Number 11, (Nov 1974), pages 120-122.

2. "Data General Corporation Introduces New Eclipse Line of Small Computers," SIGMICRO Newsletter, Volume 5 Number 3 (October 1974), pages 101-119.

CHAPTER 6

COMPUTERS WITH HORIZONTAL MICROINSTRUCTIONS

6.1 Introduction

In computers which allow parallel execution of many microoperations, the microinstructions have to be large enough to contain information about all these microoperations. This type of microinstruction is classified as horizontal. The parallelism in machines using horizontal microinstructions makes them rather powerful, but the cost of such organizations is usually high as they often make inefficient use of control store. Microprogramming is much more complex, to the extent that efficient horizontal architectures and ways of using them are topics of active research in the field. Many of the machines with horizontal microinstructions were developed and are used by research groups. Of the seven computers described in this chapter, only the first three (the California Data Processors machine, the PRIME 300, and the Varian 73) are primarily small-to-medium scale systems for end users. These systems do not show radical design departures from the systems in the preceding chapters. The NANODATA QM-1, a medium-to-large scale system, was designed for use in research as well as in commercial applications. The Burroughs Interpreter, while designed as a general purpose machine for emulating a variety of computers, is being marketed (using an inexpensive memory implementation) as a small business machine. The AMP (Argonne Microprocessor*) and MATHILDA computers, developed by research

* Here microprocessor means microprogrammable processor.

groups investigating microprogramming applications, exemplify very general horizontal architectures.

6.2 The Cal Data Processor

6.2.1 Cal Data Background

The California Data Processors (Cal Data) family of minicomputers was marketed to give large volume computer users fully compatible replacement systems that are efficient and economical. Initial models in the series are based on the basic Cal Data processor, a microprogrammable system for users who wish or need to develop custom firmware for specific applications or system enhancements. When microprogrammed to emulate the PDP-11, the Cal Data processor is marketed as the Cal Data 1/35, a low cost machine that matches the performance of a PDP-11/35 and provides interfaces for DEC-compatible peripherals and controllers. The Cal Data 5/1 represents the Cal Data processor microprogrammed to emulate the TEMPO I. Because the basic Cal Data processor was designed to be a general purpose computer for hosting the emulation of a variety of the commercially available mini- and midi-computers, it is the topic of discussion here.

6.2.2 Cal Data Architecture

6.2.2.1 Cal Data Functional Components

At the system level, the architecture of the Cal Data illustrates the use of a single bidirectional data bus to connect system components (see Figure 6.2-1). This MACROBUS is time shared by all elements of the system, including the CPU. This scheme considers data on I/O devices to be part of a large

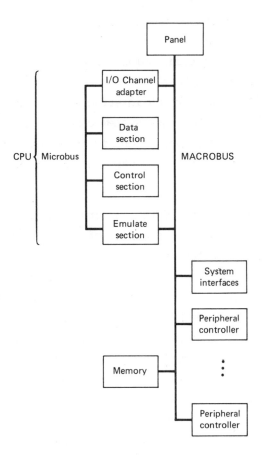

Figure 6.2-1. System level architecture of the Cal Data Processor.

data space, i.e., only the address of data is needed to reference it, and knowledge of the device type is unnecessary. Main memory is thus treated as another I/O device. One of the I/O devices may be an adapter that interfaces with another MACROBUS to facilitate multiprocessor systems. Within the CPU, a microbus provides a communication link among the CPU sections:

1. the data section, which contains the ALU/shifter and general purpose registers,

2. the control section, which contains the control store and its associated registers,

3. the I/O section which interfaces with the MACROBUS to send and receive data to other system components, and

4. the emulate section, which is an optional extension to the control section that assists in emulating a specific machine architecture.

Figure 6.2-2 presents the detailed structure of the Cal Data CPU and illustrates the relation of the MACROBUS and the microbus to the other functional units.

The Cal Data provides some special features to facilitate use of control store, which is an array of up to 4,096 forty-eight bit words with a 150-n sec cycle time. Associated with the twelve bit control store address register (the CS register) is a stack containing 16 twelve bit registers for storing microprogram addresses. The forty-eight bit control store data register (the CR register) normally holds the microinstruction read from control store that is to be executed, however, the microinstruction read from control store can be modified prior to entry into the CSDR by the contents of the emulate register. In addition, the Cal Data provides a thirty-two word block of special memory that may functionally replace designated thirty-two word blocks in control store. This feature permits testing firmware corrections and inserting diagnostic microprograms temporarily, even when the control store is a read only memory.

The Cal Data ALU performs the fifteen logical and eight arithmetic functions shown in Figure 6.2-3. Although the

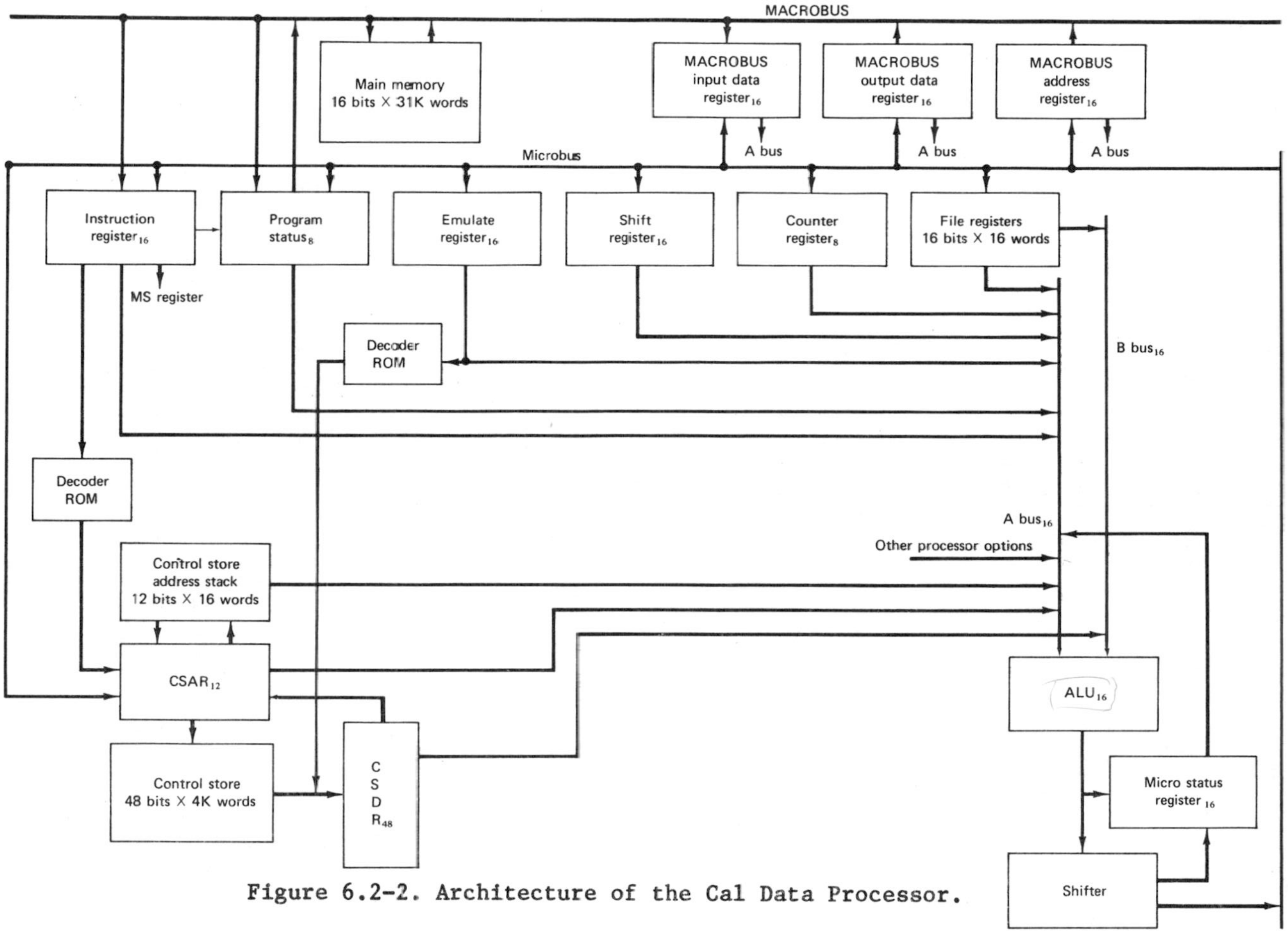

Figure 6.2-2. Architecture of the Cal Data Processor.

Logical Operations

    A

    B

    not A

    not B

    A & B

    A & not B

    not A and B

    not A & not B

    A v B

    A v not B

    not A v B

    not A v not B

    A * B   (exclusive or)

    not (A * B)

    sign extend A

Arithmetic Operations

    A + B + carry

    A - B - carry

    A + carry

    A - carry

    A + 1 + carry

    A - 1 - carry

    A + (A & B) + carry

Figure 6.2-3. CDP processor ALU operations (inputs are designated A and B).

shifter is connected serially to the ALU result, an ALU operation cannot be performed in the same microinstruction with the shift operation except in a few special purpose microoperations such as multiply step and divide step. The types of shifts that can be performed are one bit logical left shift, one bit logical right shift, one bit arithmetic right shift, and swap halves. These shifts may be single or double word and circular or end off. To perform double word shifts, the shift register (XR register) may be connected to either side of the shifter. The Cal Data provides a half-word option in which ALU/shifter operations are conditionally performed on half-words (eight bits) rather than full words. Two busses, the A bus and the B bus, provide the primary inputs to the ALU/shifter. Data assigned to these busses originates from other CPU registers as shown in Figure 6.2-2. A third input to the ALU/shifter is the carry input from a previous ALU or shift operation. Each ALU/shifter operation generates six condition codes: carry out, overflow, zero result, negative result, positive result, and odd result. These conditions may be saved in the microstatus register, however, microinstructions can test the conditions that were generated by the current ALU/shifter operation in addition to the conditions stored in the microstatus register. The result of the ALU/shifter operation is assigned to the microbus for storage in one of the CPU registers.

The sixteen bit file registers serve as general purpose local storage. Cal Data systems may contain either eight or sixteen of these file registers. The eight bit counter register (LC register) facilitates repetition of a group of one or more microinstructions. The counter register may be loaded from the microbus, and it may be tested for zero or nonzero by any microinstruction. A branch microoperation is executed if the condition is met, and the counter is decremented each time it is tested. The instruction, program status, and emulate registers enhance the performance of particular emulators by providing machine-dependent functions. Associated with the instruction register, for example, are ROM tables that translate machine language instruction codes into control store addresses of microprograms to interpret these instructions.

Owing to the MACROBUS organization of the Cal Data, a variety of memories may be used in the system. For the Cal Data 1 up to 31K words of core memory modules (with speeds of 275 n sec for access and 675 n sec for cycle or 300 n sec for access and 850 n sec for cycle) may be attached to a basic system. Capacity may be expanded to 127K with an optional memory management unit. The three registers that control main memory referencing also control I/O communication. The MACROBUS address register (AR register) stores addresses for MACROBUS operations; for the main memory it serves as the memory address register. The implementation of the MACROBUS address register permits it to be loaded with a new value after initiation of a MACROBUS operation and before the operation is complete. The sixteen bit MACROBUS output data register (DR register) stores data words that will be directed to memory and I/O devices. Like the MACROBUS address register, the MACROBUS output data register may be loaded with a new value immediately after initiation of a MACROBUS write operation. The MACROBUS input data register (RR register) is a sixteen bit register used to store data from I/O devices or from the microbus. Both the input and output data registers may, under microprogram control, operate on byte rather than word data. The instruction register and program status register may also communicate with the MACROBUS.

Fields common to all microinstruction formats

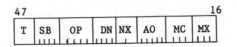

Remaining fields for specific microinstruction formats

Logical and arithmetic group microinstructions

Branch type

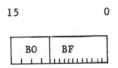

Skip type

15   0

```
┌─────────────────┐
│        LL       │
└─────────────────┘
```

Special group microinstructions

Branch type

215

```
                                   15                 0

                                   SO     BF


                                 Skip type

                                   15                 0

                                   SO     FN
```

Figure 6.2-4. CDP processor microinstruction formats.

Legend:

T (Type) - 0 specifies branch type microinstruction;
           1 specifies skip type microinstruction;
SB - branch or skip condition;
OP - basic operation;
DN - destination of ALU/shifter result;
NX - special control functions;
AO - A operand source for ALU/shifter;
MC - condition code specification;

MX - special control functions;
BO - B operand source for ALU/shifter;
BF - branch address or auxilliary control functions;
LL - literal value (B operand source);
SO - special operation control functions;
FN - auxilliary control functions.

6.2.2.2 Cal Data Microinstruction Repertoire

Although the microinstruction formats for the Cal Data may be classified into two basic groups and the formats in each group may be classified into two types, as illustrated in Figure 6.2-4 a majority of the fields in each microinstruction format are identical. Of the fields common to all microinstructions the type field indicates whether the microinstruction is a branch-type or a skip-type microinstruction. The OP field indicates the basic operations the microinstruction is to perform and may be

1. one of the operations in Figure 6.2-3,

2. emulate, which translates the operation in the instruction register into the control store address of a microprogram to execute the operation, and stores the address in the CSAR,

3. shift,

4. multiply step,

5. divide step,

6. test bit, which transfers the A bus operand to a destination via the ALU/shifter and microbus and then tests the operand bit specified by the SO field,

7. modify macrostatus, which assigns the least significant four bits of the A bus operand to the corresponding bits in the program status register,

8. conditional memory access, which performs a memory I/O operation indicated by a special emulate table, or

9. decode, which uses the ROM decode tables to modify the next microinstruction read from control store before it is assigned to the CSDR.

The AO field specifies the register to be assigned to the A bus for input to the ALU/shifter. The DN field similarly specifies

217

the register which is assigned the ALU/shifter result via the microbus. The AO field may indicate that the register it specifies also receives the ALU/shifter result. The first three bits of the SB field specify the condition to be tested for branching or skipping; the seven conditions are counter register equal zero and the six ALU/shifter conditions. The fourth bit of the SB field indicates whether the specified condition is to be tested as being true or false, and the fifth bit indicates whether the dynamic conditions (generated by the most recent ALU/shifter operation) or the static conditions (stored in the microstatus register) are to be tested. The MX field specifies which of the three fields that specify registers – AO, BO, and SO – are to be modified in the execution of the next microinstruction. The MC field specifies the modification of the microstatus register.

The logical and arithmetic group of microinstructions (indicated by an ALU operation) are of two types – branch and skip. In the branch type, the four bit BO field specifies the register to be assigned to the B bus for input to the ALU/shifter, and the BF field specifies a branch address to which control is transferred if the branch condition, indicated by the SB field, is satisfied. If no branch condition is specified, auxiliary control functions (discussed subsequently) may be executed. In the skip-type logic and arithmetic microinstructions, a sixteen bit literal field, the LL field, serves as the B operand, and when the specified condition is satisfied the next microinstruction is skipped and not executed.

The special group of microinstructions also has branch and skip-types. In the branch type, the BF field specifies a branch address as before, and the SO field specifies control functions such as the type, precision, and direction of shifts. Like the logic and arithmetic group skip-type microinstructions, when the specified condition is true the special group skip-type microinstructions do not execute the next microinstruction. Since the special group microinstructions require only one operand for the ALU/shifter, however, the remaining bits in the special group microinstructions may be devoted to auxiliary control functions (the FN field) rather than a literal value. These auxiliary control functions include activating the MACROBUS for input or output, specifying the register to receive data from the MACROBUS, specifying the byte or word mode of operation, repeating the current microinstruction (done in conjunction with the counter register), and manipulating the control store address stack.

Cal Data microinstructions have the capability to perform two distinct operations - an ALU/shifter operation and a conditional branch or skip operation. The additional capability to perform other operations simultaneously suffices to classify these microinstructions as horizontal. Two level encoding, which was a typical characteristic of vertical and diagonal microinstructions, is less prominent here. Although the interpretation of the sixteen least significant bits in each microinstruction depends on the microinstruction type (bit 47) and operation (bits 41-37), the remaining bits represent fixed fields whose interpretation is not affected by the microinstruction type or operation code.

The parallel implementation of Cal Data microinstructions has some effect on microprogram execution and performance. The basic machine clock cycle is 150 n sec, and in normal operation, a microinstruction is read from control store into the CSDR and executed in one clock cycle (there are no suboperations performed, and all operations specified by a microinstruction are executed simultaneously). When a branch or skip operation is to modify the sequential flow of control through a microprogram, the next sequential microinstruction has already been read into the CSDR; thus one machine cycle may be lost in executing a branch or skip operation. The microinstruction that has been read into the CSDR can, however, be executed conditionally under control of the NX field in the present microinstruction. The NX field specifies one of the following actions: execute the next sequential microinstruction, skip the next sequential microinstruction, skip if the branch condition is not met, and skip if the branch condition is met. This microinstruction that has been read into the CSDR is often used to modify the next microinstruction (the one at the branch or skip address).

An interesting contrast in this machine is the combination of general architecture features (file registers, microbus, general ALU/shifter operations, horizontal microinstructions, etc.) and special purpose architecture features (emulate register, instruction register and associated tables, bit testing facilities, etc.) to provide a machine that serves as a general purpose processor or as an emulator for a specific computer.

6.2.3 Cal Data Microprogrammability

The control store in the Cal Data may be implemented as read only, programmable read only, or writable memory. The 256 word writable control store modules may be interchanged with ROM and PROM modules to a maximum of 4,096 words. The writable control store can be loaded and read via the MACROBUS using I/O commands. To support microprogram development, Cal Data provides a microprogram assembler and a so called ACM Software Operating System that provides debugging capabilities.

Hexadecimal representation	Assembler language representation
73BF00000013	ADD CMA
	BRU FNI
7E1016F08004	ADD RR,X8,DR; USLO
	WRT

Figure 6.2-5. Cal Data microprogram to execute an add instruction.

Comments

The first microinstruction is a branch unconditional (BRU) type microinstruction (the type field is zero, and the SB fields specifies no condition). Control is to be transferred to the microinstruction at address 13 (hexadecimal), which is the address of the Fetch Next Instruction (FNI) routine, however, the NX field is zero so the next sequential microinstruction is to be executed before the branch takes effect. The OP field specifies Conditional Memory Access (CMA), which initiates a read/write or read/modify/write operation depending on a bit in the emulate table. The DN field has a default value for this operation which indicates that no data is to be written into a destination register.

The second microinstruction is also a branch type microinstruction, since the type field is zero. The SB field indicates a branch if the true condition (unconditional branch) is false, so the twelve least significant microinstruction bits constitute the FN (special functions) field rather than the BF field. The Op field in this microinstruction indicates addition (specified by the ADD subcommand). The two source

registers are the MACROBUS Input Register (RR register), which has
received the memory operand specified by the previous microinstruction,
and general purpose register eight (X8). The destination register is the
MACROBUS Output Register (DR register). Following the ALU operation, the
microstatus register is to be updated, as specified by the USLO
subcommand. Finally the WRT subcommand indicates that the data in the
MACROBUS Output Register is to be written back into memory. In the
microinstruction the bit set in the FN field indicates this action.

6.2.4 Cal Data Microprogram Example

Figure 6.2-5 illustrates a routine of two
microinstructions to execute an add instruction. As can be seen
from this example, the horizontal microinstructions allow a
very compact program to be written for some problems.

6.3 The PRIME 300

6.3.1 PRIME 300 Background

The PRIME 300 is the top of PRIME's present line of
compatible minicomputer systems. Featuring virtual memory and a
comprehensive set of 164 machine language instructions, the
PRIME 300 may be configured in a variety of systems with
special options, a range of memories, and a variety of
peripheral devices. An interesting standard feature on the
PRIME 300 is the microdiagnostic capability.* These
microprograms are called the Microverification routines, and
are used to test the operation of all data registers, memory
and I/O bus lines, and the CPU logic.

* See Chapter 8 for a detailed discussion of microdiagnostics.

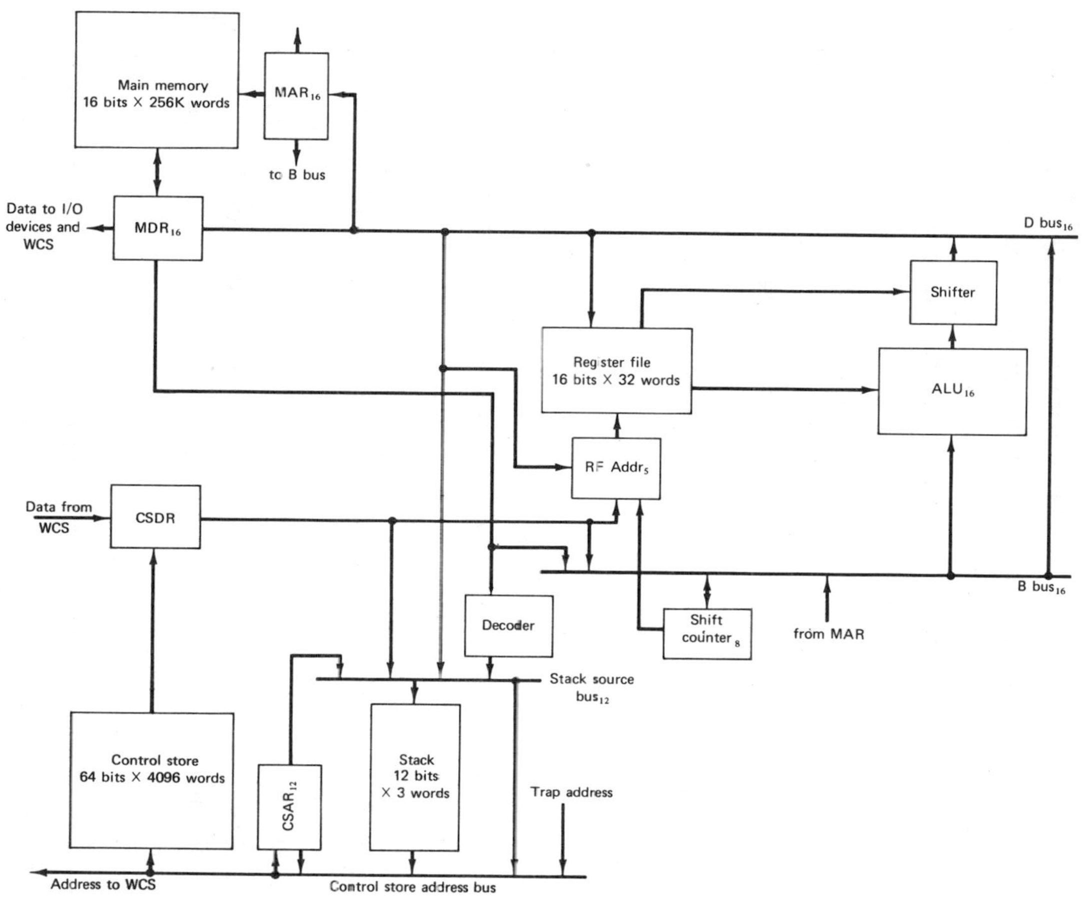

Figure 6.3-1. Architecture of the PRIME 300.

6.3.2 PRIME 300 Architecture

6.3.2.1 PRIME 300 Functional Units

The PRIME 300 provides a control store addressing capability of 4,096 sixty-four bit words. The standard processor utilizes 512 microinstruction words, implemented as fast programmable read only memory, to emulate the machine language instruction set. The standard control store may be augmented with PROM and writable memory to provide extended features, such as floating point arithmetic instructions and user microprogramming. In addition to the control store address register and the control store data register, there is a three word stack associated with the control store for saving control store addresses. The use of two busses, the stack source bus and the control store address bus shown in Figure 6.3-1, provides a flexible control store addressing scheme.

The PRIME 300 ALU is a standard commercially available unit which can perform such operations as addition, subtraction, incrementing, and sixteen logical functions. The principal ALU inputs are two busses: the B bus, whose sources originate from a variety of CPU locations, and the A bus, whose source is one of the thirty-two file registers. A third ALU input is a carry bit which may be specified as zero, one, or the one bit C register. A one bit shifter, which can also swap bytes of the ALU result, is serially connected to the ALU output. The shifter may also receive input directly from a file register. Three registers associated with the ALU/shifter indicate its status and assist in its operation. The one bit C register may indicate ALU overflow, ALU carry, the high-order (sign) bit of the result on the D bus, divide overflow, and shift overflow. The two bit condition code register indicates the high-order bit of the ALU result and whether or not the ALU

224

result is zero. The one bit link register facilitates double word shifts with its capability to store the bit lost in shifting and introduce it in later shift operations.

To facilitate efficient operation of multiply algorithms, the PRIME 300 provides special hardware that permits the shifter to select as input either the ALU output or the specified file register depending on the link register contents. The example in a later section illustrates the use of this capability. Special hardware is also provided to facilitate divide operations.

The primary local storage medium is a set of thirty-two file registers. Although the register file can be read and written during the execution of each microinstruction, only one of the thirty-two registers may be referenced in each microinstruction. An eight bit shift counter register, which can be incremented and tested independently from the ALU, facilitates multiple bit shifts and microprogram looping.

The fast main memory of the PRIME 300 has a read access time of 440 n sec and a write time of 880 n sec. The right and left bytes of a word may be written independently into memory. The memory address register and memory data register serve to address peripheral as well as main memory storage; 256K words of storage may be referenced in an absolute or paged mode.

The PRIME 300 provides a variety of facilities for microinstruction sequencing in addition to the normal sequential flow and the subroutine capability implemented, using the three word control store address stack. A conditional jump facility, in which the next address is contained in the microinstruction, offers sixty-four selectable conditions including ALU result equals zero, sign of ALU result, ALU carry, shift counter equals minus one, CPU interrupts, and I/O interrupts. The sixteen-way-branch operation is similar to a

225

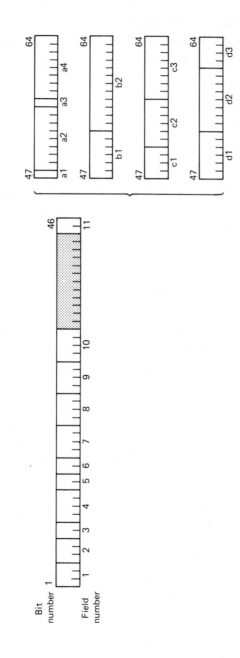

Figure 6.3-2. PRIME 300 microinstruction format.

conditional jump operation except that the low-order four bits of the jump address are taken directly from the D bus while the high-order bits are specified in the microinstruction itself. In the multi-way-branch operation the next microinstruction address is the value of the least significant twelve bits on the D bus.

6.3.2.2 PRIME 300 Microinstruction Repertoire

As illustrated in Figure 6.3-2, PRIME 300 microinstructions are sixty-four bits long but only fifty-two bits are used. The microinstructions consist of twelve fields.

1. Field one specifies the source for the D bus as either the shifter result or the B bus value. In addition it specifies shifter input (a file register or the ALU result), the type of shift to be performed (left one bit, right one bit, or swapping bytes of the ALU result), and the bit that is to replace the one vacated in shifting.

2. Field two selects the source for the B bus — the MAR, the MDR, the CSDR, the shift counter (and other flags), or the data or address from an I/O bus.

3. Field three controls the masking of traps. When a trap that is not masked occurs, a control store address is automatically loaded into the CSAR effecting a subroutine branch to a trap-handling microprogram. Conditions causing microprogram traps include memory parity error, CPU parity error, page fault (page address not in content addressable memory), write protection errors, and read or write address errors.

4. Fields four and five specify the ALU operation. The ALU operations are almost identical to those listed in Figure 5.2-2 except that the PRIME 300 operands, one of the file registers and the B bus, contain sixteen bits as does the result. In the

227

PRIME 300, field five performs the function of bits ten and eleven in the microinstruction in Figure 5.2-2, and field four performs the function of bits 12 - 15.

5. Fields six and seven indicate the file register to be used.

6. Field eight selects the registers into which data from the D bus and the memory busses is to be written.

7. Field nine indicates the condition that will cause the one bit C register to be set or the memory action, which may be virtual or absolute read, write, or write the most or least significant byte in the MDR.

8. Field ten specifies some independent action such as jumping to the instruction fetch routine, loading the shift counter, incrementing the shift counter, setting the condition code register, setting the two high-order memory address bits to facilitate addressing 256K words of memory, and pushing the data from the D bus onto the top of the control store address stack.

9. Field eleven selects one of the four formats for field twelve. When field eleven has the value zero, field twelve is a literal value that is assigned to the B bus. In this case subfields a2 and a4 indicate the two data bytes, and fields a1 and a3 indicate the parity bits for the two bytes. (The specification in field two determines whether or not the parity bits are checked.) When field eleven is one, field 12-b1 specifies a condition which, if true, causes control to be transferred to the address in field 12-b2, i.e., field 12-b2 is assigned to the CSAR. When field eleven is two, field 12-c1 indicates special actions like using the special multiply and divide logic, loading the content addressable memory used in implementing the virtual memory organization, and clearing special condition flags; field 12-c2 permits special condition

228

Operations	Minimum time (nsec.)
Register to register	240
ALU (destination is not MAR)	240
Multiply step	240
Shifts	240
Conditional branch	280
Divide step	280
ALU (destination is MAR)	280
Sixteen-way branch	480

Figure 6.3-3. PRIME 300 microinstruction times using writable control store

flags to be changed; and field 12-c3 specifies the special condition flags. When field eleven is three, field twelve controls microprogram branching and related operations. Field 12-d1 specifies a condition like field 12-b1. Field 12-d3 specifies an operation to be performed if the condition is true. These operations include decoding a machine language instruction, popping the control store address stack, sixteen-way-branch, and multi-way-branch. Field 12-d2 serves as a mask for a set of conditions that determine whether the B bus or the ALU result should be the data source for the D bus.

With its twelve fields defining a variety of operations, PRIME 300 microinstructions are classified as horizontal. As exemplified by fields four and five, six and seven, and eleven and twelve, two level coding is often used. It is usually the case, however, that one field determines the interpretation of only one other field, a departure from the typical vertical

229

scheme in which the operation code field determines the interpretation of the remaining fields.

A somewhat unique feature of the PRIME 300 is the specification by each microinstruction of the time required to execute the microinstruction. This time, specified in field eight which also indicates bus destinations, normally ranges from 160 to 280 n sec but may be extended until the completion of a memory read or write operation. Figure 6.3-3 shows some minimum execution times for microinstructions in writable control store, which is slightly slower than the fast PROM containing microprograms to interpret the machine language instruction set.

6.3.3 PRIME 300 Microprogrammability

Part of the PRIME 300 control store can be a writable memory developed for user microprogramming. Microprograms residing in main memory may be loaded into the writable control store by a microinstruction loop in which the first two microinstructions read sixteen bits from main memory into a CPU register, and the remaining part of the loop writes the data into control store. The writable control store control logic automatically packs four sequential sixteen bit words into one 64 bit microinstruction. The PRIME 300 machine language instruction set includes four "jump to writable control store" instructions that transfer control to a microprogram whose control store address is specified in the instruction and additionally change execution mode. The transfers, which are privileged instructions to permit executive checking, take approximately 2.5 microseconds.

PRIME's Macro Assembler (PMA) can be used to create special mnemonic representation for microprograms so that they may be referenced like standard PRIME 300 instructions. The

```
       * PRIME 300 MICROPROGRAM TO PERFORM A BLOCK MOVE INSTRUCTION
       *    REGISTER USAGE:
       *         X - START OF OLD BLOCK
       *         A - END OF OLD BLOCK
       *         B - START OF NEW BLOCK
       *         S - MASK (1 IN A POSITION MEANS MOVE THAT BIT)
       *
              ORG     $C00
   1   IN     RR      RX => RY
   2          CPU     BB   RY   NONE   XOR    L     M      RA ;
                      RMMRDY     AREAD  SETCC
   3          ALU     RS AND RM => RM
   4          CPU     RF   ,    NONE   ,      ,      M     RB ;
                      RY200     NOP    JAMF   JUMP ON NE TO MOVE
   5   MOVE   ALU     INC RX => RX C= AWRITE
   6          ALU     INC RB => RB ,GO TO IN
              END
```

Figure 6.3-4. PRIME 300 microprogram to perform a block move
instruction.

Comments

1. The RR "macro" indicates a register to register move, transfer the
   X register (one of the file registers) to the MAR (the Y register).
   Thus, the address of the word to be moved is assigned to the MAR.

2. The "CPU" macro lists all the microinstruction fields. The A register
   (one of the file registers, indicated by M and RA) is selected. The
   MAR (Y register, indicated by RY) is assigned to the B bus. The ALU
   performs an exclusivee or operation (indicated by XOR and L - for
   logic) thus comparing the address of the word to be moved and the
   address of the last word to be moved, and sets the condition code

231

(SETCC). Data assigned to the D bus (from the B bus) is not used. A memory read operation is initiated (AREAD) and the microinstruction waits until data is assigned to the MDR (the M register, indicated by RMMRDY).

3. In this ALU "macro" the MDR (the M register, indicated by RM) is anded with the S register (one of the file registers). Now the masked data word from the old block is in the MDR.

4. In this CPU "macro" the commas indicate default values of the field. Move the B register (one of the file registers, indicated by M RB) to the D bus (the RF specifiation). If the condition code indicates not equal (not all words have been moved from one block to the other), transfer control to the microinstruction labelled MOVE, otherwise return to the instruction fetch routine (specified JAMF). The RY200 indicates that the next microinstruction is not to be executed until completion of a memory cycle, and that the D bus data is to be assigned to the MAR. Thus, this step returns control if the routine is finished and puts the address at which the word is to be written into the MAR.

5. Increment the X register to pint to the next word to move, and write the present word into its new location in memory.

6. Increment the B register to point to the address at which to write the next word, and trransfer control to the beginning of the routine.

micro assembler permits symbolic representation of microprograms as illustrated in Figures 6.3-4 and 6.3-5. PRIME also provides a Micro Debug Package to assist in microprogram development.

```
* PRIME 300 MICROPROGRAM TO PERFORM A MULTIPLY INSTRUCTION
*    MULTIPLY RB * RA
1        RR      RA => RM
2        CPU     AL   RCM  NX    ZERO    L     M     RA ;
                 RF   NOP  LOADRSC;
                 DATA -15
3        CPU     RFRS 5    NX    6       0     M     RB ;
                 RF   LINK
* MAIN MULTIPLY LOOP - 2 MICROINSTRUCTIONS
4        CPU     ALRS RM   NX    ADD     0     M     RA ;
                 RF   LINK NOP
                 EAC  MPYLOGIC
5        CPU     RFRS 0    ALL   6       0     M     RB ;
                 RF   LINK INCRSC;
                 JUMP ON RSCNEM1 TO *-1
* CLEAN UP
6        ALU     RA MINUS RM => RA C= AOVFL;
                 NOP  EAC MPYLOGIC
```

Figure 6.3-5. PRIME 300 microprogram to perform a multiply instruction.

Comments

1. Move the A register (one of the file registers), which contains one of the operands, to the MDR.

2. Set the A register to zero (M RA selects the A register, ZERO L generates zero from the ALU, AL assigns it to the D bus, and RF assigns the value to the A register). Set the shift counter (LOADRSC) to -15 (DATA -15).

3. Shift the B register (which originally contains the second operand) right one bit (M RB and RFRS), reset the vacated bit, and set the

233

link register to the shifted out bit.

4. If the link bit is 1 then add the A and MDR registers, shift the
   result right one bit, and store the result in register A. If the link
   bit is 0 then shift the A register right one bit and store the result
   in the A register. This special multiply step is indicated by
   EAC MPYLOGIC and other fields. Set the link bit to the bit that was
   lost in shifting.

5. Shift the B register right one bit, set bit 2 of the B register to
   the value of the link bit, and reset the vacated bit. Set the link
   bit to the bit that was lost in shifting. Test the shift counter. If
   it is equal to -1 go to step 6, otherwise increment the shift counter
   (INCRSC) and go to step 4.

6. If the link bit is 1, then subtract the MDR from the A register and
   store the result in the A register. Set the carry bit if there was an
   overflow. At this point registers A and B contain the product. Note
   that bit 1 of the B register contains the zero shifted in by step 3.
   Step 5 does not alter bit 1 (the most significant bit) of the
   B register because the double word integer mode on the PRIME 300 does
   not use bit 1 of the second word.

6.4 The Varian 73

6.4.1 Varian 73 Background

The Varian 73 is a general purpose minicomputer designed
for use in a variety of scientific, commercial, and industrial
applications. The machine language instruction repertoire has
150 instructions which feature several addressing modes -
direct, multilevel indirect, immediate, indexed/indirect,
relative, and extended with preindexing - for memory which may

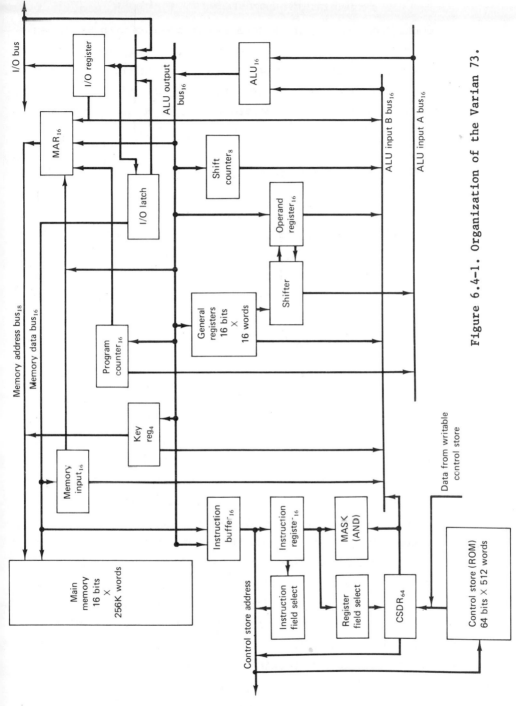

Figure 6.4-1. Organization of the Varian 73.

235

be configured from 4 or 8K core memory modules with 660-n sec
cycle time and 1, 2, 4, or 8K semiconductor memory modules with
330-n sec cycle time. These times are even multiples of the
processor and normal microinstruction time of 165-n sec. Core
memory modules can be interleaved to yield an effective cycle
time of 450-500 n sec.

6.4.2 Varian 73 Architecture

6.4.2.1 Varian 73 Functional Components

As illustrated in Figure 6.4-1 the basic Varian 73 CPU
contains a 512-word control store implemented in read only
memory. The microinstructions in this control store, which has
a 165 nanosecond cycle time, emulate the machine language
instructions of the Varian 620/f. To enhance execution of
application programs and to facilitate user microprogramming
the ROM control store may be augmented by 256- or 512-word
modules of writable control store, which have a cycle time of
190 n sec. Varian provided microprograms in the writable
control store perform double word arithmetic, floating point
arithmetic, Fortran oriented routines, byte manipulation, and
stack manipulation. These optional microprograms interpret
instructions that are generated by the Fortran compiler when
the F option to the compiler is specified. The control store
capacity is 2048 words which constitute four 512-word "pages."
Associated with the writable control store modules is a stack
which can store sixteen control store addresses. An interesting
feature of the Varian 73 control store scheme is the ability to
load control store fields which specify general register
selection (in the microinstruction in the control store data
register) with data from the instruction register. This
operation facilitates machine language instruction decoding

because the updated microinstruction operates on those registers specified in the machine language instruction.

The thirty-two operations which the Varian 73 ALU can perform are the same as those listed in Figure 5.2-2 except that the input operands and output result contain sixteen bits and that the CF field in the microinstruction specifies a carry of zero, one, the carry flag stored from a previous ALU operation, or the complement of the carry flag. The ALU communicates with the rest of the CPU via three busses. The two input busses are not symmetric in that the same information is not available to both busses. The inputs to the A bus of the ALU are the program counter, a general register, a word all of whose bits are zero, or a word all of whose bits are one. The general register input may optionally be shifted left or right one bit on its way to the ALU. This preshift capability is somewhat unusual. B bus ALU inputs include a sixteen bit control store literal, the instruction register masked by a sixteen bit control store literal, the memory input register, a general register, the operand register, the I/O register, or one of the operand register bytes (optionally sign extended). Another B bus input to the ALU is the sixteen bit PSW (program status word) which indicates conditions like ALU result zero, ALU result negative, ALU result all ones, ALU overflow, and ALU carry; and also contains five bits of the shift counter and the four bits of the processor key register. The PSW may also be altered by the ALU operation. Shifting a general register on its way to the A bus has been discussed, however, the operand register may additionally be shifted left or right one bit independently or in conjunction with the shifting of a general register, to provide double word shift capabilities.

Most of the local store registers have been mentioned, but many have associated transformation facilities such as the shifting associated with the sixteen general registers and the operand register. The sixteen bit program counter can be used as a memory address, and it can be incremented independently from the ALU operation. The eight bit shift counter may be incremented and tested independently from the ALU operation.

A variety of facilities associated with main memory improve the efficiency of interpreting machine language instructions on the Varian 73. Two sixteen bit registers, the instruction buffer register and the memory input register, serve as memory data registers. The Varian 73 provides two types of memory read operations. It can read data from memory into the memory input register alone, and it can read data into the memory input register and into the instruction buffer register. Memory write operations write the ALU output data (or one of the two bytes in the word) to memory. The memory address for these operations is specified by the memory address register (which may be loaded from the memory input register, the I/O register, the program counter, or the ALU output bus) and the key register, which contains the high-order bits of the the address. The instruction register holds the machine language instruction being executed. When used together, the instruction buffer register and the instruction register form a pipeline, i.e., before the completion of the execution of the current machine language instruction the next machine language instruction is read from memory into the instruction buffer register. Upon completion of the current instruction, the instruction register can be immediately loaded from the instruction buffer rather than from the slower main memory.

In the Varian 73 every microinstruction specifies the address of the next microinstruction to be executed. The addressing scheme is quite involved so we delay its description until the explaination of the use of some microinstruction fields.

238

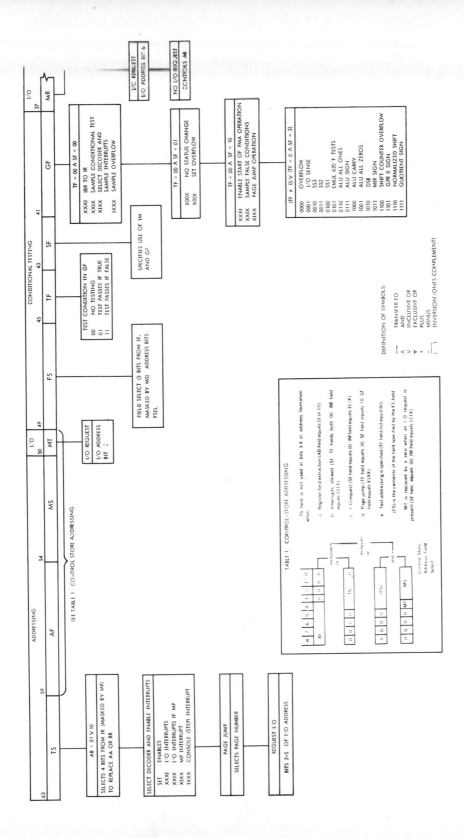

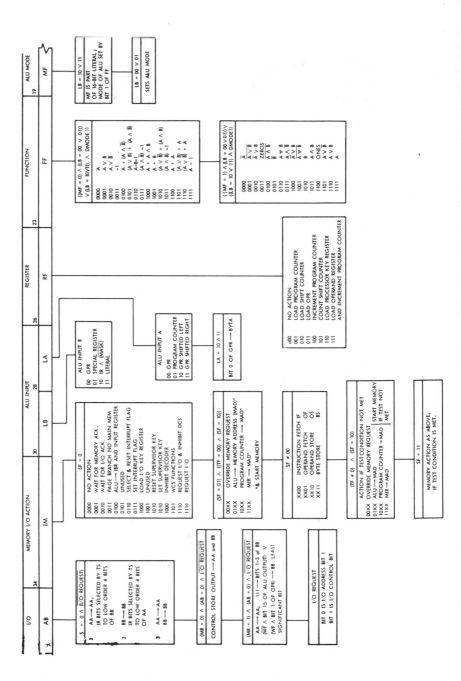

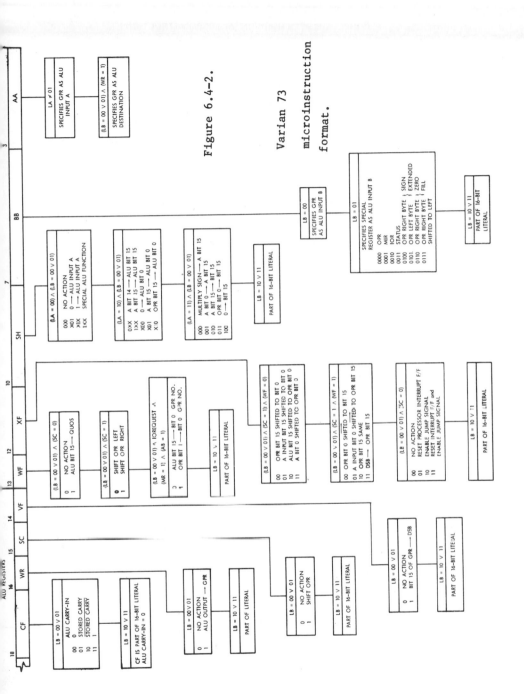

Figure 6.4-2.

Varian 73 microinstruction format.

241

6.4.2.2 Varian 73 Microinstruction Format

The Varian 73 microinstruction format, shown in Figure 6.4-2, is quite complex due to the large number of fields and the multiple level encoding of fields, i.e., the interpretation of a microinstruction field may depend on the values of two or more other fields and special conditions. While Figure 6.4-2 indicates the complete microinstruction repertoire, it gives little insight into how to microprogram the Varian 73.

To use the ALU it is necessary to specify the A bus source, the B bus source, the ALU operation, and the destination. The ALU A bus input is specified primarily by the LA field. If the input is one of the general registers, the AA field specifies the register. If the register is to be shifted, the SH field specifies the shift operation. The ALU B bus input is specified primarily by the LB and BB fields. When the B bus input is a sixteen bit control store literal, the literal comprises bits four through nineteen of the microinstruction, i.e., fields MF, CF, WR, SC, VF, WF, XF, SH, and BB. The ALU operation is specified by three microinstruction fields: the FF field which indicates one of sixteen functions (like bits 12-15 in Figure 5.2-2), the MF field which indicates that the arithmetic or logical function is to be performed (like bits 10-11 in Figure 5.2-2), and the CF field which specifies the carry input as zero, one, the stored carry, or the complement of the stored carry. The destination of the ALU result is specified by the RF field which indicates the program counter, operand register, shift counter, or key register; the LB, WR, and AA fields which indicate a general register; and the SF and IM fields which indicate memory data bus, memory address bus, memory input register, or instruction buffer register. Operand register shifting is controlled by the LB and SC fields which indicate whether or not shifting is to be performed, the WF field which indicates shift direction, and the XF field which specifies the value for the bit vacated by the one bit shift.

Several fields contribute to the formation of the next control store address. Table 1 in Figure 6.4-2 specifies the normal combination of microinstruction fields to form the next control store address. The FS field may specify a value or it may specify which five consecutive bits from the instruction register are to be used. Conditional branching is specified by the TF field which indicates no condition testing, test for false condition, or test for true condition. The GF field specifies the condition to be tested. If the condition test is successful the next control store address is that indicated previously, otherwise formation of the next control store address uses only the AF and TS fields. Jumping to another page in control store is specified by the TF, SF, GF, and IM fields. In this case the nine least significant address bits are determined as before and the TS field specifies the new page. A bit in the GF field may specify initiation of a memory operation in conjunction with the page jump. When interrupts are enabled, the next control store address may be constructed from the AF field which constitutes the high-order five bits and from the interrupt logic which constitutes the low-order four bits. The three control store address stack operations, branch and push, branch and pop, and branch and delete, are indicated by fixed values in the TF, SF, IM, and LB fields and different values in the AA and BB fields. The address pushed onto the stack is thirteen bits of the control store literal described earlier.

The IM field specifies the memory operation and the source for the memory address register. The microinstruction following a microinstruction that initiates a memory operation may change

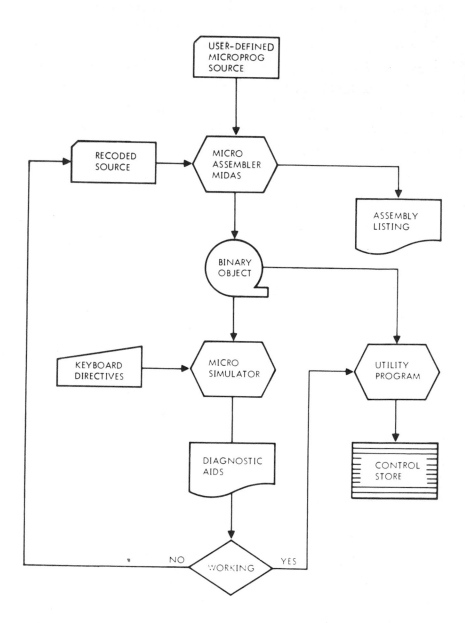

Figure 6.4-3. Varian 73 microprogramming support software.

	IDENT	MBM			MBMA			MBMB
MEMORY FUNCTION		word 0 page 1			storing data	fetching data	fetching data	
REQUEST					ØF		TESTF ØS	IF
ADDRESS		P			P		ALU	ALU
ALU INPUT A			R0	R1	—	R2	R0	R7
INPUT B					MIR			
OUTPUT		TRANA	DECA	DECA	TRANB	DECA	INCA	INCA
DESTINATION		R7	R0	see below	—	R2	R0	see below
STATUS SAMPLE						ALU	ALUS	
TEST							TESTT	
ADDRESSING MODE		PJMP						PJMP to 0
ADDRESS		MBM					P-MBMB F-MBMA	SS3M (02D)
OTHER SPECIAL ACTIONS				POUT	INCP			POUT

Figure 5.4-4. Varian 73 flow diagram for memory-to-memory block move instruction.

245

the type of operation. Through the SF and TF fields, both the initiation and overriding of memory operations may be conditioned upon a test specified by the GF field.

6.4.3 Varian 73 Microprogrammability

The Varian 73 may contain 1,536 words of writable control store. The writable control store may be loaded from main memory or general registers zero and one using I/O instructions. In addition, data from writable control store can be read into main memory or into general registers zero and one. Since the writable control store physically comprises separate modules, loading one module may proceed simultaneously with the execution of microinstructions from another module. Transfer of control between different control store modules may be accomplished via the page jump microoperation, however, the protocol between the instruction fetch microprogram and the microprogram to interpret the instruction must be maintained by new microprograms in the writable control store.

As illustrated in Figure 6.4-3, Varian provides a comprehensive software package to support development of user microprograms. To simplify the development of efficient microprograms using the sixty-four bit horizontal microinstructions, Varian encourages the use of "flow diagrams," like the one shown in Figure 6.4-4, to represent microprograms. In this diagram each vertical column represents a microinstruction, and the rows indicate the basic capabilities in a microinstruction. The translation from such a flow diagram into the machine readable assembler language is relatively straightforward.

Figure 6.4-5 shows the assembler language version of the microprogram diagrammed in Figure 6.4-4. The microinstruction

```
         1   *
         2   *
         3   *        MEMORY-TO-MEMORY BLOCK MOVE
         4   *
         5   *        CALL: BCS TO WORD 0
         6   *
         7   *        PARAMETERS:   A REG - 'TO' ADDRESS
         8   *                      B REG - 'FROM' ADDRESS
         9   *                      X REG - BLOCK LENGTH
        10   *
        11   *

0001    13   R1       EQU       1
        14   *
        15   *        THE FOLLOWING ARE SUPPLEMENTAL OPCODES
        16   *        FOR USE WITH THE MICRO ASSEMBLER
        17   *
        18   *
0009    19   ADD      EQU       9
0008    20   ALUC     EQU       8
0006    21   ALUO     EQU       6
0007    22   ALUS     EQU       7
0009    23   ALUZ     EQU       9
000B    24   AND      EQU       X'B
0002    25   AONE     EQU       2
0001    26   AZERO    EQU       1
0000    27   A$GPR    EQU       0
0002    28   A$GPRL   EQU       2
0003    29   A$GPRR   EQU       3
0001    30   A$P      EQU       1
0000    31   A$SPEC   EQU       0
0007    32   BS$ALU   EQU       7
000F    33   BS$MIR   EQU       X'F
0003    34   BS$OVR   EQU       3
000B    35   BS$P     EQU       X'B
0000    36   B$GPR    EQU       0
0001    37   B$SPEC   EQU       1
0003    38   CRY1     EQU       3
000F    39   DECA     EQU       X'F
0009    40   DECB     EQU       9
0004    41   DECODE   EQU       4
0005    42   DECOD$   EQU       5
0006    43   EOR      EQU       6
0003    44   FT       EQU       3
0001    45   GPROUT   EQU       1
000D    46   GPRS     EQU       X'D
0001    47   IBR$I    EQU       1
0004    48   IF$ALU   EQU       4
000C    49   IF$MIR   EQU       X'C
0000    50   IF$OVR   EQU       0
0008    51   IF$P     EQU       8
0000    52   INCA     EQU       0
0001    53   INCB     EQU       1

0004    54   INCP     EQU       4
0005    55   INCSC    EQU       5
0002    56   IOR      EQU       2
0001    57   IOSR     EQU       1
0006    58   KOUT     EQU       6
0000    59   LFT      EQU       0
0003    60   LIT      EQU       3
0001    61   LOG      EQU       1
0001    62   MEMC     EQU       1
0002    63   MEMC$    EQU       2
0001    64   MIR      EQU       1
000B    65   MIRS     EQU       X'B
0002    66   MSK      EQU       2
000E    67   NORM     EQU       X'E
0000    68   NOTA     EQU       0
0005    69   NOTB     EQU       5
0005    70   OF$ALU   EQU       5
000D    71   OF$MIR   EQU       X'D
0001    72   OF$OVR   EQU       1
0009    73   OF$P     EQU       9
0007    74   OLZF     EQU       7
```

247

```
                                         131   *      FOLLOWING ARE ROM STANDARD STATE ADDRESSES
                                         132   *
                                         133   *
                            013E  SS1M   134   EQU   X'13E            RESTART PIPELINE @ P
                            0092  SS2M   135   EQU   X'092            MAINTAIN PIPELINE
                            002D  SS3M   136   EQU   X'02D            DECODE NEXT INSTRUCTION (IN IBR)

                            0000         138   ORG   0

                                         140   *      FOLLOWING IS BCS ENTRY POINT
                                         141   *
0000  180800018000000               143   GEN   /N(MBM),10(PJMP),1(1)    BRANCH TO BLOCK MOVE ROUTINE

                                         145   *      FOLLOWING IS ACTUAL BLOCK MOVE ROUTINE
                                         146   *
                                         147   *
                            0101         149   ORG   X'101

                                         151   *      SAVE P IN R7
                                         152   *
0101  0810000008F90007   MBM  154   GEN   /*,12(A$P),14(TRNA),15(LOG),17(GPROUT),24(R7)

                                         156   *      DECR 'TO' ADDR
                                         157   *
0102  0818000000F10000         159   GEN   /*,12(A$GPR),24(R0),14(DECA),17(GPROUT)

                                         161   *      DECR 'FROM' ADDR ; PUT IT IN P
                                         162   *                              (continued)
```

```
0005   75  OLSE     EQU   5
0003   76  ONES     EQU   3
0000   77  OPR      EQU   0
0003   78  OPROUT   EQU   3
0001   79  OR       EQU   1
0004   80  ORSE     EQU   4
0006   81  ORZF     EQU   6
000E   82  OS$ALU   EQU   X'E
0002   83  OS$MIR   EQU   X'2
000A   84  OS$OVR   EQU   X'A
0000   85  OS$P     EQU   0
0003   86  OVFL     EQU   3
000F   87  PJMP     EQU   X'F
000F   88  PJMP$    EQU   X'F
0000   89  POUT     EQU   0
0002   90  QUOS     EQU   2
0000   91  R0       EQU   0
0002   92  R2       EQU   2
0003   93  R3       EQU   3
0004   94  R4       EQU   4
0005   95  R5       EQU   5
0006   96  R6       EQU   6
0007   97  R7       EQU   7
0008   98  R8       EQU   8
0009   99  R9       EQU   9
000A  100  RA       EQU   X'A
000B  101  RB       EQU   X'B
000C  102  RC       EQU   X'C
000D  103  RD       EQU   X'D
000E  104  RE       EQU   X'E
000F  105  RF       EQU   X'F
0001  106  RGHT     EQU   1
0000  107  SCOUT    EQU   0
000C  108  SFTC     EQU   X'C
000C  109  SHFA     EQU   X'C
000A  110  SHFT     EQU   X'A
0001  111  SHFTOP   EQU   1
0004  112  SPEC     EQU   4
0003  113  SSW1     EQU   3
0003  114  SSW2     EQU   3
0003  115  SSW3     EQU   3
0006  116  STAT     EQU   6
0002  117  SUB      EQU   2
0006  118  S$ALU    EQU   6
0001  119  S$OVFL   EQU   1
0002  120  S$SHFT   EQU   2
0003  121  TCB      EQU   3
0002  122  TESTT    EQU   2
0005  123  TESTF    EQU   5
000F  124  TFIR     EQU   X'F
0002  125  TRNA     EQU   2
0001  126  TRNB     EQU   1
0003  127  TT       EQU   3
0001  128  WAITMD   EQU   1
0003  129  ZERO     EQU   3
```

```
0103  0820000001F00001  164       GEN    /*,12(A$GPR),24(R1),14(DECA),13(POUT)
                         166    *
                         167    *   FIRST LOOP MICROWORD; STORE AT 'TO'; REQUEST FETCH OF INCR 'FROM'
0104  08280404A4A80010  169  MBMA  GEN    /*,10(OF$P),6(MEMC),11(B$SPEC),23(MIR),14(TRNB),15(LOG),
                         170                 C13(INCP)
                         172    *
                         173    *   SECOND LOOP MICROWORD; DECR BLOCK LENGTH;  SAMPLE RESULT FOR TEST
0105  0830008000F10002  175       GEN    /*,12(A$GPR),24(R2),14(DECA),17(GPROUT),7(S$ALU)
                         177    *
                         178    *   FINAL LOOP MICROWORD; EXIT OR CONTINUE THE LOOP WITH REQUEST
                         179    *   FOR A STORE AT INCREMENTED 'TO' ADDR
0106  283829C300070000  181       GEN    /T(MBMB,MBMA),5(TT),10(OS$ALU),6(TESTF),
                         182                 C12(A$GPR),24(R0),14(INCA),16(CRY1),17(GPROUT),7(ALUS)
                         184    *
                         185    *   EXIT MICROWORD ; RESTORE P AND THE PIPELINE
0107  0168090201060007  187  MBMB  GEN    /N(SS=M),7(PJMP$),1(0),10(IF$ALU),6(MEMC$),5(0),
                         188                 C12(A$GPR),24(R7),14(INCA),16(CRY1),13(POUT)

                         19C       END
```

SYMBOLS
0000 A$GPR	0002 A$GPRL	0003 A$GPRR	0001 A$P	0000 A$SPEC
0009 ADD	0008 ALUC	0006 ALUO	0007 ALUS	0009 ALUZ
000B AND	0002 AONE	0001 AZERO	0000 B$GPR	0001 B$SPEC
0007 BS$ALU	000F BS$MIR	0003 BS$OVR	000B BS$P	0003 CRY1
000F DECA	0009 DECB	0005 DECB$	0004 DECODE	0006 EOR
0003 FT	0001 GPROUT	000D GPRS	0001 IBR$I	0004 IF$ALU
000C IF$MIR	0000 IF$OVR	0008 IF$P	0000 INCA	0001 INCB
0004 INCP	0005 INCSC	0002 IOR	0001 IOSR	0006 KOUT
0000 LFT	0003 LIT	0001 LOG	0101 MBM	0104 MBMA
0107 MBMB	0001 MEMC	0002 MEMC$	0001 MIR	000B MIRS
0002 MSK	000E NORM	0000 NOTA	0005 NOTB	0005 OF$ALU
000D OF$MIR	0001 OF$OVR	0009 OF$P	0005 OLSE	0007 OLZF
0003 ONES	0000 OPR	0003 OPRCUT	0004 OR	0004 ORSE
0006 ORZF	0006 OS$ALU	000E OS$MIR	0002 OS$OVR	000A OS$P
0000 OVFL	0003 PJMP	0004 PJMF$	0001 POUT	000F QUOS
0000 R0	0001 R1	0002 R2	0003 R3	0004 R4
0005 R5	0006 R6	0007 R7	0008 R8	0009 R9
000A RA	000B RB	000C RC	000D RD	000E RE
000F RF	0001 RGHT	0002 S$ALU	0006 S$OVFL	0001 S$SHFT
0002 SCOUT	000C SFTC	000A SHFA	000A SHFT	0001 SHFTOP
0000 SPEC	013E SS1M	0092 SS2M	002D SS3M	0004 SSW1
0002 SSW2	0002 SSW3	0003 STAT	0006 SUB	0002 TCB
0002 TESTF	0003 TESTT	0005 TFIR	000F TRNA	000A TRNB
0002 TT	0001 WAITMD	0003 ZERO		

0 ERRORS ASSEMBLY COMPLETE

Figure 6.4-5. Assembler language version of the Varian 73 microprogram for the memory-to-memory block move instruction.

Detailed Comments on Microinstructions

1. 12($AP) indicates that field 12 (LA) has the value 1, i.e., the program counter (P register) is the ALU A input. 15(LOG) indicates that field 15 (MF) has the value 1, i.e., the ALU mode is logical. 14(TRNA) indicates that field 14 has the value F (hexadecimal), i.e., the ALU operation is pass the A input through and do not change it. 17(GPROUT) indicates that field 17 (WR) has the value 1, i.e., the ALU output is to be assigned to a general register. 24(R7) indicates that field 24 (AA) has the value 7, i.e., the general register addressed is number 7. /* indicates sequential addressing. Thus, this microinstruction assigns the P register to the A bus, passes it through the ALU, assigns it to general register 7, and goes to the next microinstruction.

2. Assign general register 0 to the A bus, decrement it, and assign the result back to general register 0. Thus the address to which the block will be moved is decremented because the microinstructions which request memory operations increment the address.

3. Assign general register 1 to the A bus, decrement it, and put the result in the program counter.

4. Increment the program counter to address the next word to be moved (indicated by 13(INCP)). Initiate a memory read to bring the data into the memory input register (indicated by 10(OF$P) and 6(MEMC)). The present memory input register, which contains data read during the last time through the loop, is assigned to the B bus (indicated by 11(B$SPEC) and 23(MIR)) and passed through the ALU (indicated by 14(TRNB) and 15(LOG)) so that it will be written into memory by the

250

operation indicated by the previous microinstruction in the loop
(microinstruction number 6).

5. Assign general register 2 to the A bus, decrement it, put the result
   back into general register 2, and sample the ALU output for testing
   by the next microinstruction. This microinstruction thus decrements
   the block length.

6. Assign general register 0 to the A bus, increment it, and store the
   result in general register 0, i.e., increment the address at which to
   write data. Test the sign of the previous ALU operation (indicated by
   7(ALUS)), i.e., see if the necessary number of words have been moved.
   If the condition (indicated by 5(TT)) is true, exit the loop, i.e.,
   branch to the microinstruction labelled MBMB. If the condition is
   false, initiate a memory write operation to the updated address
   (indicated by 10(OS$ALU) and 6(TESTF)) and branch to the
   microinstruction labelled MBMA to determine the data to be written
   and continue looping.

7. At this point the specified number of words has been moved, so
   general register 7 is incremented and stored in the program counter
   so it points to the next machine instruction, operations are
   performed to maintain the pipeline, and cntrol is transferred back to
   the instruction fetch and decode routine.

   statements in this language contain fields for a label, an
   operation, operands, and comments. The operations may indicate
   pseudoinstructions or microinstructions. Pseudoinstructions in
   Figure 6.4-5 include EQU which assigns a value to the symbol
   specified in the label field, ORG which sets the location
   counter, and END which indicates end of the microprogram. For
   microinstructions the operation field contains the name of a
   format which defines the interpretation of the operand fields.

251

The predefined GEN format, used for all the microinstructions in Figure 6.4-5, defines fields as in Figure 6.4-2, except that the AF and MS fields are considered to be a single address field. Another predefined format, GMSK, is similar except that the MF, CF, WR, SC, VF, WF, XF, SH, and BB fields are combined into a sixteen bit MK (mask) field. Users may define additional formats with the FORM pseudoinstruction. The operands in a statement specify values for the fields in the microinstruction. In the example in Figure 6.4-5 most operands are of the form i(A), where i is the number of the field in the microinstruction format and A is a symbol whose value is to be assigned to field i. Another possible representation is Fj, where F names the microinstruction field and j is the value to be assigned to that field. The first operand in each microinstruction in Figure 6.4-5 specifies addressing. The format for the addressing operand is

/mode(address1,address2)

where mode specifies type of addressing: N for normal, T for test, F for field select, S for test and field select, P for page jump, and * for implicit (sequential); address1 is the address of the next microinstruction in situations not involving testing, or the next address if the condition is satisfied in test situations; and address2 is the next address if the condition is not satisfied in testing situations. The assembler also provides facilities for macro definition and use.

The microprogram simulator for the Varian 73 provides many facilities for microprogram testing. Simulator commands fall into three classes – simulator and storage initialization, storage examination and changing, and execution control. The execution control commands include dumping control store, setting and removing trace points (addresses at which the values of a fixed set of registers, conditions, and microinstruction related data are printed), and entering or leaving single step mode.

The microprogram utility routine MIUTIL loads microinstructions into the writable control store and provides commands for on-line microprogram debugging. MIUTIL uses two classes of commands. The basic command set includes loading writable control store, examining and changing microinstructions, and dumping microinstructions. The debugging command set includes setting and removing trace points (addresses at which the program prints the microinstruction address before executing the microinstruction), executing a specified number of microinstructions, and terminating the program. All the programs in the support software package run on the Varian 73.

6.4.4 Additional Varian 73 Features

Two interesting optional features of the Varian 73 are the writable instruction decoder control store and the writable I/O control store which are available with writable control store modules. The instruction decoder control store, which consists of two arrays with 16 sixteen bit words, in conjunction with the instruction decode logic translates a sixteen bit machine instruction into a nine bit control store address to interpret the instruction. Setting the second bit of the GF field to one and setting the TF and SF fields to zero enables the decoders. The simulator and debugger both allow interaction with the instruction decoder control store.

The I/O Control Section of the Varian 73 performs I/O routines under control of I/O microprograms that reside in a 256-word I/O control store which has its own address register and data (command) register. The sixteen bit microinstruction words control such operations as selecting the source for the I/O register, assigning the I/O register to the I/O bus, initiating control signals for direct memory access, requesting main memory cycles, and indicating wait and busy states. The I/O Control Section is initiated by a control store microinstruction with the starting address in the MT, MR, and TS fields or by external events such as program interrupts or direct memory address transfers. It operates concurrently with central control.

6.5 The NANODATA QM-1

6.5.1 QM-1 Background

The NANODATA QM-1 is a general purpose digital computer that offers great flexibility through a variety of interesting architectural features - a two level control store, three arrays of local storage registers (one of which provides residual control functions), twelve busses which connect the various functional units to the central local store array, and several units that simultaneously perform data transformations. The purpose of this flexible architecture is to provide efficient emulation of a variety of computers. Thus the QM-1 serves as a research vehicle as well as a general purpose applications computer. Indeed the first production machine was shipped to a large computer manufacturer for use in future machine research.

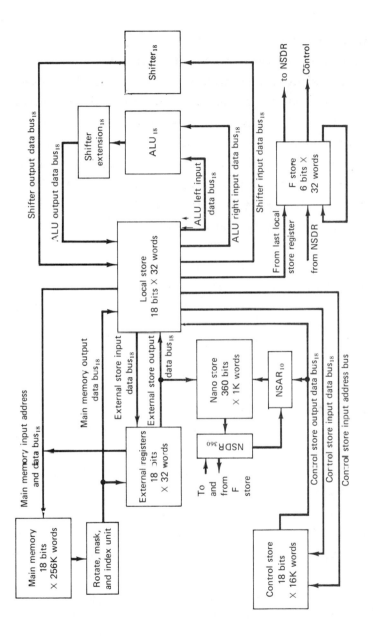

Figure 6.5-1. Architecture of the NANODATA QM-1.

255

6.5.2 QM-1 Architecture

6.5.2.1 QM-1 Functional Units

The most unusual feature of the QM-1 architecture is the two level control store illustrated in Figure 6.5-1. The higher level control store, which corresponds to the usual control store concept, is a fully readable and writable general purpose memory whose word length is eighteen bits, the standard QM-1 word size. Implemented in semiconductor memory with a 150 n sec cycle time, control store is available in blocks of 1,024 words and may be expanded to a maximum size of 16,384 words. Control store input comes from any of the central local store registers via the Control Store Input Data Bus. Control store output may be directed to a local store register or it may be used in addressing the lower level control store. Addresses for the control store read and write operations are generally supplied by the Control Store Input Address Bus, which is assigned the value of a local store register. Other sources for control store addresses are the Control Store Output Data Bus, one of four local store registers that serve as microprogram counters (control store address registers), and the value of a local store register as modified by the INDEX ALU, which will be discussed subsequently.

The lower level control store, called the nanostore, is a writable semiconductor memory with a 75 n sec access time. Nanostore is available in 256-word blocks to a maximum of 1,024 words. The word size of the instructions in nanostore, called nanoinstructions, is 360 bits. A priority selection scheme provides nanostore addresses from a list of potential addresses. Associated with each address is a condition. When nanostore is to be read, the selected address corresponds to the pending condition of highest priority that is not masked.

256

The condition with highest priority is a program check
condition such as main memory parity error, main memory address
error, attempt to execute a privileged operation, or a
nanoinstruction time out - the same nanoinstruction has been
continuously repeated for 1 sec. When a program check condition
arises, a service routine is initiated by loading the first
words from a special read only memory into the nanostore data
register (called the Control Matrix). The condition with the
next highest priority is the execution of a branch
nanooperation (which NANODATA calls a nanoprimitive) in the
current nanoinstruction. The next nanostore address is then
taken from a ten bit field in the Control Matrix. The next 30
conditions are external interrupts. The last 10 external
registers (see Figure 6.5-1) contain 30 six bit address fields
that correspond to the 30 interrupts. To transform a six bit
address field to a ten bit address field a zero is inserted
before the first bit and three zeros are inserted after the
second bit, e.g., 111111 becomes 0110001111. If none of these
conditions are true, then the nanostore program counter (which
can be incremented independently of the ALU) supplies the
nanostore address.

In the two level control store scheme in the QM-1, machine
language instructions in main memory are executed by
microprograms in control store, and the microinstructions in
control store are in turn executed by nanoprograms in
nanostore, rather than by hardwired logic. The
microinstructions in control store are typically vertical, with
one operation code and two or more operand fields within one or
more eighteen bit words, and may be defined by the user. The
nanoinstructions in nanostore are horizontal. The reason for
using two storage levels was to provide flexibility. Indeed,
since the control store is general purpose it can be used as

257

main memory, and the main memory may be used as secondary backup storage. Using both vertical and horizontal schemes makes available the advantages of both - the parallelism in horizontal microinstructions and the simplicity and smaller storage required for vertical microinstructions.

The central local storage facility is an array of 32 eighteen bit words (see Figure 6.5-1). Each of these local store registers may be connected, under nanoprogram control, to any of the twelve busses, and there is no restriction on the number or identity of busses that may be connected to any one local store register at a time. If two or more busses attempt to assign data to the same local store register simultaneously, the logical or of the two values appears in the register. Associated with the local store registers are several special purpose capabilities. Register 31, the last local store register, serves as the control store data register. It has three separate six bit fields - C (six most significant bits), A (middle six bits), and B (six least significant bits). These fields are used in conjunction with the F Store and other QM-1 operations. Registers 24 - 27 serve as control store address registers. Any one of them may, independently of the ALU, be incremented by 1, 2, the B field of register 31, or the number formed by concatenating the A and B fields of register 31.

All the local store registers except for registers 24 - 27 may be manipulated by a special INDEX ALU unit, which operates independently of the main ALU and shifter. Sources for the INDEX ALU are a local store register and one of twelve external registers (registers 8 through 19), a word all of whose bits are one, the data on the Main Memory Output Data Bus, or the data on the Control Store Output Data Bus. The INDEX ALU operations are the same as those in Figure 5.2-2 except that the operands are eighteen bits long and the carry is a constant. A local store register receives the output from this special manipulator. The sources, transformation, and destination involved in the operation of the INDEX ALU are selected by fields in a nanoinstruction and registers in the F Store.

The External Store, another local store array with 32 eighteen bit registers, comprises several groups of registers, each of which is mainly devoted to a special function. The first eight external store registers are used in I/O operations. The next twelve external store registers serve as source operands for the INDEX ALU. Each of the last ten registers provides 3 six bit addresses that correspond to external interrupts.

The third local store array is the F Store which contains 32 six bit registers. The F Store provides residual control over a variety of hardware resources. The first fourteen F registers control the busses – in addition to the twelve busses shown in Figure 6.5-1 there are two busses that provide addresses for external store input and output. The value of an F register generally indicates the local store register to which the corresponding bus is connected, however, the F register value indicates an external register for the External Store Address busses and for the Main Memory busses when the address value is greater than thirty-one. The next six F registers provide special control functions – auxiliary control actions (enable and disable external interrupts, loading parameters for the RMI Unit, etc.), specifying which of the local store registers 24 – 27 is to serve as microprogram counter, indicating machine mode (sixteen or eighteen bit ALU mode, user or supervisor mode, normal or read only nanostore mode, etc.) and saving status flags. The last twelve registers in the F Store, called the G fields, do not control machine functions but may store data that will later be assigned to another F register. Source data for the F Store registers comes from fields called the Auxiliary fields in the current nanoinstruction and from the three fields in the microinstruction register. Data from the F Store may also be assigned to the nanoinstruction in the Nano Store Data Register thus affecting the execution of the nanoinstruction.

The QM-1 ALU performs the operations indicated in Figure 5.2-2 except that the input operands are normally eighteen bits in length. Four bits in the nanoinstruction field KALC perform the function of bits twelve through fifteen in Figure 5.2-2, another bit in the KALC field specifies one of the two columns in Figure 5.2-2, and a carry bit specifies the carry to be added. While the normal ALU mode handles eighteen bit numbers in twos complement notation, the ALU can also handle sixteen bit numbers, and ones complement, unsigned, and decimal representations. The eighteen bit ALU result is directed to the shifter extension, which may shift the result before assignment to a local store register. In addition to the eighteen bit result the ALU generates the following testable conditions:

1. carry out,
2. overflow,
3. result equal zero,
4. result sign.

These conditions may be stored in one of the F registers for later interrogation. In general, the ALU requires two basic clock cycles, a total of 150 n secs, to perform an operation.

The QM-1 shifter performs the following types of shift operations: left and right logical, left and right arithmetic, and left and right circular. When no shift operation is specified, the shifter provides a convenient mechanism for transferring data from one local store register to another. To perform double length shift operations, the shifter extension is joined to the shifter to shift the number formed by joining the ALU output and the shifter input. The double length shift operations may be left or right, and arithmetic, logical, or circular. The shifter generates two testable conditions - high bit and low bit of the result on the Shifter Output Data Bus. Single and double shift operations normally require two clock cycles for completion, however, three clock cycles are required when performing an ALU operation and then a double shift. operation.

Main memory on the QM-1 is an eighteen bit wide core memory with a 750 n sec cycle time and a 600-n sec read access time. Available in 16K modules, core memory may be expanded to 256K words. The Main Memory Input Address and Data Busses and the Main Memory Output Data Bus may be connected to the first eight external registers in addition to the local store registers. In addition to its normal read-write operation, the memory may, under nanoprogram control, perform a read-modify-write operation in which the data read from memory is transformed (modified) before the regeneration (write) operation puts data back into the word from which it was read. Main memory output may optionally be transformed by a special RMI (Rotate, Mask, and Index) Unit before assignment to a local store or external register. The RMI Unit is a general data transformation device that is especially useful in extracting fields from a machine language instruction. The RMI Unit performs three operations: doing a right circular shift, masking the shift result, and adding the mask result to an eighteen bit index. Another option facilitates main memory protection. External registers 16 and 17 (or 20 and 21) serve

261

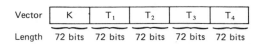

Figure 6.5-2. Format of QM-1 nanoinstruction.

as base and length registers. The main memory address is added to the base register to form an absolute address. If this absolute address is greater than the sum of the base and length registers, a main memory address violation program check is generated.

6.5.2.2 QM-1 Nanoinstruction Repertoire

Since the QM-1 microinstructions may be designed by the user, we examine the nanoinstructions which interpret microinstructions. The QM-1 nanoinstruction format, illustrated in Figure 6.5-2, is quite unusual; the 360 bits constitute five "vectors." When a nanoinstruction is read from nanostore into the control matrix (nanostore data register) the K vector and the T1 vector become active. The fields of the K vector, shown in Figure 6.5-3, generally do not perform specific actions, but rather indicate conditions and operations that may be initiated by one of the T vectors. The fields of each T vector, shown in Figure 6.5-4, initiate specific operations. In normal operation, the four T vectors are activated in succession and circularly in the order T1, T2, T3, T4, T1, etc. Each of the T vectors normally remains active for one clock cycle of 75 n secs. This time may be "stretched" to 150 n secs to allow certain operations, like ALU operations, to complete before activation of the next T vector. The K vector remains active

5.2 SUMMARY OF NANOPRIMITIVE CONTROLS

5.2.1 K-VECTOR CONTROL FIELDS

The control function of each of the fields in the K-vector is summarized in the table below, along with references to sections in which the function is described. (The number of bits in the field is shown in parentheses.)

CONTROL FIELD	[Bits]	SUMMARY OF CONTROL FUNCTION	References
KN	(10)	Address of possible successor nanoword. Nanobranch address and source for NPC load.	4.5.2.3
SUPERVISOR	(1)	Program Check if on when this word is invoked while not in Supervisor Mode.	4.5.2.2
LEGAL MICRO ENTRY	(1)	Program Check if not on when this word is invoked by a microinstruction.	4.5.3
BRANCH	(1)	Must be on if nanobranch planned from this word. Complemented after each READ NS when ALTERNATE is on.	4.5.2.3
ALTERNATE	(1)	Causes BRANCH to be complemented after each READ NS.	4.5.2.3
HOLD	(1)	Inhibits automatic loading of KALC, KSHC, KSHA, and KS from next nanoword to be executed, unless executed by microinstruction or Program Check.	4.5.2.4 4.5.4.2
HOLD 2	(1)	Inhibits automatic loading of KA and KB from next nanoword to be executed, unless executed by microinstruction or Program Check.	4.5.2.4 4.5.4.2
ALLOW NANO INTERRUPT	(1)	Allows higher-priority interrupts at end of execution of this word, if nanobranch is not taken.	4.5.2.4 4.5.4.2

263

Name	Bits	Description	Reference
ALLOW MICRO INTERRUPT	(1)	Allows lower-priority interrupts at end of execution of this word, if nanobranch is not taken.	4.5.2.4 4.5.4.2
GENERATE INTERRUPT	(1)	Generates or clears an interrupt level according to GIGSPEC] in T1.	4.5.2.4 5.8.1
ALU STATUS ENABLE	(1)	Enables move of C,S,R,O bits from local to global upon GATE ALU; C treated specially.	5.6.2
SH STATUS ENABLE	(1)	Enables move of SHB, SLB bits from local to global upon GATE SH.	5.6.3
DIRECT MS ACCESS	(1)	Inhibits MS base addressing and field length protection in this nanoword.	4.2.6.3
KA	(6)	Constant and/or scratch field for nanoword; source and destination AUX.	4.3.3
KB	(6)	Constant and/or scratch field for nanoword; source and destination AUX.	4.3.3
KALC	(6)	ALU control; destination AUX.	5.6.2
KSHC	(6)	Shift control; destination AUX.	5.6.3
KSHA	(6)	Shift amount; destination AUX.	5.6.3
KS	(6)	Global condition (and general) test mask; source and destination AUX.	4.6 5.7.1
KT	(6)	Local condition test mask (also constant and/or scratch); source and destination AUX.	5.7.1
KX	(6)	Special condition test mask (also constant and/or scratch); source and destination Aux.	5.7.1
SPARE	(2)	Reserved for future use	

----

72 BITS

264

5.2.2 T-VECTOR CONTROL FIELDS

The control function of each of the fields in the active T-Vector is summarized
in the table below, along with references to sections in which the function is
described. A code showing the characteristic timing of the action associated
with the function is given; LE = Leading Edge, TE = Trailing Edge. (The number
of bits in the field is shown parenthetically.)

CONTROL FIELD	BITS	SUMMARY OF CONTROL FUNCTION	TIME	Refs.
===	===	===	===	===
STRETCH	(1)	Stretches time of this T-step from one T-period to two.		4.4
WRITE NS	(1)	Writes 18 bits from EOD bus into Nanostore	LE	4.7 5.4.1.2
XIO	(1)	Sends pulse to external interface; one of eight external ports selected by KA.	LE	4.6
RIO	(1)	Clears Port Register and sends pulse through port, then gates external data word into Port Register; selected by KA.	LE	4.6
MSGO	(1)	Initiates MS operation; split-cycle if alone. full-read if MSRS simultaneous.	LE	4.2.6.2 5.4.3
MSRS	(1)	If alone, requests second half-cycle of MS split-cycle operation; if with MSGO, initiates full-read.	LE	4.2.6.2 5.4.3
GATE MS	(1)	Gates MOD bus into Local Store or Port Registers; modified by RMI SELECT.	TE	4.2.6.1 5.4.3
RMI SELECT 00 BYPASS 01 PARAMETER SET A 10 PARAMETER SET B 11 PARAMETER SET C	(2)	Selects RMI parameters for GATE MS, including BYPASS. If RMI not installed all encodings are BYPASS	LE	4.2.6.4
GATE ES	(1)	Gates EOD bus into Local Store.	TE	4.2.5

LOAD ES   (1) Loads an External Store register   TE   4.2.5
                    from EID bus.

TXX   (1) Halts T-Clock with Program Step Switch. TE   5.8.3

READ CS   (1) Reads Control Store; uses CS ADDR   LE   4.2.4
                    SELECT.   5.4.2.2

WRITE CS   (1) Writes Control Store; uses CS ADDR   LE   4.2.4
                    SELECT.   5.4.2.3

CS ADDR SELECT (3) Selects address for READ CS, WRITE   LE   4.2.4
  000 CIA   CS. (MPC is selected by FMPC)   5.4.2.1
  001 COD   A and AB are sign extended operands.
  010 MPC   INDEX is output of INDEX ALU.
  011 MPC+1
  100 MPC+2
  101 MPC+B
  110 MPC+AB
  111 INDEX

GATE CS   (1) Gates COD bus into Local Store.   TE   4.2.4
                                                                   5.4.2
                                                                   4.2.3

GATE ALU   (1) Gates AOD bus into Local Store.   TE   4.2.3

GATE SH   (1) Gates SOD bus into Local Store.   TE   4.2.3

CARRY CTL   (3) Controls Carry operation within the   TE   4.2.3.4
  000 NO OPERATION   ALU and Shifter components.
  001 CLEAR CIH
  010 SET CIH
  011 ALU TO BOTH
  100 ALU TO COH
  101 SET COH
  110 CLEAR COH
  111 SH TO COH

INDEX   (1) Gates INDEX ALU output into Local   TE   4.2.2.3
                    Store, selected by G(GSPEC).   5.6.4

266

INC MPC   (1) Increments MPC selected by FMPC;   TE   4.2.2
                 modified by GSPEC.   5.4.2.1
                                                             5.6.5

LOAD NPC   (2) Loads or sequences NanoProgram   TE   4.5.3
  00   NO OPERATION   Counter.   4.5.4
  01   (CS)
  10   (KN)
  11   (SEQUENCE)

READ NS   (1) Reads NS; address is from priority- LE   4.5
                 select mechanism. Influences BRANCH.   5.4.1.1

GATE NS UNCON- (1) Causes the nanoword last read to be TE 4.5.1
DITIONALLY   gated into the Control Matrix.   5.5.1
                     Independent of any TEST ACTION in T.

TEST ACTION (1) Conditional Action based on   TE   4.5
  0   SKIP   Test Specifier   4.5.1
  1   GATE NS   5.7.2

TEST SPECIFIER (3) Specifies the conditions under   LE   5.7.1
  000 NEVER   which TEST ACTION is to be executed
  001 ALWAYS
  010 If FIST AND KS = 0
  011 If FIST AND KS NOT = 0
  100 If LOCAL CONDS AND KT = 0
  101 If LOCAL CONDS AND KT NOT = 0
  110 If SPECIAL CONDS AND KX = 0
  111 If SPECIAL CONDS AND KX NOT = 0

LOAD R31   (1) Enables R31 to be loaded with micro- TE   4.5.3.2
                 instruction parameters.   5.3.4

AUXILLARY ACTION (1) Initiates Action specified by the LE 4.3.2.3
                       contents of FACT (F register 14).   5.8.2

267

```
G.SPEC                                                          (4)   Selects a G or pseudo-G for 6-bit         5.5.2
        0000    GO                                                    transfers, right input to ALUF,
        ----    ---                                                   used in GENERATE INTERRUPT, External
        1011    G11                                                   Interface G-lines; also used with
        1100    KSHA                                                  INC MPC.
        1101    B
        1110    KS
        1111    KT

FSEL0                                                           (5)   Selects F register for 6-bit transfers    5.5.2
FSEL1                                                           (5)   in Group 0, 1, and 2 respectively.
FSEL2                                                           (5)

AUX0                                                            (3)   Selects AUX for 6-bit transfers in
AUX1                                                            (3)   Group 0, 1, and 2 respectively.
AUX2                                                            (3)   (AUX2 applies to Group 2 input,
AUX3                                                            (3)    AUX3 applies to Group 2 output.)

IN0                                                             (1)   Commands AUX into F register transfer
IN1                                                             (1)   using AUX0, AUX1, AUX2 to FSEL0,
IN2                                                             (1)   FSEL1, FSEL2 respectively.

OUT1                                                            (1)   Commands F register output to AUX
OUT2                                                            (1)   transfer using FSEL0, FSEL1, FSEL2 to
OUT3                                                            (1)   AUX0, AUX1, AUX3 respectively.

                                                                      ---
                                                                      72 Bits
```

Figure 6.5-4. QM-1 nanoinstruction T vector fields.

268

for the entire nanoinstruction execution. The execution of successive T vectors continues until the occurrence of a program check interrupt, the execution of a GATE NS nanooperation, or the execution of a SKIP nanooperation. In the first two of these three cases, a new nanoinstruction is read into the control matrix. In the third, the next T vector is not activated (it is skipped) even though it consumes one 75-n sec clock cycle. Both the GATE NS and SKIP nanooperations may be executed conditionally.

QM-1 nanoinstructions are archetypical horizontal - operations that may be performed simultaneously include ALU operations, shifter operations, INDEX ALU operations, incrementing microprogram counters, extracting a field from a main memory output word, reading or writing control store, reading or writing main memory, and conditional branching or skipping. The K and T vectors shown in Figures 6.5-3 and 6.5-4 exhibit little use of two level encoding among fields. Single level encoding is normal, and the large number of one bit fields suggests no encoding. The READ NS and GATE NS nanooperations provide a parallel implementation of nanoinstruction sequences, i.e., there is no delay in activating the T1 vector of a new nanoinstruction following the deactivation of the last T vector of the present nanoinstruction. The execution of a nanoinstruction involves the activation of one or more T vectors and hence may be considered polyphase. In addition, nanooperations may be classified "leading edge" (LE) or "trailing edge" (TE) depending on whether they take effect at the beginning or end of a clock cycle. Leading edge nanooperations often initiate processes that require one or more clock cycles, and knowledge of operation duration is required to prevent race conditions with trailing edge nanooperations.

269

6.5.3 QM-1 Microprogrammability and Nanoprogrammability

As described earlier, the QM-1 control store may be read and written, and these operations are performed under nanoprogram control. With this implementation, it is easy for the nanoprogram to read the next microinstruction into the microinstruction register (the last local store register) while completing the execution of the present microinstruction. NANODATA has developed a general purpose microinstruction set and an assembler to assist in its use. Since microinstructions may be designed by the user, however, let us consider the nanoprogrammability aspects of the QM-1.

The nanostore is writable under nanoprogram control. For the purpose of writing, each 360 bit nanoinstruction comprises 20 eighteen bit fields. Data to be written into nanostore originate from the External Store Output Data Bus. The address of the word in nanostore to be written is specified by the ten least significant bits of the number formed by joining the C and A fields of the microinstruction register. The address of the eighteen bit part of the nanostore word to be written is specified by the B field of the microinstruction register. The WRITE NS nanooperation initiates the write operation.

A register transfer language has been developed to facilitate nanoprogramming the QM-1. Source statements of this register transfer language consist of single records and fall into one of the following statement classes: comment, label, command, and control. Comment statements begin with an asterisk, however, comments may be included in other types of statements by enclosing the comment between a pair of double quotation marks. Control statements provide information to the translator - end of nanoprogram, listing control, and end of nanoinstruction. A label statement identifies the beginning of a nanoinstruction and provides a name for it so that it may be

270

FETCH:
```
....  LEGAL MICRO OP ENTRY, ALLOW NANO INTERRUPT, ALLOW MICRO INTERRUPT
X...  READ CS (MPC+1)
.X..  LOAD NPC (CS)
..X.  READ NS, MPC PLUS 1
...X  GATE NS, LOAD R31
```

figure 6.5-5. QM-1 nanoprogram to Fetch a microinstruction.

Comments

Assume that upon entry to this one nanoinstruction nanoprogram, the MPC (microprogram counter) points to the currently executing microinstruction in control store. One of the F registers indicates which of the local store registers is serving as the MPC.

The K vector commands (those preceded by ....) indicate that this nanoinstruction may be invoked by microinstruction execution, and that nano and micro level interrupts are enabled.

The T1 vector command (preceded by X...) initiates reading control store at one plus the MPC, i.e., the next microinstruction.

The T2 vector command (preceded by .X..) loads the nanoprogram counter (NPC) with the operation code from the new microinstruction. The high order bits of the new nanostore address are indicated by one of the F regiters.

The T3 vector commands initiate readng the nanostoe at the new address and increment the microprogram counter.

The T4 vector commands indicate assignment of the new nanostore word to the control matrix (to initiate execution of the new microinstruction) and assignment of the new microinstruction to the microinstruction register (to provide operands for microinstruction execution). At the end of the activation of T4, the next nanoinstruction has been read into the control matrix and its T1 vector is activated.

271

```
LD:   "LD A,B"
*          REGISTER B CONTAINS CONTROL STORE ADDRESS FROM WHICH
*          DATA IS TO BE LOADED INTO REGISTER A
....  FETCH
X...  A->FCOD, B->FCIA
..X.  READ CS (CIA)
...X  GATE CS
```

Figure 6.5-6. QM-1 nanoprogram to load a word from control store into a local store register.

Comments

The K vector command FETCH causes all the commands in the FETCH nanoinstruction (Figure 6.4-5) to be inserted into the present nanoinstruction. Hence this nanoinstruction performs a fetch in addition to the load.

The T1 vector commands connect the control store address bus to the B register and the control store output data bus to the A register.

The T3 vector command initates reading control store at the address on the control store address bus (the address in the B register).

The T4 vector command assigns (gates) the data read from control store into the A register.

referenced symbolically. A label statement comprises a label (possibly null) followed by a colon. Sets of command statements define a nanoinstruction; they indicate the nanooperations and the vectors in which they appear.

There are three classes of commands: pseudo command operators, nanooperation commands, and six bit data transfer commands. Pseudo command operators permit access to the

```
ADD:    "ADD A,B   ADD LOCAL STORE REGISTER A TO B, RESULT IN A"
....    FETCH, KALC = ADD, ALU STATUS ENABLE
X...    A->FAIL, B->FAIR, A->FAOD, CLEAR CIH
.X..
..X.    GATE ALU, ALU TO COH
...X
```

Figure 6.5-7. QM-1 Nanoprogram to add two local store registers and assign the result to the first register.

Comments

The K vector command FETCH inserts commands from the FETCH nanoinstruction into the present nanoinstruction. The second K vector command indicates that the ALU operation in this nanoinstruction will be an addition, and the third command indicates that conditions generated by the ALU command may be saved in the appropriate F register for later testing.

The first three T1 vector commands connect the ALU Left Input Bus to the A register, the ALU Right Input Bus to the B register, and the ALU Output Data Bus to the A register. The fourth command clears the carry input to the ALU operation.

The T3 vector commands assign the generated ALU result to local store register A and save the ALU generated conditions.

nanostore location counter, describe microinstruction attributes, and specify the vector to which the following commands will be assigned. To indicate that K vector commands follow, four periods are used. To indicate that T1 vector commands follow, an X followed by three periods is used. Commands for vectors T2, T3, and T4 are similarly preceded by

273

```
*        UMULT  A,B   [ R(A).R(B)=R(A)*R(B) ]
UMULT:   "MULTIPLY A TIMES B"
....     LEGAL MICRO OP ENTRY, BRANCH (UMULT2), KA = ZERO, KB = LS.WORK,
         KT = 18., KX = PASS LEFT, KALC = PASS LEFT,
         KSHC = RIGHT+SINGLE+LOGICAL+RIGHT CTL
X...     A->FAIL,  KB->FAOD, B->FSID,  CLEAR CIH
.S..     KB->FAIR, A->FAOD,  B->FSOD,  GATE ALU,   READ CS (MPC+1), MPC + 1
                                                   LOAD NPC (CS)
..S.     KA->KALC, KX->F.PASS,          SH TO COH, READ NS
...S     KT->F.COUNT,                   GATE ALU,  GATE NS


: UMULT2 = N.  "CONTINUATION OF UNSIGNED MULTIPLY"
....     BRANCH (N.+1), KALC = PASS LEFT, KSHC = RIGHT+DOUBLE+LOGICAL,
         KSHA = 1, KT = CARRY, KX = F ZERO, KB = ADD
S...     KB->KALC,   SKIP (NOT T)
.X..     F.PASS->KALC
..S.     ALU TO COH, READ NS, GATE NS (X), DECF->F.COUNT
...X     SH TO COH,  GATE ALU, GATE SH


:        "COMPLETION OF UNSIGNED MULTIPLY"
....     ALLOW INTS, KSCH = LEFT+DOUBLE+LOGICAL+RIGHT CTL, KALC = PASS LEFT
         ALU STATUS ENABLE
X...
.S..     ALU TO COH, GATE ALU, GATE SH, READ NS, GATE NS, LOAD R31
```

Figure 6.5-8. QM-1 nanoprogram to perform an unsigned multiply.

Comments

In the initialization word, T1 prepares the ALU to pass the multiplicand to local store register LS.WORK for use as the multiplicand source during additions. Carry-in-hold is also cleared for the add operations that will follow. T2 executes the GATE ALU, saving the multiplicand. The ALU and SHIFTER bus connections are completed. All microinstruction fetch actions are completed: READ CS (MPC+1), LOAD NPC (CS), and MPC PLUS 1. The next nanoprogram address is now selected, but will not be referenced until the READ NS in the completion word. T3 changes the ALU function to ZERO, which will clear the initial product value in R(A). An F register named F.PASS is initialized with the value of the ALU pass function. COH is set to the value of the rightmost bit of the multiplier, taken from SID bit 0 using the "RIGHT CTL" function of the SHIFTER. Nanostore location UMULT2 is read. Finally, T4 sets an F register named F.COUNT to the value 18 (decimal), which will be used by UMULT2 as a counter during its 18 loops. Register R(A) is zeroed via the ALU, and control is transferred to T1 of UMULT2.

UMULT2 performs the actual multiplication. This requires it to repeat its full 4 T-steps 18 times. T1 is used to set the ALU control to ADD mode, and to determine whether to change the function to PASS LEFT. If the current rightmost bit of the multiplier is a 1 then T2 will be skipped, leaving the ALU set for an add operation. If a 0 then T2 is executed and the ALU will not alter the result during this loop cycle. T3 transfers the ALU carry-out condition to the carry-out-hold, as required before the actual GATE ALU is performed, to preset carry-out-hold with the correct value to be propogated into the SIGN bit position of AOD. T3 also reads the next nanostore location, and makes the decision to terminate the multiplication when F.COUNT is decremented to zero. T4 now completes the cycle by gating the new partial product into R(A) and R(B) along with the shifting of the multiplier right one bit position. The SH TO COH operation sets COH to the value of the new rightmost bit on SOD, to be used for the ADD/PASS decision in T1 for the next loop cycle.

The completion word is required only if it is desired to set FIST to accurately portray the SIGN and RESULT of the final 36 bit product. T1 is empty, allowing for interrupt address selection and for ALU-SHIFTER propagation. T2 gates the ALU and SHIFTER back into their

275

current registers, unmodified, only to cause the correct setting of SIGN, RESULT, OVERFLOW and CARRY in FIST. CARRY and OVERFLOW are meaningless in an unsigned multiply operation.

Since UMULT2 is actually a complete multiply routine any nanoprogram requiring a multiplication operation as its last procedure may use it. With minor alterations, UMULT2 may also be used as the fin. phase of a signed multiply routine.

periods and an   X in the position corresponding to the vector number. To stretch a T vector execution to two clock cycles, an S replaces the X. Examples in the next section illustrate these conventions.   The nanooperation and six bit transfer commands indicate the use   of fields in the nanoinstruction and use register transfer format.

In addition to   the register transfer language, NANODATA has   a debug package that also runs on   the QM-1 and allows nanoprogram execution to be monitored.

6.5.4 QM-1 Examples

Owing to the complexity of QM-1 nanoinstructions, we give examples of several nanoprograms. The examples in Figures 6.5-5 through 6.5-8 start with simple operations and proceed to more difficult ones.

6.6 The Burroughs Interpreter

6.6.1 Interpreter Background

To provide a nucleus for a variety of computer systems,* the design objectives of   the Burroughs Interpreter included simplicity, versatility, and modularity. Some of the reasons

*Interpreter based systems are also known as D machines.

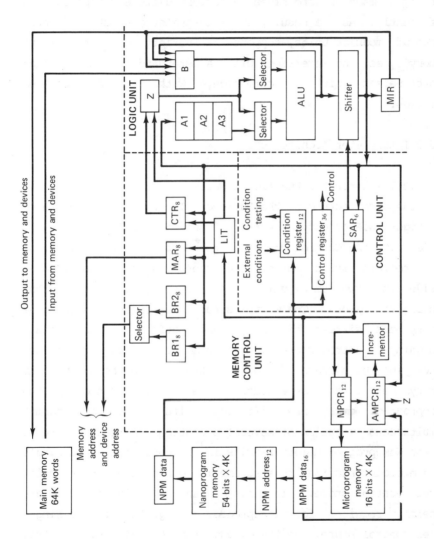

Figure 6.6-1. Architecture of the Burroughs Interpreter.

277

for these objectives were a desire to provide general purpose, as opposed to special purpose, functions that could be readily adapted to a variety of applications, a desire to provide smooth and unlimited system growth, and a desire to provide a variety of machine word sizes to support different applications efficiently. As a result, the Interpreter consists of three types of modular units, supports a variety of control store memory types, and interfaces with a standard switch interlock (Port Select Unit) to communicate with I/O devices and memories.

6.6.2 Interpreter Architecture

6.6.2.1 Interpreter Functional Units

The architecture of the Burroughs Interpreter, illustrated in Figure 6.6-1, comprises three types of modular units - the Logic Unit, the Control Unit, and the Memory Control Unit. The microprograms which control the operation of these modules reside in two memory units - the Microprogram Memory and the Nanoprogram Memory. The microinstructions in the Microprogram Memory are sixteen bits long and perform two functions - assigning a control store literal to a local store register and specifying the address of a microinstruction in the Nanoprogram Memory that is to be executed. The microinstructions in the Nanoprogram Memory are fifty-four bits long and permit simultaneous execution of several operations. As each reference to the Nanoprogram Memory results in the execution of a single long microinstruction, this scheme is classified as a split level control store. In this organization fewer bits are generally required for microprogram storage than in a single level control store. As the disadvantage of this split control store organization is the time delay inherent in two memory accesses when executing a long microinstruction, a single level

278

Number	Operation
0	X + Y
1	not X & not Y
2	not X & Y
3	X + Y + 1
4	not X v not Y
5	X + (X v Y)
6	(X & not Y) v (not X & Y)
7	X & not Y
8	not X v Y
9	(X & Y) v (not X & not Y)
10	X + (X & Y)
11	X & Y
12	X + not Y
13	X v not Y
14	X v Y
15	X + not Y + 1

Figure 6.6-2. Interpreter ALU operations. Notations: x - left input; y - right input; & - logical and; v - logical or; + - addition.

control store organization may be used. In this case, there is one large control store whose word length is fifty-five bits. The first bit of each word indicates whether the microinstruction is a short or a long microinstruction. If it is a long microinstruction the remaining fifty-four bits constitute the microinstruction; if it is a short microinstruction the next sixteen bits constitute the

279

microinstruction, and the remaining thirty-eight bits are generally not used.

Associated with the memories that hold the microprograms are several registers in the Memory Control Unit and the Control Unit. The MPCR (microprogram counter register) serves as control store address register that may be loaded from the AMPCR (alternate microprogram counter register) or incremented by zero, one, or two. The thirty-six bit control register in the Control Unit serves as a control store data register in controlling the operation of the Logic Unit and to some extent the other units.

The Logic Unit of the Interpreter performs arithmetic, logic, and shifting operations and provides several registers for data storage. The Logic Unit is an eight bit wide module, i.e., the registers and transformation units handle eight bit data. Up to eight Logic Units may be joined together, however, providing data manipulation capabilities for words up to sixty-four bits long. The ALU can perform the sixteen operations shown in Figure 6.6-2. The shifter, called a barrel switch due to the appearance of the circuit diagram, consists only of combinational logic and can shift an input word any number of places in a right end off, left end off, or right circular manner. There are several registers associated with the ALU and shifter in the Logic Unit. The three A registers hold information for input to the ALU. The B register serves as another ALU input. Logically the B register has three sections – the most significant bit, the least significant bit, and the remaining central bits. When the B register is selected as an ALU input, each of the three sections may independently be sent directly to the ALU, complemented before being sent, set to zero before being sent, or set to one before being sent. The Z input to the ALU facilitates manipulation of other

Intepreter registers. The shift amount register (SAR) in the Control Unit indicates the length of the shift to be performed by the shifter. The SAR may be assigned a literal value by a short microinstruction or the output of the shifter.

Several registers in the Memory Control Unit and the Logic Unit effect the interface between the Interpreter and external storage – memory and I/O devices. The address of a data word is formed by concatenating the value in one of the two base registers (BR1 or BR2) and the value in the memory address register (MAR). This address contains sixteen bits so that normally 64K words of memory and 64K words on I/O devices may be addressed. A second Memory Control Unit may be added, however, to provide an addressing capability of 4096K words of memory and 4096K words on devices. For write operations, the data originates from the memory information register (MIR), which receives its input from the shifter. For read operations, the data are read into the B register. There are twelve different I/O operations: two memory read operations, two memory write operations, two I/O device read operations, two I/O device write operations, two I/O device unlock operations, and two operations which request status information from the highest priority locked and unlocked devices. The generality of this scheme permits the attachment of peripherals ranging from fast registers to slow I/O devices with equal facility.

The counter (CTR) register in the Memory Control Unit is an eight bit register that facilitates microprogram looping. The counter register may be loaded with the complement of the value in the literal (LIT) register or with the complement of the shifter result. In addition, the counter may be incremented and tested independently of the ALU operation.

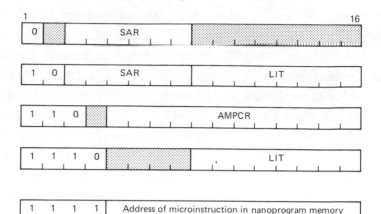

Figure 6.6-3. Formats of Interpreter 16 bit microinstructions.

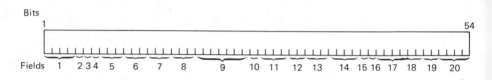

Figure 6.6-4. Format of Interpreter 54 bit microinstructions.

6.6.2.2 Interpreter Microinstruction Repertoire

The operation of the Interpreter is controlled by two types of microinstructions. One of the sixteen bit microinstructions is read from the Microprogram Memory during each major clock cycle. The formats of these sixteen bit microinstructions, shown in Figure 6.6-3, fall into two classes. The first class uses four microinstruction formats which assign literal values to specified registers. The second class contains one microinstruction format which specifies the address of a microinstruction in the Nanoprogram Memory.

When a sixteen bit microinstruction references a microinstruction in Nanoprogram Memory, the specified fifty-four bit microinstruction is immediately read from Nanoprogram Memory and executed. As shown in Figure 6.6-4, the fifty-four bit microinstructions have twenty fields.

1. Field 1 specifies a condition to be tested. The sixteen conditions include counter overflow, ALU overflow, all bits in ALU result are one, least significant bit in ALU result is one, most significant bit in ALU result is one, read operation complete, no memory operation in progress (or no memory operation that still requires the MIR and MAR registers), and four types of external and I/O interrupts. In addition there are three local condition bits that may be changed under microprogram control by field 5 and two global condition bits (for lock out and interrupts) that may be set by other Interpreters in a multiprocessor system.

2. Field 2 indicates whether the specified condition is to be tested for being true or false.

3. Field 3 indicates whether or not the operation of the Logic Unit, specified by fields 8 through 20, depends on the result of condition testing. If the Logic Unit operation depends on condition testing and the condition does not hold, the Logic Unit performs the same operations as in the previous microinstruction.

4. Field 4 indicates whether or not condition adjust (specified by field 5) and memory and I/O operations (specified by field 20) depend on condition testing.

5. Field 5 specifies the adjustment of local and global condition bits.

6. Fields 6 and 7 secify microprogram sequencing. Field 6 specifies the address of the next microinstruction in Microprogram Memory if the tested condition holds, and field 7 specifies the next address otherwise. Figure 6.6-5 lists the eight sequence operations.

Number	Command	Action
0	WAIT	Use same microinstruction
1	STEP	Go to next microintruction
2	SAVE	Store microinstruction address in AMPCR and go to next microinstruction
3	SKIP	Go to microinstruction after next
4	EXEC	Execute microinstruction whose address is one plus value in AMPCR, but do not alter MPCR
5	JUMP	Go to microinstruction whose address is one plus value in AMPCR
6	CALL	Store microinstruction address in AMPCR, and perform JUMP
7	RETN	"Return" to the microinstruction whose address is two plus value of AMPCR

Figure 6.6-5. Interpreter sequencing operations.
The action implies changing the value of the MPCR except where noted otherwise.

7. Field 8 specifies the left input to the ALU.

8. Field 9 specifies the right ALU input including the interpretation of the B register sections if it is selected.

9. Field 10 indicates whether or not carries are to be propogated between the eight bit ALU modules.

10. Field 11 specifies the ALU operation, and field 12 specifies the shifter operation.

11. Field 13 specifies which, if any, of the three A registers are to receive the shifter result.

Microinstruction Number	Type	Clock 1	Clock 2	Clock 3	Clock 4	Clock 5
1	Long	FM DM FN DN	AS AO SO AR			
2	Long		FM DM FN DN	AS AO SO AR		
3	Short			FM DM AL		
4	Short				FM DM AL	
5	Long					FM DM •••

Figure 6.6-6. Timing characteristics for the execution of microinstructions on the Burroughs interpreter.

Legend:

FM – Fetch short microinstruction from Microprogram Memory;

DM – Decode short microinstruction;

FN – Fetch long microinstruction from Nanoprogram Memory;

DN – Decode long microinstruction;

AS – ALU operand selection;

AO – ALU operation;

SO – Shifter operation;

AR – Assign results to destination registers;

AL – Assign control store literal to register.

12. Field 14 specifies input for the B register. In addition to input data, shifter result, ALU result, and MIR contents, the B register may be assigned the result of the logical or operation of the shifter result with the input data, the ALU result, or the MIR contents. The B register may also be assigned the complements of certain carry bits (for decimal arithmetic operations) from the ALU operations.

13. Fields 15 and 16 indicate whether or not the MIR and AMPCR are to be assigned the shifter result.

14. Field 17 specifies changes in the BR1, BR2, and MAR registers.

15. Field 18 specifies the change to be made to the counter register.

16. Field 19 specifies SAR input.

17. Field 20 specifies a memory operation.

The two types of Interpreter microinstructions illustrate contrasting characteristics. The sixteen bit microinstructions are vertical, use two level encoding, and are executed in a serial monophase manner. The fifty-four bit microinstructions, in contrast, exemplify the horizontal and single level encoding characteristics. These horizontal microinstructions require two major clock cycles for completion – one for fetch (which is done in the same cycle in which the short microinstruction was fetched from microprogram memory) and one for execution. As the two phases are distinct, they may be overlapped. As shown in Figure 6.6-6, the execution phase of one microinstruction proceeds simultaneously with the fetching of the next one. The determination of the next microinstruction and the conditional execution of certain operations depends on conditions generated by the previous microinstruction. The execution of a long microinstruction itself has at least four distinct phases:

1. selection of ALU inputs,

2. performing the ALU operation,

3. performing the shift operation, and

4. assigning results to destination registers.

An interesting consequence of this parallel polyphase implementation is that the effect of executing a long microinstruction may depend on the execution of the next microinstruction, when the next microinstruction is a short microinstruction that assigns a literal to a local store register. In microinstructions 2 and 3 in Figure 6.6-6, the literal value in microinstruction 3 is assigned to a register before other destination registers are assigned in microinstruction 2, so the literal value in microinstruction 3 may be used in microinstruction 2. An example of this anomaly is illustrated in the microprogram in Figure 6.6-8 in lines 0300 and 0400. Microinstruction execution speed depends on the speeds of the Microprogram Memory, the Nanoprogram Memory, and the type of logic circuits. The clock cycles of various realizations range from one microsecond down to around 150 n sec.

6.6.3 Interpreter Microprogrammability

The Microprogram Memory and Nanoprogram Memory have been implemented in a variety of memory types. When these control store memories are writable, they may be loaded directly from an external device, such as a card reader or disk, or a sequence of commands may overlay the control store memories with microinstructions from main memory.

A register transfer language, TRANSLANG, and a translator have been developed to assist in preparing microprograms for the Interpreter. The translator has been implemented in ALGOL to run on the Interpreter itself. There are also ALGOL (B5500)

```
000   PROGRAM FIB;
100   A1=:MAR1;
200   B001=:B,MIR;
300   B001=:A3; MW1;
400   A2=:CTR; SAVE;
500   LOOP: IF SAI THEN A1+1=:A1,MAR1,
              INC, STEP ELSE WAIT;
600   A3+B=:MIR;
700   B=:A3; BMI,MW1; IF NOT COV
              THEN JUMP ELSE STEP;
```

Figure 6.6-7. Interpreter microprogram to compute Fibonacci series.

Comments

General – The Fibonacci series is the sequence of integers 1, 1, 2, 3, 5, 8, 13, 21, ... in which successive terms are formed by adding the previous two. Assume that the A1 register contains the starting address in memory for storing the series, and A2 contains the number of terms to be computed.

000 – Program header

100 – Pass A1 through the ALU and shifter and assign it to the BR1 and MAR registers. Note that the destination register in the assignment is on the right of the operator.

200 – Pass a 1 from the B register through the ALU and shifter and assign it to the MIR and B registers. Note that the notation B001 means use zero for the most significant bit, zeros for the central bits, and one for the least significant bit of the B register.

288

300 – Pass a 1 from the B register through the ALU and shifter and assign it to register A3. Initiate a memory write to write the data from MIR into memory at the address specified by BR1 and MAR. At this point B, MIR, and A3 contain 1, and the first term is being written into memory.

400 – Pass the A2 register (containing the number of terms) through the ALU and shifter and assign its complement to the counter register. Save the address of this microinstruction in the AMPCR.

500 – If the memory write operation is complete (SAI), then add one to the A1 register, assign the result to the A1 and BR1–MAR registers (i.e., increment the memory address for the next term), increment the counter, and go on to the next microinstruction. If the memory write operation is not complete, repeat this microinstruction, in effect, wait until the write operation completes.

600 – Add the contents of the A3 and B registers (compute the next term in the series) and assign the result to MIR.

700 – Pass the B register through the ALU and shifter and assign it to the A3 register. Assign the MIR register to the B register. (Now the A3 register contains the previous term, and the B register contains the present term.) Initiate a memory write as in 300. If the counter has not overflowed (reached 0) then go back to the microinstruction labelled LOOP to compute additional terms.

```
0000    PROGRAM BIMULT;
0100    A3 XOR B=: ; IF LC1;
0200    B0TT=:A2; IF MST THEN SET LC1;
0300    B000=:B,LCTR;
0400    16=:LIT; 1=:SAR;
0500    A3 R=:A3; SAVE;
0600    LOOP: IF NOT LST THEN B00T C=:B; SKIP ELSE STEP;
0700    A2+B0TT C=:B;
0800    A3 OR BT00 R=:A3,INC; IF NOT COV THEN
                                    JUMP ELSE STEP;
0900    IF NOT LC1 THEN B0TT=:B; SKIP ELSE STEP;
1000    B1TT=:B;
```

Figure 6.6-8. Interpreter microprogram to perform binary multiply.

Comments

General — Assume sign magnitude representation with 16 bit multiplier in
A3 and 16 bit multiplicand in B. The product will be put into
B (most significant part) and A3 (least significant part).

0000 — Program header.

0100 — Perform the exclusive or of A3 and B to generate conditions.
Reset local condition one by testing it.

0200 — Pass the B register through the ALU and shifter and assign it to
A2. The notation B0TT means that from the B register zero is used
for the most significant bit and that the other bits are not
changed (True). If the previous ALU operation (in 0100) had a
result whose most significant bit was one (the signs of the

290

multiplier and multiplicand were different), set local condition one.

0300 — Pass zeros through the ALU and assign them to the B register. At this point A2 contains the unsigned multiplicand, B contains zero, and A3 contains the multiplier.

0400 — This is a 16 bit microinstruction that assigns 16 to the literal register and 1 to the shift amount register. The LCTR operation in microinstruction 0300 now loads the value -16 from the literal register into the counter. Note that this unusual construct arises from the overlapped execution of the two types of microinstructions and the polyphase implementation of the 54 bit microinstructions.

0500 — Shift register A3 right one bit and store the result in A3. Save the address of this microinstruction.

0600 — If the least bit of the ALU result (the bit lost in shifting) was not one, then shift the B register value (with the most significant bit set to 0) right circurlarly one bit, assign the result to the B register, and skip the next microinstruction.

0700 — Add the multiplicand to the B register (with a zero sign), shift the sum right circurlarly one bit, and assign it to the B register. At this point, the most significant bit of B has the next bit in the accumulated partial product (least significant part).

0800 – Set the most significant bit of the ALU result with the most significant bit of B and right shift. Assign the result to A3. Now the second most significant bit of A3 contains the next bit of the product (least significant part). Increment the counter. If the counter is not zero, continue looping at 0600.

0900 – If the signs were originally identical (LC1 equals zero), then set the sign of B to zero and skip the next microinstruction.

1000 – Set the sign of B to one.

and COBOL (B3500) versions of the translator. The figures in the next section demonstrate TRANSLANG constructs. To assist in microprogram debugging, Burroughs has developed a simulator of the Interpreter that runs on the Interpreter itself.

6.6.4 Interpreter Examples

Figures 6.6-7 and 6.6-8, microprograms to compute Fibonacci series and perform binary multiplication, illustrate Interpreter capabilities and TRANSLANG constructs.

6.6.5 Interpreter Applications

Designed as a general purpose machine, the Interpreter has been used in a variety of applications. Emulators for several military and commercial computers have been developed. The Interpreter has been used for higher level language execution. In this application, higher level language programs are translated into an intermediate language which is then interpreted. The Interpreter has been microprogrammed to perform the functions of a peripheral controller. With its Microprogram Memory implemented as part of main memory, Nanoprogram Memory implemented as read only memory, and two Logic Units, the Interpreter is marketed as the B700 family of commercial computers. Burroughs has done some "tuning" studies with the Interpreter. These involve augmenting an emulator with microprograms to interpret routines that are frequently executed in an application program.

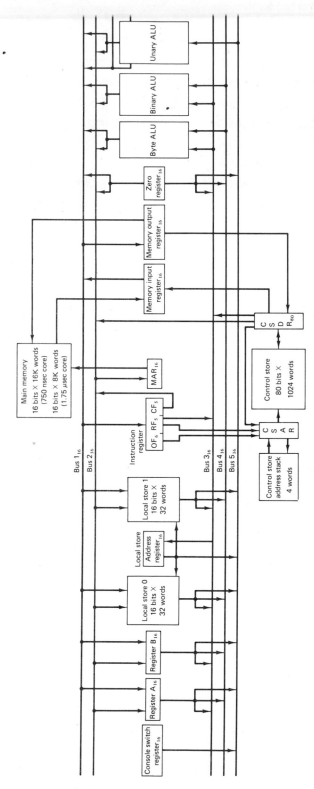

Figure 6.7-1. Architecture of the AMP.

6.7 The Argonne Microprocessor* (AMP)

6.7.1 AMP Background

AMP was designed and constructed at the Argonne National
Laboratory as   a tool for research in microcontrol, processor
design, and language design.   It   has been   used in   an
experimental raster graphics system called MIRAGE. Featuring a
general multiple bus structure, a large high-speed local store,
and three ALUs, AMP provides substantial low level parallelism.
The general design permits hardware modification to be easily
accomplished, which further supports the experimental nature of
the machine.   As   a research tool, AMP has been used to
investigate the efficiency of low   level parallelism in
effecting programs expressed in machine language and
microprogrammed directly.

6.7.2 AMP Architecture

6.7.2.1 AMP Functional Components

Central to the architecture of AMP are the five busses,
illustrated in   Figure   6.7-1,   that connect the various
functional components.   The two upper busses, Bus 1 and Bus 2
are primary routes for ALU results, and the three lower busses
provide inputs to the ALUs. In addition to permitting selection
of up to three data sources and providing up to two results in
the execution of   each microinstruction, this general bus
structure allows register-to-register transfers and a variety
of connections among resources. It also facilitates interfacing
additional hardware, such as local store registers and ALUs, to
increase processing power.

*Here, microprocessor means microprogrammable processor.

The large number of local store registers constitute the fastest of the four levels of memory in AMP. The other three levels are control store, and two types of main memory. Two local store arrays, each containing 32 sixteen bit words, constitute the majority of the local storage capability. Normally used for temporary storage of operands generated by the CPU or obtained from main memory, each of the two local store arrays may be addressed directly by fields in a microinstruction. In addition, the two local store arrays may be considered to be a sixty-four word array addressed by the six bit local store address register. Each microinstruction can thus address up to three registers in the two local store arrays. The local store address register may be set or incremented independently of the ALU operations. The sixteen bit A and B registers also serve as general purpose storage. The sixteen bit instruction register comprises three subregisters which are used to facilitate the interpretation of machine language instructions. The first two subregisters, the six bit OF field and the five bit RF field, may serve as addresses or address offsets for control store. The RF field and the five bit CF field may serve as parameters, i.e., operands, to the microprograms that execute the machine language instructions. The zero register provides a word all of whose bits are zero to any bus. The console switch register permits introduction of external input onto Bus 5.

AMP control store is an array of 1,024 120-bit words. At present microinstructions use seventy-four of these bits. In addition to the control store address register and the control store data register, there is a four word control store address stack to facilitate micro-subroutine linking. Control store cycle time is 150 n sec.

Figure 6.7-2. AMP microinstruction format.

Main memory on AMP consists of a 16K core memory with a 750-n sec cycle time and an 8K core memory with a 1.75-microsecond cycle time. The word length for both memories is sixteen bits. The two core memory modules actually constitute the first 24K words in a 64K address space. This address space contains an area reserved for peripheral I/O devices (including control store), so data on I/O devices are addressed like main memory. The asynchronous communication between the CPU and devices in the 64K address space (including main memory, control store, and data on I/O devices) is effected by the memory address register, the memory input register, the memory output register, and by the capability of a microinstruction to alter the timing of its execution.

To facilitate low level parallel processing, AMP provides three separate arithmetic and logic units, called manipulators, two of which may be used by each microinstruction. The unary manipulator may be used by any microinstruction to perform unary operations such as incrementing, decrementing, and shifting. The binary manipulator may be used by word mode microinstructions to perform common unary and binary arithmetic and logic functions. The byte manipulator may be used by I/O mode microinstructions to perform byte (eight bits) operations such as packing, unpacking, and swapping. The first bit of each microinstruction identifies the microinstruction mode as word or I/O.

6.7.2.2 AMP Microinstruction Repertoire

Figure 6.7-2 illustrates the format of AMP microinstructions. These microinstructions have twenty-four fields.

1. Field 1 specifies the mode and determines the interpretation of field 11.

298

2. Field 2 is a control store literal used as a control store address or as data to be assigned to a bus.

3. Field 3 controls input to register A.

4. Field 4 controls input to the memory address register.

5. Fields 5 through 9 specify inputs for the five busses.

6. Field 10 controls input to the memory output register.

7. Fields 11-a1, 11-a2, and 11-a3 control input to register B, input to the instruction register, and the operation of the binary manipulator. Fields 11-b1 through 11-b4 control I/O, an interrupt mask register, input to the control store address register, and operation of the byte manipulator.

8. Field 12 controls the operation of the unary manipulator.

9. Field 13 specifies addressing for the local store address register.

10. Field 14 specifies addressing for Local Store 1, or it may be an extension of the control store literal in Field 2.

11. Field 15 selects the input for Local Store 1.

12. Fields 16 and 17 control addressing and input selection for Local Store 0.

13. Field 18 controls addressing for both local store arrays.

14. Fields 19 through 24 control microinstruction sequencing. Fields 19 and 21 specify the conditions under which a jump to the control store address in field 2 or a skip the next microinstruction are to be performed. The conditions are tests of the data assigned to Bus 1 or Bus 2 (selected by field 23) during the present microinstruction: less than zero, equal to zero, greater than zero, all bits one, and least significant bit equal one. Fields 20 and 22 manipulate the control store address stack – popping the stack and assigning the address to the CSAR, and pushing the address of the next

299

sequential microinstruction onto   the stack. When neither the
jump nor skip conditions is true and popping the control store
address stack is not specified, the next microinstruction to be
executed is simply the next sequential microinstruction in
control store.

With the large number of operations that can be performed
in parallel, AMP microinstructions are clearly horizontal.
While most fields employ single level encoding, the use of two
level encoding (the mode bit of field 1 controls interpretation
of field 11) reduces the number of bits required for each
microinstruction. With a sequence of ten timing signals AMP
implements microinstructions in a polyphase manner. Among the
phases normally executed are

1. selecting data from registers and assigning it   to
busses,

2. selecting inputs from busses for the manipulators,

3. performing the manipulator operations,

4. assigning data to the result busses,

5. transmitting data to destination registers, and

6. determining the address of the next microinstruction.

Microinstructions specifying conditional sequencing lengthen
the normal microinstruction execution time of 430 to 700 n sec.
Using field 24 a microinstruction may also specify that the
next microinstruction is   not to begin execution until the
completion of   an   I/O event. This facilitates asynchronous
communication with main memory and I/O devices.

6.7.3 AMP Microprogrammability

Since AMP control store is part of the 64K address space
it   can be read and written just as main memory is read and
written.   To assist in the preparation of microprograms, a

300

register transfer language, MIRAGER, has been designed to represent microprograms. The translator that converts the register transfer representations into the actual microprograms has been written in PL/I. With some exceptions the syntax of MIRAGER resembles that of a higher level language. MIRAGER statements fall into two general categories – pseudoinstructions and microinstructions. Pseudoinstruction statements include

1. EQU, which assigns a user defined name to an AMP register, bus, or functional unit,

2. NO OPERATION and RESERVE, which reserve one or more microinstructions for later use, and

3. ORIGIN, which specifies the starting control store address for the following microinstructions.

Microinstruction statements specify, on separate cards, the microoperations of a microinstruction. The microoperations include arithmetic and logic operations, in which the operation is enclosed in angular brackets (<,>); move operations, which specify the busses over which information is to be transferred; branch and skip operations, which may be conditional; miscellaneous operations, such as setting microinstruction mode, manipulating the control store address stack, interrupting the microinstruction to await input, performing an I/O operation, and incrementing the local store address register; and field assignment operations, which explicitly assign bits to microinstruction fields. An interesting construct of MIRAGER is the special processing "stack" which is initialized with a set of microoperations for each microinstruction. The microoperations in a microinstruction statement are added to the stack until encountering a stack flushing operation – a RESERVE, NO OPERATION, or ORIGIN

```
*******************************************************************************
*.....BRANCH TABLE INSTRUCTION FOR THE MOVE THROUGH MASK AND SHIFT RIGHT.......*
*******************************************************************************
ORIGIN=B'CCC0001'
                  <BYPASS5>SPE0--B2-->BMAR,SPE17
                  INCREMENT SPAR
                  READ                              *GET THE FIRST SOURCE WORD
                  GO TO #MASKSHIFTR
                  ...                                                   *DET
--------- --------- --------- --------- --------- --------- --------- ---------
                                        .
                                        .
                                        .
*******************************************************************************
*.....*.....*.....*.....*.....*.....*.....*.....*.....*.....*.....*.....*.....*
*.....*.....*.....*.....*.....*.....*.....*.....*.....*.....*.....*.....*.....*
*....MICRO ROUTINE TO PROCESS THE MOVE THROUGH MASK AND SHIFT RIGHT INS........*
*.....*.....*.....*.....*.....*.....*.....*.....*.....*.....*.....*.....*.....*
*.....*.....*.....*.....*.....*.....*.....*.....*.....*.....*.....*.....*.....*
*******************************************************************************
$RA<-----------WDCNT              *WORD COUNT
$RB<-----------MASK               *AND MASK
$SPE16<--------AS                 *CONTENTS OF MEMORY TO MOVE AND MSK
$SPO16<--------CFIELD             *SHIFT COUNT
$SPE17<--------SOURCE ADDRESS
$SPO17<--------DESTINATION ADDRESS
#MASKSHIFTR:      <UNPASS5>SPE0--B1-->SPO17
                  INCREMENT SPAR
                  WAIT
                  PUSH
                  GO TO #MASKSHIFTINIT
                  ...                                                   *DET
--------- --------- --------- --------- --------- --------- --------- ---------
#MASKSHIFTR2:     SPE16<AND>RB--B1-->SPE16         *AND MASK WITH SOURCE WORD
                  <SUB1>RA--B2-->RA                *DECREMENT WORD COUNT
                  ...                                                   *DET
--------- --------- --------- --------- --------- --------- --------- ---------
#MASKSHIFTR3:     <RGT1>SPE16--F1-->SPE16,MDRO     *SHIFT RIGHT 1 BIT
                  <BISUB1>SPO16--B2-->SPO16        *DECREMENT SHIFT COUNT
                  IF B2 > 0 TO TO #MASKSHIFTR 3
                  ...                                                   *DET
--------- --------- --------- --------- --------- --------- --------- ---------
                  SPO17--B4-->BMAR
                  <ADD1>SPO17---B1--->SPO17
                  <BYPASS3>RA--B2-->
                  WRITE                            *STORE MASKED AND SHIFTED WORD
                  WAIT
                  IF B2 = 0 GO TO #USUPERVISOR     *EXIT WHEN WORD COUNT = 0
                  ...                                                   *DET
--------- --------- --------- --------- --------- --------- --------- ---------
                  <ADD1>SPE17---B2--->BMAR,SPE17   *INCREMENT THE SOURCE ADDRESS
                  READ                             *GET NEXT SOURCE WORD
                  WAIT
                  ...                                                 *JONES
--------- --------- --------- --------- --------- --------- --------- ---------
                  IRCF---B2--->SPO16               *RE-INITIALIZE SHIFTCOUNT
                  MDRI---B1--->SPE16               *STORE NEW SOURCE WORD IN SPE16
                  GO TO #MASKSHIFTR2               *DO IT ALL AGAIN
                  ...                                                   *DET
--------- --------- --------- --------- --------- --------- --------- ---------
                                        .
                                        .
                                        .
```

```
****************************************************************************
*......*......*......*......*......*......*......*......*......*......*......*
*......*......*......*......*......*......*......*......*......*......*......*
*....*MICRO CODE COMMON TO BOTH RIGHT AND LEFT MASK AND SHIFT INSTRUCTIONS......*
*......*......*......*......*......*......*......*......*......*......*......*
*......*......*......*......*......*......*......*......*......*......*......*
****************************************************************************
#MASKSHIFTINIT:   MDRI--B1-->SPE16              *PUT 1ST SOURCE WORD IN SPE16
                  <BYPASS3>SPE0---B2--->RA      *STORE N=NUMBER OF WORDS IN RA
                  INCREMENT SPAR                *SET SPAR TO R3 = MASK
                  ...                                              *JONES
--------- --------- --------- --------- --------- --------- --------- ---------
                  <BIPASS3>SPE0---B1--->RB      *STORE MASK IN RB
                  IPCF---B2--->SP016            *STORE THE SHIFTCOUNT IN SP016
                  IF B2 = 0 GO TO #MASKNOSHIFT
                  ...                                              *DET
--------- --------- --------- --------- --------- --------- --------- ---------
                  POP                           *RETURN
                  ...                                              *JONES
--------- --------- --------- --------- --------- --------- --------- ---------

                                    .
                                    .
                                    .
****************************************************************************
*........COMMON ROUTINE USED TO PROCESS INSTRUCTIONS WITH NO SHIFT.............*
****************************************************************************
#MASKNOSHIFT:     SPE16<AND>RB--B1-->MDPO       *AND SOURCE WORD WITH MASK
                  INCREMENT SPAR                *SET SPAR TO R1:DESTINATION ADD
                  ...                                              *DET
--------- --------- --------- --------- --------- --------- --------- ---------
                  <SUB1>RA--B1-->RA             *DECREMENT WORD COUNT
                  <BYPASS3>SP017---B2--->BMAR
                  WRITE                         *STORE MASKED WORD
                  WAIT
                  IF B1 = 0 TO TO #USUPERVISOR  *EXIT IF WORD COUNT = 0
                  ...                                              *DET
--------- --------- --------- --------- --------- --------- --------- ---------
                  <ADD1>SPE17---B2--->BMAR,SPE17 *INCREMENT THE SOURCE ADDRESS
                  READ                          *GET THE NEXT SOURCE WORD
                  WAIT
                  ...                                              *DET
--------- --------- --------- --------- --------- --------- --------- ---------
                  MDRI--B1-->SPE16              *PUT NEXT SOURCE WORD IN SPE 16
                  <ADD1>SP017--B2-->SP017       *INCREMENT DESTINATION ADDRESS
                  GO TO #MASKNOSHIFT
                  ...                                              *DET
--------- --------- --------- --------- --------- --------- --------- ---------
```

303

Figure 6.7-3. AMP microprogram to perform a move through mask and shift right instruction.

Comments

1. The instruction format has three parts:
   a) the operation code - 000001,
   b) the address of the first parameter register R, which must be between 0 and 31, and
   c) the shift count, which must be between 0 and 16.

2. There are four parameter registers, arranged consecutively in the local store memory array:
   a) the first register contains the beginning address of the block of words to be moved,
   b) the second register contains the beginning address of the block to which the words will be moved,
   c) the third register contains the number of words to be moved, and
   d) the fourth register contains the mask pattern.

3. The operation of the instruction is the following. The first word in the source block is anded with the mask pattern in the fourth parameter register. This result is then shifted right by the shift count. This result is then moved to the first word in the destination block. The process is then repeated for the remaining words in the block.

	Implemented by directly microprogramming	Implemented by microprogrammed machine lang.
Microoperations per microinstruction (mean)	2.72	2.58
Bits utilized per microinstruction (mean)	31.1	29.2
Local store references per microinstruction (mean)	1.00	0.99
Percent of microinstructions using control store literal for microinstruction address	25	42
Percent of microinstructions using control store literal for constant data	43	10
Number of seconds required to perform 1000 matrix additions of 126 by 126 matrices with 16 bit integer elements	1	11*

Figure 6.7-4. Experiences with AMP in implementing a graphics system. (* - Assuming the machine language does not have an add vector instruction).

pseudoinstruction; the label of the next microinstruction; or the stack flushing pseudoinstruction, which is simply three consecutive periods. When a stack flushing operation is encountered, the microoperation statements on the stack are translated, unused fields are assigned from the default microoperations, and the stack is reinitialized. Statements that contain a percent sign in column one alter the default microoperations with which the stack is initialized.

6.7.4 AMP Example

Figure 6.7-3 shows an AMP microprogram to perform a "Move Through Mask and Shift" instruction. The machine level instruction is a form of block move instruction with masking and shifting added. If the mask is all ones and the shift count is zero, then a straight block move is accomplished.

6.7.5 AMP Experiences

AMP was designed for research in microprogramming applications, and some results have been reported. The graphic system MIRAGE was implemented directly by microprograms and also by a machine language instruction set of forty-two instructions that required 248 microinstructions to implement. Figure 6.7-4 presents some observations on the two different implementations.

6.8 MATHILDA

6.8.1 MATHILDA Background

MATHILDA is a dynamically user micrprogrammable processor developed by a group at the University of Aarhus, Denmark. Because MATHILDA was intended for use as a tool in emulator and and processor design research, the following design criteria were quite different from criteria assumed in the design of most commercial computers:

1. modularity and homogeneity - to reduce the number of different features, implement different features by standard architectural constructs, and permit system growth;

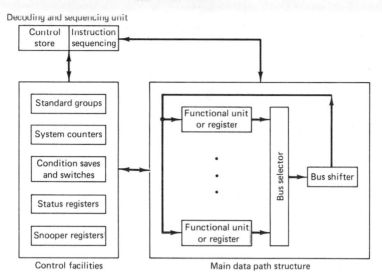

Figure 6.8-1. The MATHILDA Processor.

2. to provide general techniques for controlling system resources;

3. the ability to define virtual machines through several levels;

4. the ability to multiprogram virtual machines at the microprogram level;

5. to have a clean and consistent technique of handling timing problems.

The result of these considerations was a computer with a very "reasonable" microprogram level architecture that is not influenced by any machine language. Despite its complexity in terms of number of components, MATHILDA is relatively easy to use in systems implementation.

307

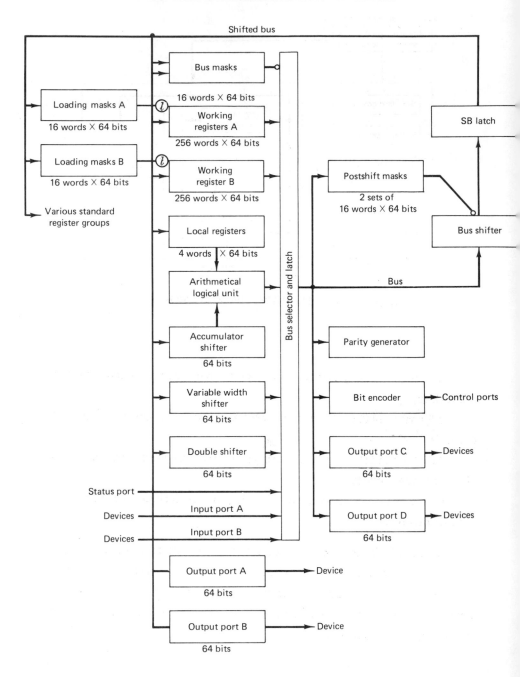

Figure 6.8-2. MATHILDA Main Data Path.

6.8.2 MATHILDA Architecture

6.8.2.1 Upper Level Design of MATHILDA

Figure 6.8-1 shows the major elements of MATHILDA:

1. the Main Data Path,

2. Control Facilities, and

3. the Decoding and Sequencing unit.

The Main Data Path element serves as the primary data handling
facility and consists of a variety of sixty-four bit registers,
data paths, and transformation units. The Control Facilities
element contains components like those in the Main Data Path,
however, they exercise control over the components of the Main
Data Path.   The Decoding and Sequencing element decodes the
sixty-four bit microinstructions and selects   the   next
microinstruction to be executed.

6.8.2.2 MATHILDA Functional Units

Figure 6.8-2 presents a detailed diagram of the Main Data
Path. During the execution of each microinstruction, the Main
Data Path can perform the following operations:

1. select a sixty-four bit input (via the Bus Selctor and
Latch) from one   of   the units connected to the bus (the A
Working Registers, B Working Registers, ALU, Variable Width
Shifter, etc.),

2. mask that input (via the Bus Masks),

3. shift the masked input (via the Bus Shifter),

4. mask the result of step 3 (via the Postshift Masks),
and

5. assign the result of step 4   to one of the units
connected to the bus.

In performing the mask operations in steps 2 and 4, the input
to   the operation is masked independently with two   mask
registers, and the logical or of the two mask operations yields

309

the final result. The local storage units labeled Working Registers A and Working Registers B in Figure 6.8-2 each contain 256 words of sixty-four bits. The writing of data from the bus into these local storage units may be masked by the A and B Loading Masks so that only selected bits of the chosen working register will be loaded. This feature is useful, for example, in constructing the result of a floating point operation in which one word has several distinct fields. The four Local Registers provide one input to the ALU. To provide flexibility in using Local Registers, the register selected for input to the ALU and the register selected to receive the bus result may be different. The standard sixty-four bit ALU can perform the operations listed in Figure 5.2-2. The other ALU input is the Accumulator Shifter, a sixty-four bit register whose contents can be shifted left or right one bit position. The bit position vacated as a result of shifting can be loaded by any bit of the Accumulator Shifter itself, so that cyclic shifting of any word size up to sixty-four bits can be performed. The Variable Width Shifter is a sixty-four bit register that is logically identical to the Accumulator Shifter. The Accumulator Shifter and Variable Width Shifter may be combined, so that cyclic shifting of word sizes up to 128 bits can be performed. The Double Shifter, another sixty-four bit register, is similar to the Accumulator Shifter except that its associated shift mechanism shifts two bits at a time. The Status Port may select data from one of sixty-four locations and assign it to the bus. The selected data may originate from the current microinstruction, system counters, etc. The Input Port and the Output Port Registers provide communication with I/O devices. For generality, memory is treated as an I/O device.

310

In the operation of the Main Data Path, many resources require some sort of control specification. For example, addresses are required to select the two bus masks, the A Working Register, the B Working Register, the Local Register, the two Postshift masks, etc. Control information is also required in the specification of operations that the ALU and shifting mechanisms are to perform. While this information can be specified by each microinstruction (immediate control), MATHILDA also provides several residual control sources that may specify control information:

1. an external register,
2. the least significant bits from the shifted bus in the Main Data Path,
3. the output of the Bit-Encoder (see Section 6.8-5), and
4. the value of a Save register.

These control sources are typically combined to form a "standard group" as shown in Figure 6.8-3. Another part of the control facilities unit is the system counters. Associated with each of the 2 sixteen bit counters is a standard group. The sixteen Register Group registers in each of these standard groups are used to save the contents of the counter register, so that each counter can control up to sixteen levels of nested loops. The counters themselves can be independently loaded, incremented, decremented, and cleared. As MATHILDA executes microinstructions, a large number (almost 128) of system conditions may arise and be selected for testing. These conditions indicate the status of the ALU, shifters, Bit-Encoder, counters, I/O, bus parity, etc. Selected conditions may be saved in a register group of 128 one bit registers.

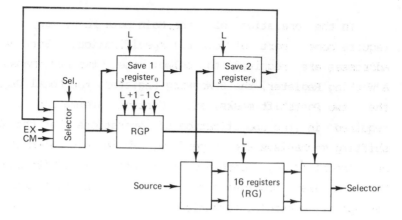

Figure 6.8-3. Typical MATHILDA standard group.

The control store in MATHILDA is an 80-n sec sixty-four bit wide memory that may contain up to 4096 words. A register called the Control Store Address Buffer addresses the control store. As shown in Figure 6.8-4, several resources are associated with this register to facilitate microinstruction sequencing. These facilities include:

1. two sixteen word stacks,

2. arithmetic and logic units for address calculation,

3. inputs from the current microinstruction (the B input in Figure 6.8-4),

4. input from the Main Data Path (labeled SB(0:11) in Figure 6.8-4), and

5. input from an external register.

When a hardware interrupt occurs, the Current Address and the Control Store Address Buffer registers are set to zero, and the Interrupt Recovery Address Register is assigned the address of the microinstruction that would have been executed had the interrupt not occurred. This address may be stored in one of the Status Registers for later use.

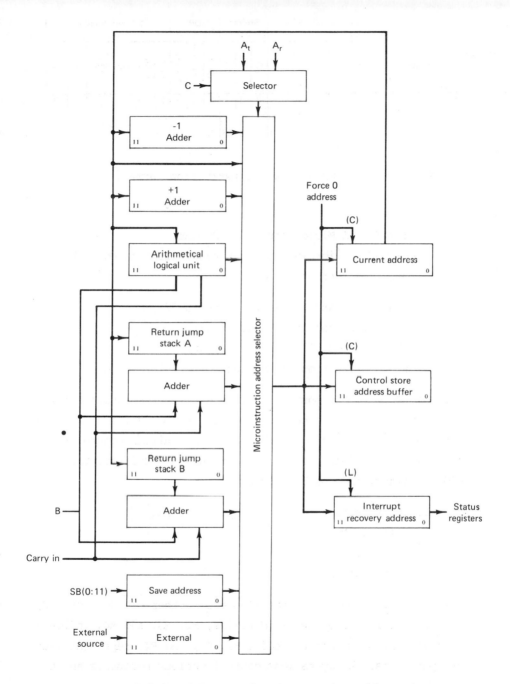

Figure 6.8-4. MATHILDA microinstruction address bus.

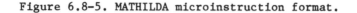

Operations and data				Shifter control				MDP transport		Microinstruction sequencing					Major field
Operations F₁	Operations and data S₁ | M₂ | F₂	Operations and data M₃ | F₃	Operations and data S₃ | M₄ | F₄	AS	VS	DS	Shift	Destination	Source	BISB	CISB	Condition selection	A_F	A_T	Subfield
7	10	8	10	2	2	2	1	3	3	2	1	7	3	3	Subfield w
63				29	28		23	22		16	15			0	Bit number

Figure 6.8-5. MATHILDA microinstruction format.

6.8.2.3 MATHILDA Microinstruction Format

The MATHILDA microintruction format, illustrated in Figure 6.8-5, comprises four basic parts:

1. Main Data Path transport (bits 16-22),
2. operations and data (bits 29-63),
3. shifter control (bits 23-28), and
4. microinstruction sequencing (bits 0-15).

The Main Data Path transport field specifies the source for the bus, whether or not the bus data is to be shifted, and the destination of data on the bus. The shifter control field specifies operations for the Accumulator Shifter, Variable Width Shifter, and Double Shifter:

1. shift left,
2. shift right,
3. load, or
4. no operation.

The operations and data subfields are further divided into F, S, and M fields. The one bit M fields, M2, M3, and M4, indicate whether the seven bit F fields, F2, F3, and F4, represent data or operations. The operations control various resources and the

314

standard groups associated with them - the ALU, counters, mask registers, input and output ports, etc. The operations may move literal data to registers or register pointers. The subfields in the microinstruction sequencing field select a condition to be tested, specify the sequencing calculation to be used if the condition is true (At) or false (Af), and indicate the inputs to the address calculation routine.

Since MATHILDA microinstructions specify several independent operations they are classified as horizontal. Most fields employ single level encoding. The M fields, however, determine the interpretation of the F fields and thus are examples of two level encoding. The microinstructions are implemented in a polyphase manner. The logical phases of microinstruction execution are the following:

1. performing the data transport on the Main Data Path,

2. executing shift and other operations, and

3. calculating the address of the next microinstruction to be executed.

In one microinstruction, data can be loaded into a register in a register group, and then the register group pointer can be changed. To provide flexibility in testing conditions, MATHILDA can run in both serial and parallel modes.

1. In the long cycle mode, any condition arising as a result of performing Main Data Path transport, shifter control, and other operations can be tested and used for sequencing in the same microinstruction. In the long cycle mode, microinstructions require 370 nanoseconds for execution.

2. In the short cycle mode, conditions used in microinstruction sequencing are those devolved from previous microinstructions. In the short cycle mode, microinstructions require 280 nanoseconds for execution.

```
1                         .C O R E  A D D I T I O N  (UNPACKED FORMAT).
2                         .MATHILDA (16 BITS)-SHORT CYCLE.
3                         *R=8
4                         *V
5                         LA:1-2=100000,77777
6                         WA: 0-1=50,26
7                         *E
8                         *R=10
9                         *T.1
10                        WAP
11                        *E
12                        .FETCH OPERANDS.
13                        .TEST WHETHER X=0.
14                        .TEST WHETHER SIGNS ARE EQUAL.
15                        .ADD MAGNITUDES.
16                        *D.1
17 START1: VS,LR:=WA ;WAP+1,   BSS:=CM, PGS:=CM, KD:=SC ; IF FALSE THEN
R+1.
18         DS,AS:=WA ;LAP+1,   SETALF+, SCUALF+          ; IF BUS THEN
R+EXIT1.
19                   ;LAP+1                        ; IF AL(15) THEN
R+SUB.
20                        .LOAD SUM INTO WA. DETERMINE SIGN.
21 LOAD1:  WA:=AL    ;LAP-1                  ; IF KD THEN R+1 ELSE
R+EXIT1.
22         WA:=VS    ;PAP+1                  ; IF BUS THEN R+1 ELSE
R+EXIT1.
23         WA:=VS    ;LAPC,   PG>16                ; R+EXIT1.
24                        .SUBTRACT MAGNITUDES.
25 SUB:              ;PAP+1, SETALF-,         SETKD
26         AS:=DS    ;        PG>1
27         LR:=VS    ;LRIP+1, PG>1
28         LR:=DS    ;PAPC,   PG>16          ; IF AL(15) THEN R+1 ELSE
R-LOAD1.
```

316

```
29          AS:=AL      ;ALF:=    (AV-B)+A+1,        LROP+1
30          WA:=AL      ;LAPC
31                      *D.1
32 EXIT1:               ;PAPC,              LRPC,    LAPC
```

Figure 6.8-6. MATHILDA microprogram to add 2 sixteen bit integers in sign magnitude representation.

Assumptions

1) First operand in Working Register A0
2) Second operand in Working Register A1
3) Result left in Working Register A1
4) Working Register A Pointer = 0
5) Local Register Input Pointer = 0
6) Local Register Output Pointer = 0
7) Loading Mask A0 = 177777 (base 8)
8) Loading Mask A1 = 100000 (base 8)
9) Loading Mask A2 = 077777 (base 8)
10) Loading Mask A Pointer = 0
11) Short cycle
12) Word size = 16 bits

Abbreviations

AL – ALU result
AS – Accumulator Shifter
DS – Double Shifter
LA – Loading Mask A
LAP – Loading Mask A Pointer
LR – Local Register
PAP – Postshift Mask A Register Pointer
R – Relative (for relative addressing)
VS – Variable Shifter
WA – Working Registers A
WAP – Working Registers A Pointer

317

Comments

Lines 1-2: Introductory comments

Line 3: Pseudoinstruction to indicate that base 8 will be used for subsequent numeric data

Lines 4-7: Pseudoinstruction to initialize LA1, LA2, WA1, and WA2 for the simulator run

Line 8: Pseudoinstruction to indicate that base 10 will be used for subsequent numberic data

Lines 9-11: Pseudoinstructions to define Table 1 for the simulator. Table 1 contains the WAP and the register it addresses.

Lines 12-15: Comments for the microinstructions in lines 17-19.

Line 16: A pseudoinstruction that will cause the simulator to print the values of the registers in Table 1 when execution reaches this point.

Line 17: Load VS and LR0 with WA0 (the first operand). Increment the WAP to 1. 'BSS:=CM' indicates that the microinstructions will specify bus shifts. 'PGS:=CM' indicates that the microinstructions will specify Postshift Masks. Set the KD switch to the Selected Condition (FALSE). Proceed to the next microinstruction.

Line 18: Load DS and AS with WA1 (the second operand). Increment the LAP (to 1). Set the ALU function to addition. Set the Sequencing and Control Unit ALU function to addition. If the Bus has value 0 (the first operand, which was assigned to the Bus in the previous microinstruction, was 0) then branch to EXIT1 (because the second operand is the sum).

Line 19: Increment the LAP (to 2). If bit 15 (the sign bit) of the ALU result is 1 (the operands have different signs) then branch to SUB (the subtract magnitudes routine).

Line 20: Comment for lines 21-23.

Line 21: Load WA1 with the ALU result masked by LA2. (Thus WA1 is loaded with the sum of the magnitudes of the operands if the operands had the same sign or with the difference of the magnitudes if the operands had different signs; the mask leaves the sign bit unchanged.) Decrement the LAP to 1. If switch KD is FALSE (the signs of the operands were the same and so there is no need to change the sign in WA1) then branch to EXIT1.

318

Line 22: Load WA1 with VS masked by LA1 . (This sets the sign of the result to the sign of the first operand.) Increment PAP. If the Bus does not have value 0 (the sum of the magnitudes of the operands is not 0) then branch to EXIT1.

Line 23: Load WA1 with VS masked by the Postshift Mask of 0, indicated by PG>16. (Set WA1 to 0 because the sum of the operands is 0.) Clear the LAP. Branch to EXIT1.

Line 24: Comment for lines 25-30.

Line 25: Increment PAP. Set the ALU function to subtraction. Set the KD switch to TRUE to indicate that the operands have different signs.

Line 26: Load AS with DS (the second operand) masked by the Postshift Mask that deletes the sign bit, indicated by PG>1.

Line 27: Load LR0 with VS (the first operand) masked by the Postshift Mask that deletes the sign bit. Increment the LR input pointer to 1.

Line 28: Load LR1 with DS masked by the Postshift Mask of 0 (set LR1 to 0). If bit 15 of the ALU result is 1 (the result of subtracting the magnitude of the second operand from the magnitude of the first operand is less than 0, i.e., the magnitude of the second operand is greater than the magnitude of the first operand) then go to the next microinstruction; otherwise go to LOAD.

Line 29: Load the AS with the ALU result (the magnitude of the first operand minus the magnitude of the second operand). Set the ALU function to $(A \vee notB) + A+1$. Increment LR output pointer to 1.

Line 30: Load WA1 with the ALU result:

$(LR1 \vee notAS) + LR1+1$

$= (0 \vee notAS) + 0+1$

$= notAS + 1$

$=$ magnitude of operand 1

$-$ magnitude of operand 2

Clear the LAP.

Line 31: Same as line 16

Line 32: Reset the machine state: clear the PAP, clear the LR input and output pointers, and clear the LAP.

319

The transition from one mode to the other is made under microprogram control.

6.8.3 MATHILDA Microprogrammability

The MATHILDA control store is writable under microprogram control. A microinstruction which contains a control store load microoperation performs the following steps:

1. load the contents of the Control Store Data Buffer (actually Device number 15 associated with Output Port A) into the control store location addressed by the Control Store Address Buffer register, and

2. then proceed to the next sequential microinstruction.

Alternatively the control store may be loaded from a small PROM. Such loading is used to initialize the system.

An assembler and simulator have been developed to facilitate writing and debugging microprograms. As shown in the example in Figure 6.8-6, lines in a MARIA assembler microprogram represent microinstructions, pseudoinstructions (lines that start with asterisks), and comments (lines that start with periods). The fields in a microinstruction are coded in the order in which they are logically executed: bus transport, operations, and sequencing. Semicolons separate the three parts of microinstructions. The bus transport and other operations are written as simple assignment statements using the Algol 60 operator ´:=´ to indicate assignment. The sequencing operations are written as simple conditional statements (IF...THEN...ELSE....). Microinstructions may be labeled to facilitate sequencing. Pseudoinstructions may be used to

1. indicate the base for numerical data,

2. set the assembler microprogram counter,

3. define the address in control store at which to begin execution,

4. define external names,

5. associate names with constants,

6. assign values to register groups, and

7. control microprogram listing.

In addition to these common operations, pseudoinstructions can define tables of registers. Other pseudoinstructions indicate points in a microprogram at which to print the values of registers in a table or sections of control store during simulation. The simulator, which runs on the IBM System/360 amd other systems, thus provides tracing facilities, but it relies heavily on the assembler and is not interactive. Additional support software includes a loader and a "normalizer," which initializes machine registers.

6.8.4. MATHILDA Example

Figure 6.8-6 shows a sample MATHILDA microprogram to add two integers represented in sign-magnitude format. While this sounds like a simple problem, there are several cases that must be considered. On a less general machine such a task would be extremely difficult to microprogram. Experiences with MATHILDA indicate that substantial projects require surprisingly little microcode.

6.8.5 Additional MATHILDA Features

MATHILDA contains a special Snooper Facility to assist in performance monitoring. When the address of the next microinstruction to be executed is sent to the MATHILDA Control Store Address Buffer register, it is also sent to the Snooper Control Store Address Buffer register. While the addressed microinstruction is being executed, an instruction fetched from

321

the Snooper Control Store is executed. This instruction controls the Snooper resources: two sets of sixteen registers, counters, and comparators. A Snooper instruction can specify, for example, incrementing two registers. The Snooper Facilities can be read or written through normal I/O Ports. The Snooper Control Store is writable so that different data gathering routines can be developed for each microprogram.

A novel feature of MATHILDA is the Bit-Encoder that is part of the Main Data Path. The Bit-Encoder examines the value on the data bus and determines the left and rightmost bit positions that have the value one. These values, and various functions of them, may be saved and used in future decisions and computations.

Bibliography

A. Cal Data Processor

1. "Cal Data 1 Computer Family."

2. "CDP Processor Maintenance Manual Volume I," Document 21518003, Revision X2, May 1974.

3. "PDP-11 Emulation," Version A, June 2, 1974.
     Available from
               California Data Processors
               2019 South Ritchey Street
               Santa Ana, California 92705

B. PRIME 300

1. "PRIME 300 Computer."

2. "PRIME Writeable Control Store."

3. "Microcoders Handbook."
   Available from
   PRIME Computer, Inc.
   145 Pennsylvania Avenue
   Framingham, Massachusetts 01701

C. Varian 73

1. "Varian 73 System Handbook," June 1972.

2. "Varian 73 System Processor Manual," March 1973.

3. "Varian Microprogramming Guide," August 1973.
   Available from
   Varian Data Machines
   2722 Michelson Drive.
   Irvine, California 92664

D. QM-1

1. "QM-1   Hardware   Level   User's   Manual,"   Second   Edition,
   Revision 1,   NANODATA   Corporation,   2457   Wehrle   Drive,
   Williamsville, New York, 14221, March 31, 1974.

2. "Computer Alters Its Architecture Fast via New Control," _Electronics_, August 8, 1974, pages 39-40.

E. Burroughs Interpreter

1. E. W. Reigel, U. Faber, and D. A. Fisher, "The Interpreter - A Microprogrammable Building Block System," _1972 Spring Joint Computer Conference Proceedings_, AFIPS Press, Montvale, New Jersey, pages 705-723.

2. S. Zucker, "A Micro-Translator for the Interpreter Based Systems," TR 70-1 (Revision A), February 10, 1970.

3. H. W. Bingham, "The BD:Machine An APL Model for Micro-Instruction Execution in Interpreter Based Systems," TR 70-3, April 30, 1970.

4. "D-Machine Users Manual," April 1971.

5. H. W. Bingham _et al_, "Microprogramming Manual for Interpreter Based Systems," TR 70-8, November 1970.

> Available from
>> Burroughs Corporation
>> Federal and Special Systems Group
>> Paoli, Pennsylvania 19301

F. AMP

1. R. G. Barr, J. A. Becker, W. P. Lidinsky, and V. V. Tantillo, "A Research-Oriented Dynamic Microprocessor," _IEEE Transactions on Computers_, Volume C-22 Number 11 (November 1973), pages 976-985.

2. W. P. Lidinsky, "MIRAGE, A Microprogrammable Interactive Raster Graphics Equipment," IEEE Computer Society Conference Proceedings, September 1971, pages 15-16.

G. MATHILDA

1. B. D. Shriver, "A Description of the MATHILDA System," Department of Computer Science Report PB-13, University of Aarhus, Aarhus, Denmark, April 1973.

    This document provides a detailed description of the MATHILDA system including lists of microinstructions, test conditions, examples, etc. The redesign of a few MATHILDA features in 1974 makes some of the discussions out of date.

2. P. Kornerup and B. D. Shriver, "An Overview of the MATHILDA System," Department of Computer Science, Univesity of Aarhus, Aarhus, Denmark.

    An updated summary of the MATHILDA system and associated research work.

3. E. Lynning et al, "A Users Manual for the Simulated RIKKE-MATHILDA System on the CDC 6400," Department of Computer Science, University of Aarhus, Aarhus, Denmark, February 1974.

    A description of the system assembler and simulator and how to use them.

4. P. Kornerup, "Concepts of the MATHILDA System," Second Annual Symposium on Computer Architecture Proceedings, IEEE, January 1975, pages 159-164.

    A brief overview of the MATHILDA system.

CHAPTER 7

DEVELOPMENTS IN MICROPROGRAMMING LANGUAGES

7.1 Introduction

With the commercial availability of several user microprogrammable computers, low level microprogramming languages (such as assembler and flowchart languages) and simulators have become available and are widely used. There has been little development of register transfer and higher level languages for microprogramming commercially available computers, even though microprogramming is conceptually similar to programming. In general, the development of microprogramming languages has lagged far behind the development of programming languages. With an increasing desire on the part of end users to experiment with and utilize microprogramming, there is a need for higher level microprogramming languages in which the user can express microprograms easily and efficiently. This chapter surveys and comments on recent work in the area of microprogramming languages.

7.2 Register Transfer Microprogramming Languages

One of the first register transfer languages was ML, a language developed for Lincoln Laboratory's LX-1 Microprocessor* [Hornbuckle 1970]. The LX-1 Microprocessor, a prototype computer used for studying applications in emulation

* Here microprocessor means microprogrammable processor.

Syntax for ML

The syntax for ML is based upon the extended BNF notation developed by Cheatham. The metasymbol $\Rightarrow$ is equivalent to the BNF $::=$ and means "is defined as" or "consists of." Upper case alphabetics and all other characters (other than metasymbols) are terminal symbols, whereas strings of lower case alphabetic characters (in some cases separated with dashes) are used to define nonterminal syntactic elements. Exceptions are that space, tab, and cr stand for the obvious terminal symbols. The metasymbol | is used to separate and specify alternatives, brackets enclose alternatives, and brackets with subscripts and superscripts mean the following:

$[\ ]_j^i$ choose at least j but at most i of the alternatives
$[\ ]^i$ choose none or at most i
$[\ ]_j$ choose at least j with no upper limit
$[\ ]$ is equivalent to $[\ ]^1$
$\{\ \}$ is equivalent to $[\ ]_1^1$.

The following example means that a jwak is defined as a snex followed by at most 3 zats followed by exactly one carriage return:

$$\text{jwak} \Rightarrow \text{snex}[\text{zats}]^3 \{\text{cr}\}.$$

In general, the microprogram source text may be liberally sprinkled with separators; only those places where separators are necessary are indicated in the following.

Preliminary

alphabetic-character $\Rightarrow$ A $|$ B $|$ C $| \cdots |$ Z $|$
alphanumeric-character $\Rightarrow$ alphabetic-
   character $|0|1| \cdots |9$
separator $\Rightarrow$ space $|$ tab
comment $\Rightarrow$ $_*$ [any-character-but-cr]$^\infty$
lname, cname, rname $\Rightarrow$ alphabetic-character
   [alphanumeric-character]^{15}

General Program Structure

microprogram ⇒ definition-section assignment-section END cr

definition-section ⇒ [definition-line cr]₁

definition-line ⇒ comment | definition [comment]

assignment-section ⇒ [assignment-line cr]₁

assignment-line ⇒ comment | assignment-statement [comment]

Definitions

definition ⇒ register-declaration | constant-declaration

register-declaration ⇒ rname = octal-number-modulo-16

constant-declaration ⇒ cname ≡ octal-number-modulo-2^{16} | cname ≡ label

Assignments

assignment-statement ⇒ [label] [separator]₁ assignment [/[goto]]

assignment ⇒ left-side [→ right-side]

right-side ⇒ [dregsel] [, special-bit]⁶

left-side ⇒ [aregsel [shiftop] logop] [−]
               bregsel |
               aregsel [shiftop] + [−] bregsel
               [, carryin] |
               aregsel [shiftop] − bregsel |
               [aregsel] λ bregsel |
               aregsel {x | x̲} bregsel

bregsel, aregsel ⇒ rname | cname | octal-number-modulo-2^{16}

dregsel ⇒ rname

logop ⇒ ∨ | ∧ | ∀

shiftop ⇒ {/ | *} {octal-number-modulo-16 | #}
    [, {special-bit | 0 | 1}]

carryin ⇒ {special-bit | 1 | 0}

label ⇒ lname [({1 | 0} [, {1 | 0}])]

goto ⇒ lname [({special-bit | 1 | 0}
    [, {special-bit | 1 | 0}]) [‖]]

special-bit ⇒ C | Z | H | L | S | F

Figure 7.2-1. Syntax for the microprogramming language ML for the LX-1 Processor.

```
1      0 -> COUNT
2      -XYZ -> TEMP,Z,L /L3(L,Z)
3      L3(0,0)  TEMP/1->TEMP,L,Z /L3(L,Z)
4      L3(1,0)  COUNT+1->COUNT /L3(0,0)
5      L3(0,1)  ABC*#,F->ABC
```

Figure 7.2-2. Sample ML microprogram for the LX-1 processor.

Comments

General: Rotate register ABC left an amount equal to the number of zer
        in XYZ.

1. Set the COUNT register, which will count the number of places to
   shift, to zero.

2. Complement register XYZ, so that zeros become ones and vice versa,
   and assign it to register TEMP. Store the L bit, the least
   significant bit of the result, and the Z bit, which is one if the A
   result (of the complement operation) was zero. Branch to one of the
   L3 labels depending on the L and Z bits. If both L and Z were zero,
   i.e., if a zero was shifted out and the ALU result was nonzero,
   branch to L3(0,0). If L was one and Z was zero, branch to L3(1,0).
   L was zero and Z was one branch to L3(0,1).

3. Shift TEMP right one bit and store the result back in TEMP. Save the
   L and Z bits, and branch according to their status.

4. Here the previous operation indicated a one had been in TEMP, so add
   one to the COUNT, and branch to step 3 to continue shifting.

5. At this point, all necessary bits in TEMP have been examined (as it has a zero value), so register ABC is right shifted the number of bits in the COUNT register. The F modifier indicates that the shift is circular. Note that there is no need for a label L3(1,1) because an ALU result cannot simultaneously have a least significant bit of one and a value of zero.

and real-time digital signal processing problems, employs a sixty-four bit microinstruction format. An ML program consists of a set of definitions, which assign symbolic names to registers and constants, and "assignment statements," which indicate machine operations. The syntax of ML has been defined formally. This definition is illustrated in Figure 7.2-1. The microprogram in Figure 7.2-2 illustrates ML constructs. Some of these constructs are unusual:

1. the formats of the labels,

2. the characters asterisk and slash that represent shift operations and,

3. the slash followed by a possibly variable label to indicate conditional branching, a construct reminiscent of early SNOBOL implementations.

In addition to ML, a sophisticated simulator package for the LX-1 was developed.

The register transfer language TRANSLANG for the Burroughs Interpreter was discussed in Section 6.6. The TRANSLANG microprograms shown in Figures 6.6-7 and 6.6-8 illustrate more conventional conditional operations than those of Figure 7.2-2. The TRANSLANG microprograms also illustrate the use of mnemonic auxiliary operations like LCTR (for load counter) and SAVE (save a microprogram address). AMIL [Rauscher 1975], a

```
* AMIL PROGRAM TO EXECUTE AN AN/UYK-7 DIFFERENCE INSTRUCTION,
*  C(ACCUMULATOR REGISTER A) =
*         C(ACCUMULATOR REGISTER A) - C(ACCUMULATOR REGISTER B)
*
*
.DIFF   BARA = FSU(2) + LSA(8) , ACSAR = TEMPLATE2  $
           * BARA = A(ACCUMULATOR REGISTER A)
           * TEMPLATE2 IS FORMAT OF TYPE IVA INSTRUCTION
*
        INPUT(BUF(BARA),LSB(12)) , BARB = FSU(4) + LSA(8)  $
           * LSB(12) = C(ACCUMULATOR REGISTER A)  (STORED IN MAIN MEMORY)
           * BARB = A(ACCUMULATOR REGISTER B)
*
        INPUT(BUF(BARB),LSA(12)) $
           * LSA(12) = C(ACCUMULATOR REGISTER B)  (STORED IN MAIN MEMORY)
*
        LSA(12) = LSB(12) - LSA(12)
           * LSA(12) = C(ACCUMULATOR REGISTER A)
           *               - C(ACCUMULATOR REGISTER B)
*
        OUTPUT(LSA(12),BUF(BARA)) , BARA = LSB(8) , *
        ACSAR = TEMPLATE1 , JUMP TO ACSAR  $
           * C(ACCUMULATOR REGISTER A)  (IN MAIN MEMORY)
           *  = C(ACCUMULATOR REGISTER A) - C(ACCUMULATOR REGISTER B)
           * BARA = A(NEXT INSTRUCTION)
           * JUMP BACK TO FETCH ROUTINE
*
```

Figure 7.2-3. Sample AMIL microprogram.

microprogramming language developed for the Microprogrammed Control Unit (MCU)*, followed TRANSLANG. An example of this language is illustrated in Figure 7.2-3. The nanoprogramming language for the NANODATA QM-1, illustrated in Figures 6.5-5 through 6.5-8, uses similar register transfer constructs, yet is more complex due to the unusual architecture of the machine. In the microprogramming languages for the LX-1, Interpreter, and QM-1, the destination of an assignment operation appears on the right side of the subcommand, a convention opposite to that used in most higher level programming languages. The register transfer language MIRAGER [Clark 1972], developed for the Argonne Microprocessor, was described and illustrated in Section 6.7.3.

ANIMIL [Rauscher 1975], the microprogramming language for the Signal Processing Arithmetic Unit (SPAU)** developed at the Naval Research Laboratory, uses constructs like those of the previous languages as illustrated in Figure 3.2-7. To simplify the representation and preparation of SPAU microprograms, however, ANIMIL uses some simple programming language techniques not generally found in earlier languages, for example, free-format line-independent statements and comments, cross-reference lists, macro facilities, and a syntax based on a formal parsing technique [Rauscher 1973]. The simulators developed for the MCU and SPAU use a common and fairly sophisticated command language.

The Microprogram Design System (MDS) [Dubbs 1972], was designed to "support future microprogram development activities within IBM." One component of MDS is a translator which can be tailored for application to a particular machine. This is accomplished via a translator writing system which assumes most of the responsibility for translator design and implementation.

* The MCU is described in Section 8.6.
** The Signal Processing Arithmetic Unit is described in Section 8.6.

333

```
/* MDS MICROPROGRAMMING LANGUAGE EXAMPLE */
ROUTINE RSTOR,FS=100,INCR=100,T1='REGISTER STORE ROUTINE';
BEGIN:      GOTO BOUND(**) V(3,6:7)/* TEST FOR WORD BOUNDARY          */
            :: BNDRY=8                                                 ;
BOUND(00):  ENABLE S4,Z=(UB-L)//16 /* COMPARE REG NO. TO UPPER BOUND */;
            W(V/4)=REG(L),V=V+4,    /* STORE REG AND INCR ADDRESS     */
            GOTO ENDTST(*X) S4  /* TEST FOR END                       */;
ENDTST(0X): L=L+1, GOTO BOUND(00)  /* INCR REG NO. AND LOOP           */;
ENDTST(1X): GOTO LS(RTN)            /* RETURN                         */;
 /* STORE REGISTERS WHEN ADDRESS IS INCONVENIENTLY ALIGNED */
BOUND(01):  K=1,GOTO SETUP
                                                                      ;
BOUND(10):  K=2,GOTO SETUP
                                                                      ;
BOUND(11):  K=3
                                                                      ;
SETUP:      Y1=W(V/4)               /* GET CURRENT CORE CONTENTS      */;
TSTEND(01): Y(K:K+3)=REG(L)         /* MOVE IN REG CONTENTS           */;
            W(V/4)=Y1,V=V+4         /* STORE DATA AND INCR ADDRESS    */;
            ENABLE S4,Z=(UB-L)//16 /* COMPARE REG NO. TO UPPER BOUND */;
            Y1=Y2,L=L+1,            /* SHIFT RESIDUE, INCR REG NO.    */
            GOTO TSTEND(*1)  S4  /* TEST FOR END                      */;
TSTEND(11): W(V/4,0:K-1)=Y1(0:K-1),/* STORE LAST PART                 */
            GOTO ENDTST(1X)         /* RETURN                         */;
```

Figure 7.2-4. MDS microprogramming language example.

The language for such a project had to be

1. sufficiently general to represent all microprogram functions,

2. subsettable to provide a tailored language for different machines,

3. extendable to support new features,

4. readable to aid in understanding microprograms.

As illustrated in Figure 7.2-4, the language chosen is a free form algebraic language with constructs similar to those used in PL/I. Like those previously discussed, the translator is not intended as a compiler for microprograms. It translates statements into microinstructions on a one-to-one basis. Reported innovations in the MDS translator include modifications to the LALR parsing algorithm and provisions for semantic support. This latter feature incorporates concepts of computer description languages so that the MDS system can be used for a variety of machines.

It is interesting to note that most of the computers for which register transfer microprogramming languages were developed employ horizontal microinstructions. The reason for this may have been the fact that the constructs of higher level languages are difficult to implement efficiently in computers with horizontal microinstructions because there are presently few techniques to make effective use of the available parallelism.

7.3 Higher Level Machine-Dependent Microprogramming Languages

While register transfer microprogramming languages facilitate the writing of microprograms, higher level machine dependent microprogramming languages alleviate the strict correspondence between statements and microinstructions. Statements in such languages may be translated into several microinstructions and thus provide convenient vehicles for representing arithmetic expressions, simple control blocks, etc. A simple example of such a language is the MIL language developed for the Burroughs B1700. The MIL language was

335

```
DECLARE
  <global declarations>
BEGIN
  <statements>
        DECLARE                   Inner block,
          <local declarations>    may occur
        BEGIN                     zero, one,
          <statements>            or several
        END                       times
END
```

a) Microprogram structure

        Code of outer block
                                    Outer block
        Constants of outer block

        Variables of outer block

        Code of inner block 1
                                    Inner block 1
    Unique constants of inner block 1

        Code of inner block 2
                                    Inner block 2
    Unique constants of inner block 2

                    .

                    .

                    .

336

Variable storage for all inner blocks

b) Control store allocation

Figure 7.3-1. Datasaab FCPU microprogram characteristics.

discussed and illustrated in Section 4.3. MIL differs from related languages in using English verbs (a la COBOL) rather than mathematical notation to represent common operations like assignment and arithmetic operations. BML, another microprogramming language for the B1700, was developed by a research group at the University of Michigan before Burroughs began releasing information about MIL [DeWitt 1973]. BML uses a register transfer notation and thus is a slightly different type of language.

The microprogramming language for the Datasaab FCPU (Flexible Central Processing Unit) [Lawson 1973] was designed to facilitate writing and reading microprograms because it was expected that much more microcode would be written for the FCPU than for previous medium-scale computers. The syntactical structure of the language was therefore designed to be simple to understand and utilize, yet directly related to the microinstruction repertoire of the machine. A very general structure, illustrated in Figure 7.3-1a, was chosen for microprograms. The microprogram structure of an outer block with global declarations and several inner blocks with local declarations is reflected in the organization of microprograms in control store (see Figure 7.3-1b). In a Datasaab FCPU

337

```
* DATASAAB FCPU MICROPROGRAM FOR INTERPRETING DATASAAB D23 INSTRUCTIONS
*
*   FACILITY DECLARATIONS
DECLARE AR = GR.0                    *ACCUMULATOR IN GENERAL REGISTER 0
        MR = GR.1                    *MULTIPLIER REGISTER IN GENERAL REG 1
        AU-OVERFLOW = WSBIT.37       *OVERFLOW IN WORKING STATUS BIT 37
        AU-SIGN = WSBIT.32           *SIGN IN WORKING STATUS BIT 32
        SS-S-IND = SSBIT.0           *A PROGRAMMABLE FLIP-FLOP
        VLS-I-IND = CU-BIT-VLS.0     *ANOTHER FLIP/FLOP
        TARGET = IMM 0               *IMMEDIATE VALUE 0
        INITIAL = IMM 1              *IMMEDIATE VALUE 1
BEGIN
* FIRST D23 INSTRUCTION EXECUTION
        START (INITIAL,D23OP)        *READ NEXT INSTR AND GO TO D23OP
*   OPCODE BRANCH VECTOR 128 CASES
 D23OP: DO CASE (8)
    OP00: DO

             .

             .

             .

          END

      .

      .

      .

    OP07: DO                         *EXECUTE += INSTRUCTION
          AR = ADD (AR, AUTFR.0)     *AND RETURN TO START
          SS-S-IND = AU-OVERFLOW     *TO FETCH NEXT INSTRUCTION
          FUTFR.0 = AR
          WRITE (ACR.1, FUTFR.0, LEFT) LENGTH (24)
          VLS-I-IND = AU-SIGN
          START (TARGET,D23OP)
          END
        END
END
```

Figure 7.3-2. Datasaab FCPU microprogram segment.

microprogram, global declarations are valid throughout the microprogram, but local declarations are valid only in the block in which they appear. In control store there are consequently only two areas for variables. Note that the FCPU control store permits general operand storage as well as microprogram storage. The Datasaab FCPU microprogramming language provides facilities for treating groups of statements as one. In the DO CASE statement, one of several statements is selected for execution depending on some condition. These statements may themselves be sequences of microinstructions bracketed by DO and END as illustrated in Figure 7.3-2. With the DO iteration statement, a microprogrammer can indicate repetitive execution of a sequence of microinstructions by specifying:

1. a register for counting,
2. a By Factor (a register or immediate value) for incrementing the counter register, and
3. a To Factor that indicates the terminating condition.

The translator generates the appropriate loop controlling microinstructions for the DO statement.

General Purpose Microprogramming Language (GPM) [Ostreicher 1973, Ostreicher 1974] was developed at the USC/Information Sciences Institute as the microprogramming language for the MLP-900, a dynamically user microprogrammable computer. The goal of GPM was to provide a convenient microprogramming language which did not preclude the specification of any machine operation in the MLP-900. To meet this goal, some GPM statements use low level register transfer constructs while other statements utilize higher level constructs that may represent several microoperations. The higher level statements are broken into four types:

1. syntactic block structure,
2. hardware generalization,
3. multi-instruction statements, and
4. expressions.

The block structure of GPM permits compile time specification of scope for data names and control statements. In any block, indicated by the BEGIN...END construct, data names may be applied to any MLP-900 memory cell. Blocks also define the scopes of IF and DO statements. With hardware generalization statements, a microprogrammer may ignore some hardware intricacies by specifying related operations. A simple example of a hardware generalization would be the capability to indicate branch-on-greater-than even though the only hardware conditional branch was branch-on-less-than. The branch-on-greater-than statement would be compiled into two microinstructions. Some GPM statements compile into several MLP-900 microinstructions. Examples include the case statement, which permits multi-way branching, and the assignment of one register to another through an intermediary (unspecified) register. Compound Boolean and arithmetic expressions in GPM are compiled into multiple microinstructions for the MLP-900. As one of the design decisions in GPM was to prohibit implicit changes to machine state at runtime, expression evaluation must not require the use of temporary storage. Thus, the GPM statement

$$R0 \quad \leftarrow \quad R0 \text{ AND } R1 \quad + \quad R2;$$

is valid and is translated into

$$R0 \quad \leftarrow \quad R0 \text{ AND } R1;$$
$$R0 \quad \leftarrow \quad R0 + R2;$$

while the GPM statement

$$R0 \quad \leftarrow \quad R0 \text{ AND } (R1+R2);$$

is invalid because its evaluation would require temporary

storage for the evaluation of the subexpression (R1+R2). With these higher level constructs, GPM is easy to use for a variety of purposes ranging from diagnostic microprogramming to applications microprogramming.

Like the Datasaab FCPU, the microinstruction format for the MLP-900 is essentially vertical. The higher level constructs implemented in the microprogramming languages for these computers can therefore be efficiently translated into microinstructions without great difficulty.

PUMPKIN [Lloyd 1974] is a higher level machine—dependent microprogramming language whose form is similar to that of LSD [Bergeron 1972], a systems programmers' dialect of PL/I. A sample PUMPKIN microprogram was illustrated in Figure 3.2-8. The PUMPKIN language was designed for the Microprogrammed Control Unit (MCU) under development at the Naval Research Laboratory.* With sixty-four bit horizontal microinstructions, the MCU presents a difficult target for efficient translation from high level representations, and the PUMPKIN language has not been implemented. The PUMPKIN language did however address many of the problems associated with the design of a higher level machine—dependent microprogramming language for a computer with horizontal microinstructions. In PUMPKIN there are several extensions to the constructs that indicate primitive MCU operations and facilities. For example,

1. Variables may be allocated to local store or main memory. For variables in main memory, a compiler would generate microinstructions to set up the memory address register and read data into available local store registers.

2. General arithmetic and logical expressions employing primitive operations may be used.

* The MCU is discussed in Section 8.6.

341

```
PRIME:
     PROCEDURE;                    /* A PROCEDURE TO CALCULATE THE
                                      FIRST 1000 PRIME NUMBERS */
          DECLARE
             P(1000) WORD,         /* THE ARRAY OF PRIMES */
             TEST WORD,            /* THE VALUE BEING TESTED */
             (I,J) WORD;           /* INDICES */
          P(1)=TEST:=1; P(2)=2;    /* SET INITIAL VALUES */
          DO I=3 TO 1000;          /* MAIN LOOP TO FILL THE TABLE */
L1:          TEST += 2;            /* INCREMENT THE TEST VALUE */
             J = 2;                /* INDEX FOR TRIAL DIVISORS */
             DO WHILE TEST/P(J)>=P(J);
             /* THIS LOOP USES ALL DIVISORS <= SQUARE ROOT OF TEST */
                 IF TEST MOD P(J)=0 THEN /*NOT PRIME, SO */
                     GO TO L1;    /* FOR NEXT TRIAL VALUE */
                 J += 1;
             END;
             P(I)=TEST;    /* TEST IS PRIME, SO STORE IT IN TABLE */
          END;
     END PRIME;
      /* NOTE ***
      1. THE OPERATOR ':=' SPECIFIES AN IMBEDDED
         ASSIGNMENT (WITHIN ANOTHER ASSIGNMENT STATEMENT).
         THE LEFT-HAND VALUE OF THE IMBEDDED ASSIGNMENT
         IS USED IN COMPUTING THE VALUE OF THE CONTAINING
         ASSIGNMENT.
      2. THE OPERATOR '+=' SPECIFIES AN INCREMENT OPERATION.
         THAT IS, THE VALUE ON THE LEFT OF '+=' IS
         INCREMENTED BY THE VALUE ON THE RIGHT.
      3. THE OPERATOR 'MOD' IS THE MODULO OPERATOR.  IT IS
         SIMILAR TO THE DIVIDE OPERATION EXCEPT THAT THE
         RESULTANT VALUE IS THE REMAINDER OF THE OPERATION
         AND NOT THE QUOTIENT. */
```

Figure 7.3-3. An MPL program for the Microdata 32

3. General flow of control primitives (IF...THEN...ELSE..., DO WHILE, CASE, etc.) permit conditional or repeated execution of groups of statements.

4. Simple data structures like one dimensional arrays and PL/I-like structures facilitate data addressing and manipulation.

5. Multiple level subroutine calls permit program modularity and generality.

These and other PUMPKIN features were designed by considering hardware resources. With present research efforts directed toward the investigation of code generation and optimization techniques, PUMPKIN and languages like it should become available in the future.

The primary implementation language for the Microdata 32/S computer,* is MPL (Microdata Programming Language) ([Burns 1973], [Microdata 1973], [Microdata]). "Although MPL is a high-level programming language, it is not machine independent. In fact the 32/S machine and MPL were designed symbiotically. Full access to the resources of the 32/S computer is provided through appropriate language constructs. Each construct of MPL is directly mirrored in the 32/S architecture."** As illustrated in Figure 7.3-3, MPL is a derivative of PL/I. Variables in MPL may be declared to have a length of 1, 2, 4, 8, 16, or 32 bits. Memory allocation may be controlled by the programmer. The general expression structure permits the use of constants, variables, array elements, function references, conditional expressions, imbedded assignments, arithmetic operators, logical operators, relational operators, and shift operators. Statements may be grouped in DO, BEGIN, or PROCEDURE blocks. BEGIN and PROCEDURE

* The Microdata 32/S was discussed in Section 5.5.
** [Microdata 1973], p. 1-1.

blocks may dynamically allocate storage when they are invoked during program execution. Conditional and repetitive execution of groups of statements may be specified by IF...THEN...ELSE... and DO statements as in PL/I. MPL is a more sophisticated language than previously discussed machine-dependent microprogramming languages, and accordingly its implementation differs somewhat from those implementations. MPL is not translated directly into microprograms, but rather it is translated into an intermediate language that is interpreted by Microdata 3200 microprograms. This intermediate language may be considered the machine language of the Microdata 32/S. Central to the execution of this intermediate language is a stack capability which the 32/S supports naturally. MPL therefore lies in the gray area between higher level languages for microprogramming and using microprogramming to support the execution of higher level language programs (see Figure 3.2-9).*

7.4 Higher Level Machine-Independent Microprogramming Languages

In spite of a great need, the design and implementation of higher level machine-independent languages for microprogramming continues to be a research problem. These languages fall into three basic categories:

1. Special purpose languages whose compilers have details of the computer architecture and microinstruction repertoire into which the higher level language will be translated. These languages are special purpose in that they may not provide general memory allocation, expression specification, or other features normally associated with higher level languages. As a

* Other developments in the area of microprogrammed support of higher level languages are discssed in Section 8.4.

result programmers should have a general knowledge of the architecture of the computer on which the microprograms will run. While such languages may differ only slightly from machine dependent higher level microprogramming languages (in that the operations and constructs are more general), they are amenable to optimization because the language constructs are simple, and sophisticated optimization techniques can be built into the compilers.

2. General purpose languages whose compilers have details of the microinstruction repertoire into which programs will be translated. These languages differ from those in the previous category in providing descriptive constructs to specify the architecture of a virtual machine which will be mapped into the real machine. Programs in these languages generally consist of two parts: a machine description part and an algorithm specification part.

3. General purpose languages whose compilers have knowledge of the microinstruction repertoire into which programs will be translated, but do not require programmers to define a virtual machine and then express operations in terms of that virtual machine. While this type of language corresponds to the general concept of higher level languages, it has been the type least discussed in the literature.

Several research groups have reported developments in the area of higher level machine-independent microprogramming languages.

The compiler designed for the Univac (formerly RCA) Series 70/45 [Tirrell 1973] is driven by several tables, many of which contain machine dependent information specified during compiler construction. Among these tables are

1. a substitution table which specifies the microoperations and microinstruction format,

345

```
*START
DCLG       (PS=1).
DCL        HLDA=F1%0-%1.
DCL        HLDB=F2; L=2.
DCL        CLWM = (OR#5=0).
DCL        A=FFR1; PC= (R=X'02'); STOR=HLDA.
DCL        B=FFR1+1; PC=(R=X'02'); STOR=HLDB.
*          NOTE :- OR-REG SET TO X'0C' (CLWM)
*                   OR X'2B' (SETWM) PRIOR TO
*                   ENTERING ALGORITHM.
WM01    :  RD A TO HLDA%1; IF CLWM; BR WMJ ¹
WM02    :  AND X'BF' TO HLDA%1.
WM03    :  WR A FROM HLDA%1.
WM04    :  LET A = A-1.
WM05    :  RD B TO HLDB%1.
&WM06      OR5EQ0WM13
WM07    :  RESET HLDB%1#6.
WM08    :  WR B FROM HLDB%1.
WM09    :  SUB 1 FROM B.
WM10    :  ENDA.
WM11    :  OR X'40' TO HLDA%1.
WM12    :  BR WM03.
WM13    :  SET HLDB%1#6.
WM14    :  BR WM08.
*END
```

Figure 7.4-1. A sample microprogram in the higher level microprogramming language for the Univac series 70

Notes

1. The program performs the IBM 1401 Set
   Wordmark and Clear Wordmark
   instructions

2. The declare statements (DCL)
   generally assign names to registers.

3. RD means read from memory.

4. WR means write to memory.

5. RESET means set to 0.

6. The line whose initial character is
   '&' indicates an assembler
   microprogram statement.

2. a prerequisite table which specifies operations that depend on the previous execution of other operations, and

3. an alternative table which specifies microoperations that can be substituted for other microoperations under certain conditions.

Many of the tables in the compiler are used for optimization. The language has two types of statements – declare statements and command statements. Declare statements assign symbolic names and specify initial values for hardware resources. Command statements include

1. read from main memory to local store,

2. write from local store into main memory,

3. move values (possibly computed from arithmetic and logical expressions) from one local store area to another,

4. conditional and unconditional branch, and

5. end of a sequence.

A sample program appears in Figure 7.4-1. Among the problems encountered in the project were designing the contents of the

```
begin
comment determine sign of product in R3;
R1 ∧ M1 → ACC;
R2 ⊕ ACC → ACC;
ACC ∧ M1 → R3;
comment force both operands to positive;
if R1< 0 then R0 - R1 → R1;
if R2< 0 then R0 - R2 → R2;
comment extract and determine exponent for product;
R1 ∧ M3 → ACC;
R2 ∧ M3 → R4;
R4 + ACC → ACC;
R3 ∨ ACC → R3;
comment extract mantissas and clear ACC;
R1 ∧ M4 → R1;
R2 ∧ M4 → R2;
R0 → ACC;
comment multiplication proper by shift and add;
while R2 ≠ 0 do begin
             ACC ↑ - 1 → ACC;
             R2 ↑ - 1 → R2;
             if UF = 1 then R1 + ACC → ACC;
             end;
comment if product mantissa overflows, adjust to normalize;
if ACC ∧ M5 ≠ 0 then begin
             ACC ↑ - 1 → ACC;
             R3 + M1 → R3;
             end;
comment pack exponent and mantissa into floating-point format;
R3 ∨ ACC → R3;
comment complement mantissa if product sign is negative;
if R3< 0 then R0 - ACC → ACC;
end;
```

Fig. 5. An example: a SIMPL microprogram for 64-bit floating-point multiplication.

```
sign
  ┌─┬──────────────┬──────────────────────────┐
  │ │characteristic│        mantissa          │
  └─┴──────────────┴──────────────────────────┘
  0              13 14                        63
```

Figure 7.4-2. A SIMPL microprogram for 64 bit floating point multiplication.

substitution table to facilitate identification of all the possible commands, and cataloging possible conditions that may arise during the optimization phase of compilation. Such hardware considerations led to the conclusion that "in order to construct a viable micropogramming compiler ... the concepts and technical approaches using different types of microprogrammable hardware would be required."*

SIMPL (Single Identity Microprogramming Language) [Ramamoorthy 1974] is a higher level language designed especally for computers that use horizontal microinstructions. Although the syntax of ALGOL 60 was a basis for SIMPL, there are some dfferences to facilitate microprogram optmization:

1. there is no go to statement,

2. there can be at most one operator in an expression, and the operators must be add, subtract, and, or, exclusive or, not, left shift, right shift, or circular shift,

3. there is a case statement to permit multi-way branching, and

4. read and write statements transfer data between main memory and local store.

Figure 7.4-2 illustrates a SIMPL microprogram. "By the single identity principle, a variable that has been assigned a value is considered to be defined for all the statements that appear before a statement that reassigns a new value to the variable; the same variable is not considered to be defined for statements referring to it elsewhere."** After the compiler arranges microoperations (so that microoperations with variables dependent on values of other variables are in correct order), the single identity principle is used to determine the earliest execution time of each microoperation. A large part of

* [Tirrell 1973], page 76.
** [Ramamoorthy 1974], page 793.

349

the SIMPL compiler, which was designed for a proposed research machine, is devoted to microprogram optimization. The SIMPL approach to microprogramming languages is quite interesting and appears useful in situations where the imposed constraints can be satisfied.

As a basis for a higher level microprogramming language, Eckhouse chose a dialect of PL/I because it could be used to write microprograms and also because it could be used to describe hardware ([Eckhouse 1971a], [Eckhouse 1971b]). In this higher level microprogramming language, called MPL, the computer hardware is described by declarations of various data items. There are basically six types of data items:

1. machine registers and their parts,

2. control store,

3. local store and main memory,

4. events which correspond to testable machine conditions (carry, zero result, etc.),

5. numeric constants, and

6. label and symbol constants.

Microinstructions may be written using statements in PL/I with the following modifications:

1. registers may be concatenated to indicate double length operands,

2. several arithmetic and logical operators have been changed (there is no multiplication, division, or exponentiation, but left and right shift and exclusive or have been added), and

3. IF statements can test events that correspond to machine conditions.

Figure 7.4-3 presents a segment of an MPL program to illustrate these conventions. The translation of MPL into microcode

350

```
INTERDATA3:  PROCEDURE OPTIONS(MAIN);

    DECLARE (R0,R1,R2,R3,R4,R5,R6,R7,AR,DFR) BIT (8),

            MS (0:32767) BIT (16),

            MAR BIT (16),
                    MAH BIT (8) DEFINED MAR POSITION (1),
                    MAL BIT (8) DEFINED MAR POSITION (9),

            MDR BIT (16),
                    MDH BIT (8) DEFINED MDR POSITION (1),
                    MDL BIT (8) DEFINED MDR POSITION (9),

            'LOCCNT' BIT (16),

            (CARRY,SNGL,CATN,TRUE,FALSE) EVENT;

    INITIAL:
            /* FETCH THE LOCATION COUNTER AND PUT IT INTO R0 AND R1  */
            MAR = LOCCNT; /* LOCCNT STANDS FOR SOME MS LOCATION (TO   */
    /* BE ASSIGNED DURING TRANSLATION) WHICH HOLDS THE EMULATED LC   */
            MDR = MS(MAR);
            R0//R1 = MDR;
            GO TO DISPLY;            /* GO CHECK ON CONSOLE SETTINGS  */
    /* IF THE CONSOLE RUN SWITCH IS ON, WE SHALL RETURN TO I-FETCH   */


IFETCH: PROCEDURE;
            /* INSTRUCTION FETCH, LOC CNTR UPDATE & OP CODE DECODE   */
            MAR = R0//R1;                   /* INSTRUCTION ADDRESS   */
            MDR = MS(MAR);
            R0//R1 = R0//R1+2; /* INCREMENT LOCATION COUNTER         */
            R4//R3 = MDR;                      /* GET OP CODE        */
            R7 = R3.RSH.3;             /* RIGHT JUSTIFY R1/M1        */
```

```
                AR = (R3.LSH.1)|1;    /* LEFT SHIFT REGISTERS R2/X2  */
                                      /* OF THE EMULATED 360 MACHINE */
                R2,DFR = R4.RSH.4        /* INTO AR WITH LSB SET     */
                IF CARRY THEN GO TO RXFORM;
     RRFORM:    R6 = AR&1;                   /* REG-REG FORMAT        */
                R5 = 0;
     DECODE:    IF SNGL|CATN THEN GO TO SUPORT;
     SUPRET:    R3 = R4&OPX;                 /* MASK OP CODE          */
                AR = R3+(R3.LSH.1);        */ MULTIPLY BY 3           */
                DFR = R2;
                IF TRUE THEN GO TO ILLEG;
                    ELSE IF FALSE|CARRY THEN GO TO TROUBL:
              ...
          END IFETCH;
          ...
     END INTERDATA3;
```

Figure 7.4-3. A portion of an MPL program to emulate the INTERDATA 3 computer.

consists of three phases: traslation of MPL into SML (a machine—independent intermediate language), translation of SML into virtual microcode (much like real microcode except that each operand may represent multiple data items in the machine), and optimization and the translation of virtual microcode into actual microcode. Phase 1 of the translation builds a dictionary from declaration statements that Phase 3 uses in assigning operands to machine registers. The value of MPL lies in its demonstration that one language can be used to write, test, and debug microprograms for a large class of machines.

MPGS [Hattori 1972] was designed as a microprogram generating tool for GPMS (General Purpse Microprogrammed Simulator, a hardware version of a software simulator for computers). MPGS programs consist of three parts:

1. the machine description part,
2. the function part, and
3. the microprogram part.

In the machine description part, the programmer defines the hardware of the target machine and the correspondence between the target machine and the host machine. The function part describes the rules for generating or translating programs into microinstructions. These rules are expressed as high level subroutines that are called from the microprogram part. Subroutine facilities include conditional assignment, DO groups, and macro statements. The microprogram part describes the microprograms to be generated. It consists of subroutine calls to the function part or host machine microinstructions written symbolically. With its three parts, the MPGS system is a kind of translator writing system (see [Feldman 1968]) and thus offers great flexibility in developing microprograms.

7.5 An Evaluation of Developments in Microprogramming Languages

Reviewing the language developments discussed in this and previous chapters shows little use of register transfer and higher level languages for microprogramming commercially available computers. Enough research work has been done to demonstrate the capability of developing

1. translators for register transfer languages for computers with horizontal microinstructions and

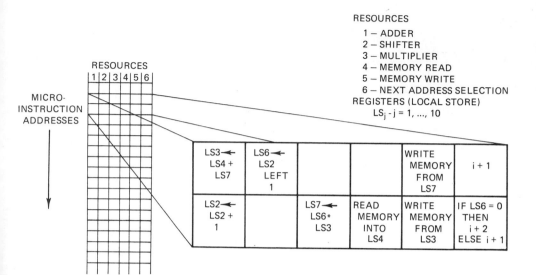

Figure 7.5-1. Two dimensional representation of a horizontal microprogram.

2. compilers for higher level machine dependent microprogramming languages for computers with vertical microinstructions.

Many manufacturers of computers became manufacturers of user microprogrammable computers essentially by retrofitting writable memories in their control stores. Very little language support is available for such machines.

A primary poblem in developing higher level languages for microprogramming lies in the design of the microprogram level architecture of microprogrammable computers. This level is generally considered as an implementation level rather than as an architecture level. As a result, there may be special

354

purpose features, timing constraints, and other anomalies that make the machines "unreasonable" for general microprogramming applications. Many computers use diagonal and horizontal microinstructions, yet few language techniques have been developed to facilitate the use of and to exploit these capabilities. One suggestion is to suffix or otherwise tag microoperations to indicate the resources they reference or affect. In this scheme the microprogramming language provides information to the microprogrammer because it reflects the computer architecture, its capabilities, and its constraints. With such information microprogramming a computer with horizontal microinstructions may be considerably simplified. Another suggestion is based on the observation that microprogramming a computer with horizontal microinstructions is essentially a two-dimensional process as illustrated in Figure 7.5-1 [Agrawala 1973]. The capability to represent microprograms for horizontal machines in a tabular form would facilitate microprogram preparation and debugging. While some microprogramming manuals use this two-dimensional technique, present languages do not accept this format; they require a linear representation of microprograms. Forcing a sequential scheme on the representation may cause the microprogrammer to lose sight of the two-dimensional aspect of the problem, making even manual optimization difficult.

The development of register transfer and higher level microprogramming languages for horizontally microprogrammed machines has necessitated corresponding development of sophisticated translators. Some programming language techniques, such as formal definition of syntax, have been applied to microprogramming languages (see, e.g., [Hornbuckle 1970]). While formal syntax provides a basis for mechanical translation, additional programming language techniques facilitate parsing, code generation, and hence translator construction. Register transfer languages for machines using horizontal microinstructions, for example, can be naturally conformed to the operator precedence scheme (see, e.g., [Rauscher 1973]). Recent studies of formal semantic models of programming languages are applicable to microprogramming languages as well. It seems that some of the differences between microprogramming and programming could be exploited in the development of techniques for representing and translating microprograms. Such analyses provide simplicity and efficiency of implementation as well as elegance of language design and definition, yet reports on such work are scarce.

Another concern in the development of higher level microprogramming languages has been the ability of compilers for microprogramming languages to generate optimal or even efficient microprograms. In this regard efficiency may be measured in terms of

1. the time required to execute the generated microprogram,

2. the amount of control store required to store the generated microprogram, and

3. to a lesser extent, the time required to compile the microprogram.

For microprograms to be run on dynamically user microprogrammable computers, the first factor is generally the most important and the other factors are constrained only by some reasonability criteria. Since the format of vertical microinstructions resembles that of machine language instructions, optimization techniques used in translating programming languages are applicable in translation of higher level microprogramming languages to vertical microcode. Kleir and Ramamoorthy [Kleir 1971] offered some early comments on this subject. For computers with horizontal microinstructions, optimization is more difficult for two reasons:

1. Several operations may be executed concurrently. Thus an optimizing compiler would have to schedule the order of execution of microoperations, yet maintain a logical ordering that does not affect the results of the computation.

2. Microinstruction implementation (see Section 2.4) may affect the execution of microinstructions. For example, since a microinstruction may select its successor depending on conditions that arise during its execution, the overlap between the execution phase of a microinstruction and the fetch phase for the next microinstruction is critical. Another example involves a polyphase implementation in which a register may serve as an input for one operation and as a destination of another operation in the same microinstruction.

Several research projects have considered the problem of microprogram optimization ([Lloyd 1974], [Tsuchiya 1974], [Yau 1974], [Kleir 1974], [Ramamoorthy 1974], [Agerwala 1974]).

Although microprogramming is almost as old as programming, the development of microprogramming languages and techniques has lagged behind their programming language counterparts. In many areas, obvious programming language techniques have not been extensively applied to microprogramming; in other areas new techniques need to be developed.

357

Annotated Bibliography

A. Register Transfer Microprogramming Languages

1. R. K. Clark, "Mirager, the ´Best-Yet´ Approach for Horizontal Microprogramming," Proceedings of the ACM 1972 National Conference, pages 554-571.

    While "Best-Yet" is an overstatement, this paper describes an interesting register transfer language developed for the Argonne Microprocessor.

2. D. J. DeWitt et al, "A Microprogramming Language for the B-1726," Sixth Annual Workshop on Microprogramming, ACM, September 1973, pages 21-29.

    Describes a register transfer microprogramming language for the Burroughs B1726, and uses it to give examples of and analyze B1726 microprograms.

3. E. W. Dubbs et al, "A Microprogram Design System Translator," COMPCON 72 Digest of Papers, IEEE, September 1972, pages 95-98.

    Overviews the design philosophies and components of the MDS system, and gives particular attention to the register transfer microprogramming language and its translator.

4. G. D. Hornbuckle and E. I. Ancona, "The LX-1 Microprocessor and Its Application to Real-Time Signal Processing," IEEE Transactions on Computers, Volume C-19 Number 8 (August 1970), pages 710-720.

    Includes a description and examples of the register transfer language ML.

5. "QM-1 Hardware Level User's Manual," NANODATA Corporation, Williamsvile, New York, March 31, 1974.

   Chapter 6 of this manual describes the register transfer language used for nanopogramming the QM-1, and Chapter 7 gives several examples.

6. T. G. Rauscher et al, "AN/UYK-17 (XB-1) (V) Signal Processing Element Micrprogramming Support Software," Naval Research Laboratory Report 7777, Washington, D. C., 1975.

   Descriptions of the AMIL and ANIMIL microprogramming languages and their preprocessor facilities.

7. E. W. Reigel et al, "The Interpreter - A Microprogrammed Building Block System," 1972 Spring Joint Computer Conference Proceedings, AFIPS Press, Montvale, New Jersey, pages 705-723.

   Introduces and gives examples of the register transfer language TRANSLANG for the Burroughs Interpreter.

B. Higher Level Machine Dependent Microprogramming Languages

1. R. D. Bergeron et al, "Systems Programming Languages - A Survey," Advances in Computers, Volume 12, Academic Press, New York, 1972, pages 175-284.

   Discusses LSD, the language on which PUMPKIN is loosely based.

2. R. Burns and D. Savitt, "Microprogramming, Stack Architecture Ease Minicomputer Programmer's Burden," Electronics, February 15, 1973, pages 95-101.
   "Microdata 32/S Computer," Microdata Corporation, Irvine, California.

Overviews of the Microdata 3200, the Microdata 32/S, and the features that support the language MPL.

3. H. W. Lawson, Jr. and L. Blomberg, "The Datasaab FCPU Microprogramming Language," Proceedings of ACM SIGPLAN-SIGMICRO Interface Meeting, May 1973, pages 86-96.

Describes the Datasaab FCPU and gives details of the machine dependent microprogramming language developed for it.

4. G. R. Lloyd, "PUMPKIN - (Another) Microprogramming Language," SIGMICRO Newsletter, Volume 5 Number 1 (April 1974), pages 45-76.

A detailed description of PUMPKIN - an unimplemented higher level machine dependent microprogramming language. An overview of PUMPKIN is presented in the paper by Lloyd mentioned in the Chapter 3 bibliography.

5. "Microdata 32/S Programming Language Reference Manual (MPL)," Microdata Corporation, Irvine, California, November, 1973.

Reference manual for MPL.

6. D. R. Oestreicher, "A Microprogramming Language for the MLP-900," Proceedings of the ACM SIGPLAN-SIGMICRO Interface Meeting, May 1973, pages 113-116.

D. R. Oestreicher, "General Purpose Microprogramming Language for the MLP-900 - Reference Manual," USC/Information Sciences Institute, Marina del Rey, California, March 1974.

An overview and a detailed description of the machine dependent microprogramming language GPM.

7. W. T. Wilner, "Microprogramming Environment on the Burroughs B1700," COMPCON 72 Digest of Papers, IEEE, September 1972, pages 103-106.

Overviews the B1700 and the MIL microprogramming language.

C. Higher Level Machine Independent Microprogramming Languages

1. R. H. Eckhouse, Jr., "A High-Level Microprogramming Language (MPL)," 1971 Spring Joint Computer Conference Proceedings, AFIPS Press, Montvale, New Jersey, pqges 169-177.

R. H. Eckhouse, Jr., "A High-Level Microprogramming Language (MPL)," Ph. D. Thesis, Technical Report 1-71-mu, Department of Computer Science, State University of New York at Buffalo, Buffalo, New York, June 1971.

An overview and detailed description of the use of higher level languages for microprogramming and the MPL language.

2. J. A. Feldman and D. Gries, "Translator Writing Systems," Communications of the ACM, Volume 11 Number 2 (February 1968), pages 77-113.

An excellent tutorial and survey.

3. D. F. Goessling and J. F. McDonald, "ISPMET - A Study in Automatic Emulator Generation," Fifth Annual Workshop on Microprogramming Preprints, ACM, September 1972, pages 90-95.

The basic concepts of the ISPMET language are similar to to those of MPL developed by Eckhouse. The language base for ISPMET is Bell and Newell's ISP. The compiler for ISPMET was based on work done by Irons.

4. M. Hattori, M. Yano, and K. Fujino, "MPGS: A High-Level Language for Microprogram Generating System," Proceedings of the ACM 1972 National Conference, pages 572-581.
A description of the MPGS system that includes a lengthy example.

5. C. V. Ramamoorthy and M. Tsuchiya, "A High-Level Language for Horizontal Microprogramming," IEEE Transactions on Computers, Volume C-23 Number 8 (August 1974), pages 791-807.
A description of the high-level language SIMPL and its compiler, which was designed to generate efficient microcode for a horizontally microprogrammed machine.

6. A. K. Tirrell, "A Study of the Application of Compiler Techniques to the Generation of Microcode," Proceedings of ACM SIGPLAN-SIGMICRO Interface Meeting, May 1973, pages 67-84.
A description of the language and compiler for microprogramming the Univac Series 70/45.

D. Evaluation of Developments in Microprogramming Languages

1. A. K. Agrawala and T. G. Rauscher, "The Application of Programming Language Techniques to the Design and Development of Microprogramming Languages," Sixth Annual Workshop on Microprogramming Preprints, ACM, September 1973,

pages 134-138.

Noting that the development of microprogramming languages has lagged far behind the development of programming languages and that terminological confusion permeates the subject of microprogramming, this paper forms the basis for some of the discussions in this chapter.

2. T. G. Rauscher and A. K. Agrawala, "On the Syntax and Semantics of Horizontal Microprogramming Languages," Proceedings of the ACM 1973 National Conference, pages 52-56.

Reviewing present languages for horizontally microprogrammable computers reveals unnatural symbolism, inflexible format requirements, and unnecessary constraints which make their use difficult. The use of formal syntax and semantics is recommended and introduced in the ANIMIL microprogramming language.

E. Optimization

1. T. Agerwala, "A Survey of Techniques to Reduce/Minimize the Control Part/ROM of a Microprogrammed Computer," Seventh Annual Workshop on Microprogramming Preprints, September 1974, pages 91-97.

2. R. L. Kleir and C. V. Ramamoorthy, "Optimization Strategies for Microprograms," IEEE Transactions on Computers, Volume C-20 Number 7 (July 1971), pages 783-794.

3. R. L. Kleir, "A Representation for the Analysis of

Microprogram Operation," <u>Seventh Annual Workshop on Microprogramming Preprints</u>, September 1974, pages 107-118.

4. G. R. Lloyd, "Optimization of Microcode for Horizontally Encoded Microprogrammable Computers," Master's Thesis, Brown University, Providence, Rhode Island, June 1974.

5. M. Tabandeh and C. V. Ramamoorthy, "Execution Time (and Memory) Optimization in Microprograms," <u>Seventh Annual Workshop on Microprogramming Preprints Supplement</u>, ACM, September 1974, pages S-19 - S-27.

6. M. Tsuchiya and M. J. Gonzalez, Jr., "An Approach to Optimization of Horizontal Microprograms," <u>Seventh Annual Workshop on Microprogramming Preprints</u>, ACM, September 1974, pages 85-90.

7. S. S. Yau, A. C. Showe, and M. Tsuchiya, "On Storage Optimization of Horizontal Microprograms," <u>Seventh Annual Workshop on Microprogramming Preprints</u>, ACM, September 1974, pages 98-106.

CHAPTER 8

APPLICATIONS OF MICROPROGRAMMING

8.1 Introduction

Microprogramming witnessed an inordinate time delay
between conception and fruition. The causes were many –
unavailable technology, dearth of experimentation and research,
tradition, etc. As these issues were overcome, an aura of
pragmatism surrounded microprogramming. With the development of
writable control stores and user microprogrammable machines,
practitioners have facilities to explore new applications, yet
in general, applications of microprogramming are still in their
infancy. Interpretation of machine language instructions
continues to be the most common application of
microprogramming. Here we consider some of the typical
applications of microprogramming.

8.2 Emulation

Historically, emulation has connoted the facilities added
to a computer system to enable it to execute with some
efficiency programs developed for another system. These
facilities included hardware components for handling special
features of the emulated machine. Adding such hardware
resources essentially changes the architecture of a computer
and generally lies outside the capabilities of most computer
users. Microprogramming, however, generally provides the

365

facilities to execute with some efficiency programs developed for other systems and lies within the potential capabilities of many computer users. Accordingly, microprogramming has become central to the modern concept of emulation.

> ... we use the term "emulator" to describe a complete set of microprograms which, when embedded in a control store, define a machine. We shall call a machine which is realized by an emulator a "virtual machine" [or target machine] and the machine which supports microprograms a "host machine."*

To "define a machine," microprograms must implement the architecture of the machine. Since the architecture of a machine consists of a conceptual structure and a functional behavior,** the microprograms of the host machine must

1. map the components of the virtual machine into those of the host machine and

2. perform the "machine language" instructions of the virtual machine.

Performing the machine language instructions is accomplished by microprograms interpreting the machine language instructions. As interpreting machine language instructions is also called simulation, emulation is sometimes called microprogrammed simulation. A simple emulator was discussed in Chapter 1.

Many applications of microprogramming are considered variations on the basic emulation concept. In these schemes, virtual machines which efficiently support programs for a particular application area are designed. The virtual machines are then emulated on some host machine. Examples of this type of application include studies of ternary computers [Frieder 1972] and block-structured architectures [Lutz 1972]. Many of the applications discussed later in this chapter may be considered from the same viewpoint. While microprograms provide

* [Rosin 1969], page 197.
** Computer architecture was discussed in Chapter 2.

flexiblity in defining virtual machines, their generality depends on the organization of the hardware resources of the host machine. The extent to which a computer serves as a universal host machine measures its capability as a general purpose emulation vehicle. A primary objective of a majority of the commercally available microprogrammable computers is the efficient emulation of a particular machine. Machine language interpretation therefore remains a primary application of microprogramming and often is used as a definition for microprogramming. The hardware resources and microinstruction repertoire of such machines are often specialized for this emulation and thus may be difficult to adapt to general emulation problems. The representation of data is of primary importance in this regard. For example, a machine whose registers and operations were designed to handle thirty-two bit integers in two's complement notation would probably not be a good host for emulating a machine whose basic data type is thirty-six bit integers in sign-magnitude representation. A subject of current research is the design of microprogrammable computers that serve as efficient hosts for a variety of virtual machines. The MATHILDA computer described in Section 6.8 is an example of such research.

In addition to being efficient it is important that emulators be correct. The correctness of emulators of machine language instruction sets on commercial computers is fundamental to the proper execution of system and user software, however, microprograms like programs can be prone to errors. As an example, one user reported an error in the machine language emulator of one of the first computers with writable control store [SIGMICRO 1971]. The special features of microprogramming and emulation make proving correctness of microprograms somewhat different from proving correctness of programs. Although automatic validation of microprograms is far from reality, significant research work has been done in the area of proving microprogram correctness ([Leeman 1973], [Birman 1974], [Leeman 1974], [Bouricius 1974], [Ramamoorthy 1974]).

8.3 Program Enhancement

In the normal exection of a program, machine language instructions are individually fetched, decoded, and executed. Machine language instructions are often grouped together (by programmers or compilers) to form commonly executed routines. In executing these routines, machines may devote a significant amount of time to the fetching and decoding of separate machine language instructions. Implementing frequently executed machine language routines directly by microprograms can save the time required to fetch and decode the individual machine language instructions. In addition, the resulting microroutine can usually be optimized for the particular application. This is especially true when the routine is CPU bound, uses many intermediate results which need not be preserved, is highly repetitive, or is awkward to implement with machine language instructions. The literature abounds with examples of simple routines which save significant amounts of time when microprogrammed. These examples include square root routines, matrix inversions, matrix multiplies, tree searches, stack handling routines, array addressing routines, and table searches. Another example was illustrated in Figure 1.3-10, a microprogram to perform a sort routine. In real-time applications, microprogramming such routines can be of critical importance to the viability of the program. While conclusions on performance improvement over machine language routines vary, improvement ratios of five and more to one are typical.

368

In some instances the computer can be "tuned"
([Reigel 1972,1973]) to particular applications. Tuning
involves monitoring the execution of application programs to
analyze usage of machine instructions and to determine which
program segments are frequently executed. Using this
information to modify the instruction set (by adding and
deleting instructions) can result in significant performance
improvement. This procedure can be automated and some very
prelminary studies have been reported on the subject.
Automatically generating microprograms to improve program
performance has the possible advantage of transportability –
moving the program to another machine does not necessitate
rewriting the program because the microprograms were generated
from a higher level representation.

8.4 Executing Higher Level Language Programs

The use of higher level machine-independent languages for
programming has become widespread in many computer
applications. Since most computers were designed to support a
particular machine language, there are often significant
incongruities between high level programming languages and the
machine languages into which they are translated. As a result
many higher level language constructs have machine language
representations which are inefficient in terms of execution
time and memory space. Microprogramming can, and has been, used
to alleviate this problem.

As illustrated in Figure 3.2-9, microprograms can be used
to implement higher level language programs in a variety of
ways.

369

1. Programs may be translated directly into microprograms; this technique is just the use of higher level languages for microprogramming and was discussed in Chapter 7.

2. At the other extreme of possible implementations, microprograms directly interpret the higher level language programs. In this case, the higher level language is essentially the machine language, so the computer is called a higher level language machine.

3. As a combination of these two approaches, the higher level language programs may be translated (via software or firmware) into an intermediate language. Microprograms may then interpret the intermediate language. The level of possible intermediate languages varies greatly. The intermediate language may be a simple encoding of the higher level language itself - blanks removed, memory addresses replace operands, subroutine addresses represent operators, etc. When the intermediate language is at a fairly high level, the computer is called a higher level language—oriented machine. Such an approach relies on a sophisticated microprogram interpreter but provides great flexibility at execution time. Thus, languages that do not bind attributes until execution time (e.g., APL, SNOBOL, and EULER) are amenable to this kind of implementation. Simpler intermediate languages include Polish notation, quadruples, triples, etc. Low level intermediate languages are conventional machine languages, the traditional vehicle for representing higher level language programs. As remarked earlier, another view of this intermediate language approach is that the intermediate language is the machine language of a virtual machine designed to support the higher level language efficiently.

Note that this area of executing higher level language programs differs somewhat from the area of program enhancement discussed in Section 8.3. The difference is that program enhancement is concerned with the improvement of particular program segments by microprogramming. Microprogrammed assistance in executing higher level language programs is concerned with the general improvement of data manipulating and control constructs used throughout programs expressed in a particular higher level language.

The area of micropogrammed execution of higher level language programs has witnessed some interesting developments. Several years ago, Weber reported a microprogrammed implementation of EULER on an IBM System/360 Model 30 [Weber 1967]. That implementation consisted of three parts:

1. a translator, written in Model 30 microcode, which translated EULER source language programs into a reverse Polish string form,

2. an interpreter, written in Model 30 microcode, which interpreted the Polish string programs, and

3. an I/O control program, written in System/360 machine language, which interfaces the translator and interpreter to the operatng system.

Broca and Merwin demonstrated that that the microprogrammed execution of the intermediate text (in the form of quadruples, triples, and duos) generated by a high-level language compiler provides improvement in the factors of storage requirements and execution time when compared to the conventional method of machine code generation and execution.*

A microprogrammed implementation of APL was developed for the IBM System/360 Model 25 [Hassitt 1973]. In this APL system, the APL emulator is loaded into the control store, and a supervisor and translator are loaded into program store (main memory). The supervisor and translator were, of course, written in APL. The translator reads in the user's program (written in APL), translates it into an internal form (that is very high level), and stores it in program memory.

* [Broca 1973], page 62.

The machine then starts to execute the program generated in the previous step."*

The area of microprogrammed execution of higher level language programs has been enhanced through developments by computer manufacturers. MPL, a machine dependent higher level language, is an example.** Programs in MPL are translated into instructions for the Microdata 32/S. These instructions are interpreted by microprograms in the host Microdata 3200. Some computer manufacturers provide microprograms to improve performance of common higher level language fuctions – conversion of data from one representation to another, subroutine calls, trigonometric functions, etc. The MCM/70, a stand alone APL desk top computer, reportedly uses microprogramming to implement APL. The Burroughs B1700 computers, discussed in Section 4.3, implement a variety of higher level languages, e.g., Fortran and COBOL, by translating programs into intermediate languages called S-languages. For each higher level language there is a special S-language, and these S-languages are interpreted by microprograms.

When using an intermediate language in the microprogrammed execution of higher level language programs, it is important to distinguish between the translation phase which generates the intermediate language program, and the intepretation phase which executes the intermediate language program. In the translation phase known compiling algorithms will be executed and microprograms can be developed specifically to support this activity. The microprograms for the execution phase must be more general because they process unknown algorithms. These microprograms should support a variety of data and control structures that reflect those in the higher level language. The efficiency of handling these structures can be a measure of the system performance.

---

* [Hassitt 1973], page 201.
** MPL is described in Section 7.3.

8.5 Operating Systems

Because "users seldom (if ever) perform a computation without assistance from the operating system,"* and operating systems execute the same routines repeatedly, they are excellent candidates for firmware assistance. Owing perhaps to operating systems' historic propensity for excessive size and unreliability, the application of microprogramming to operating system implementation has been largely experimental.

In recent years, operating systems have been described as hierarchical structures.** Each level in the hierarchy defines and implements functions which the next higher level uses to perform its tasks. Studies of microprogram applications to operating systems have sought to determine

1. the appropriate repertoire of primitive operating systems tasks,

2. the distinction of these tasks in a hierarchical structure, and

3. which primitives should employ microprogramming in their implementation.

Microprogramming can be used in two ways to assist implementation of operating system primitives. First, microprograms can directly implement the primitives, and second, microprograms can support primitives, e.g., by implementing a suitable virtual machine on which the primitives can be executed. The types of operating systems primitives that are especially amenable to microprogrammed implementation or support include those that are too specific or complex for hardware implementation yet would be too slow if implemented in software, and those which have a monolithic structure, i.e.,

* [Denning 1971], page 175.
** See, for example, [Dijkstra 1968].

which are unique yet interface cleanly with other system primitives and tasks. Some of the primitives suggested ([Werkheiser 1970], [Burkhardt 1973]) for microprogrammed implementation are

1. partial word operations that can efficiently set, reset, test, and manipulate individual bits in a word (to facilitate operations on tables and status keeping),

2. searching operations (for operating on lists and other special data structures),

3. process synchronization and gatekeeping operations (to facilitate interprocess communication and protection), and

4. interrupt handling operations.

The main logical benefits of a microcoded machine for the design of such a system are the ability to determine the machine primitives, and the capablity to economically raise the level of complexity realizable in these primitives.*

The Venus Operating System [Liskov 1972] is an experimental multiprogramming system defined by a combination of microprograms and software. Microprograms in the host Interdata 3 computer, a small computer which uses vertical microinstructions and has a 2K control store, define the Venus machine. The microprograms support both the ordinary instruction set and a number of nonstandard architectural features to assist in the implementation of the operating system. The operating system features supported by microprograms include segmentation, demand paging, multiprogramming with process communication through semaphores, an I/O channel, and procedure call and return mechanisms.

With increasing understanding of operating system design, there is a need for more microprogrammed support for operating systems. Before a substantial effort can be committed to such support, however, the extent of improvement achieved through microprogramming should be properly evaluated.

* [Balzer 1973], page 121.

8.6 Signal Processing

Computer systems developed to perform signal processing, communications processing, and related tasks are amenable to microprogrammed implementation because they utilize "special-purpose algorithms which typically have a high repetition rate, are relatively simple, have real-time implications, and represent a significant percent of the processing load."* Since efficient implementation of the special purpose algorithms used in signal processing generally requires special purpose hardware, microprogramming a general purpose signal processing architecture obviates the need for special hardwired machines for each of the algorithms.

The use of two levels of parallelism facilitates the design of an efficient programmable signal processing computer. At the system level, multiple functional units (multiprocessors) perform distinct functional tasks such as data gathering, data organization, and signal transformation. At the implementation level, horizontal microprogrammed control of parallel resources effects flexible and efficient processing.**

Using such design considerations several computers have been developed for signal processing ([Shay 1972], [Ashcraft 1973], [Fisher 1973], [Murtha 1973], [Smith 1974], [Kratz 1974], [Aiso 1974]). As examples of such systems, let's consider the AN/UYK-17 and Analyzer Unit computers.

The AN/UYK-17 (XB-1) (V) Signal Processing Element (SPE) [Smith 1974] was developed at the Naval Research Laboratory to provide a high performance digital processor for radar, sonar, and communication systems. The SPE, illustrated in Figure 8.6-1, is structured to take advantage of the distinction between the two basic signal processing functions: data

* [Kratz 1970].
** [Ihnat 1973], page 113.

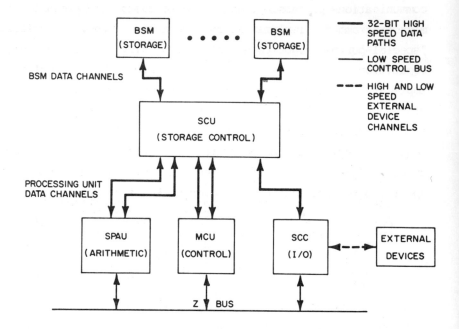

Figure 8.6-1. SPE data and control.

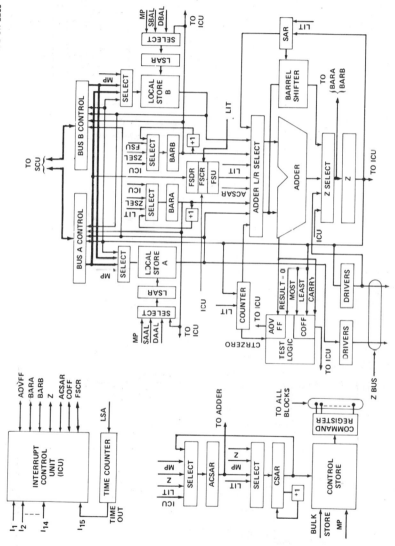

Figure 8.6-2. Microprogrammed Control Unit (MCU).

377

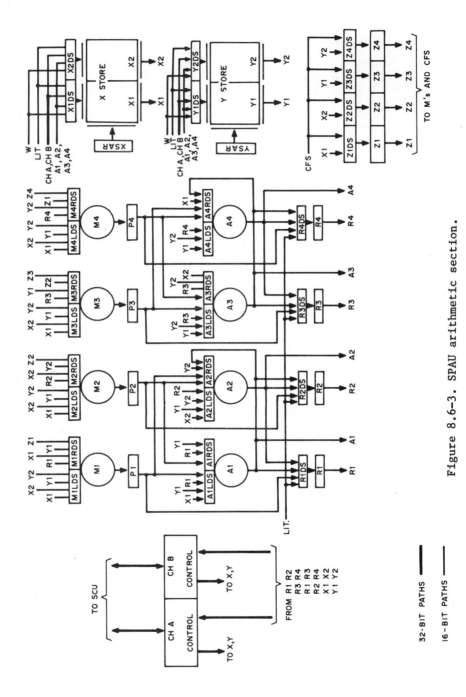

Figure 8.6-3. SPAU arithmetic section.

378

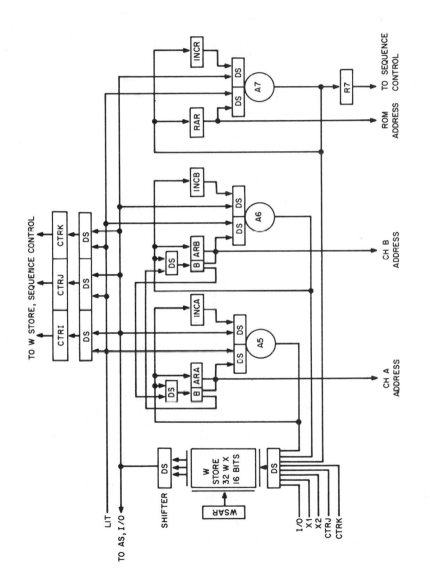

Figure 8.6-4. SPAU address generator section.

379

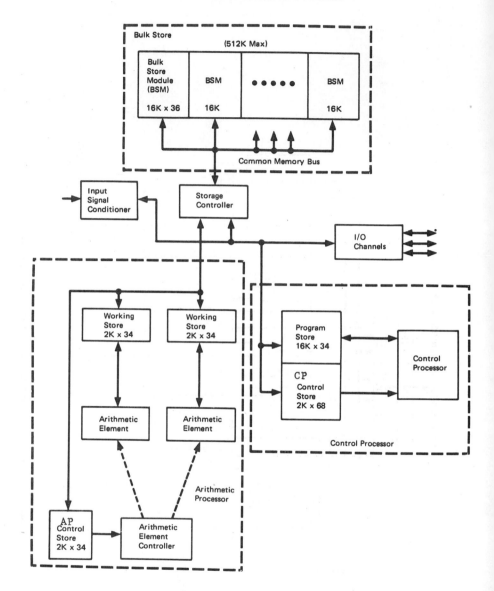

Figure 8.6-5. Analyzer Unit data flow.

management and complex arithmetic. The Microprogrammed Control Unit (MCU), shown in Figure 8.6-2, is the SPE system controller. Its functions include data management, process scheduling, I/O control, interrupt handling, and applications routine processing. The MCU is controlled by sixty-four bit horizontal microinstructions which execute in the system cycle time of approximately 150 n sec. The Signal Processing Arithmetic Unit (SPAU) is the SPE system arithmetic processor and performs signal processing algorithms on arrays of data stored as thirty-two bit words in the buffer storage modules (BSMs). The arithmetic section of the SPAU, shown in Figure 8.6-3, contains four multipliers, four adders, two memory busses, and other features which operate concurrently. The SPAU address generator section, shown in Figure 8.6-4, computes addresses for BSMs and a coefficient store, and operates in parallel with the arithmetic section. With this large number of functional components, the SPAU is controlled by 160 bit horizontal microinstructions that are executed at the same rate as microinstructions in the MCU. The storage control unit (SCU) is a hardwired switching interface between the independent BSMs and other SPE components. The selector channel controller (SCC) moves data between BSMs and peripheral devices.

Another microprogrammble digital signal processor is the Analyzer Unit (AU) [Kratz 1974]. As shown in Figure 8.6-5, the AU was designed as a system of several functional elements. Partitioning processing requirements among the different elements reduces idle time caused by one processing element requiring service from another. The control processor (CP) performs supervisory and data management functions. The CP is a microprogrammable thirty-two bit general purpose computer which hasa memory for data and programs (the Program Store) in addition to the writable control store for microprograms. ALU operations can be performed on operands with lengths of 32, 16,

381

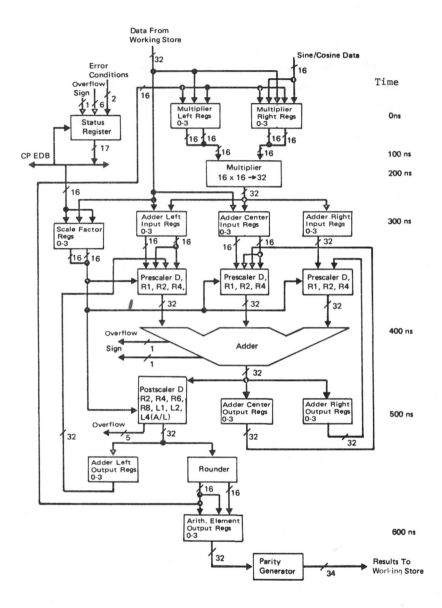

Figure 8.6-6. Analyzer Unit arithmetic element.

8, and 4 bits. Operands may be selected from a sixty-four word
local store or from 192 External Registers that contain
literals or I/O data. The Arithmetic Processor (AP) performs
the AU signal processing algorithms. The AP contains up to four
Arithmetic Elements (AEs). Each AE, illustrated in Figure
8.6-6, contains a multiplier, a three input adder, and several
local store registers. The AE operates in a pipelined fashion
at a 100-n sec staging rate, so that new operands enter each of
the six stages of the execution pipe every 100 n sec. The
sixty-four bit microinstructions which control the AEs are read
from the AP control store every 100 n sec. The Working Store
connected to each AE is composed of two 1K sections so that one
section can communicate with Bulk Store while the other
supports an AE. The Storage Controller which interfaces the
Bulk Store to other AU elements can perform a variety of
operations on data transferred between Working Store and Bulk
Store: compression, scaling, bit reversal, and demultiplexing.
The Input Signal Conditioner provides the analog sensor
interface for acoustic data for the AU.

8.7 Graphics

In contemporary graphics systems, pictures "must be
transformed (translated, rotated, scaled, projected in
orthographics or perspective views, windowed, etc.) and edited
(inserted and deleted, reconnected and reconfigured) at the
console."* Although performing such manipulations may require
significant computation time, "delays are intolerable in
interactive design."* Microprogramming has therefore been
utilized to facilitate realization of graphics systems.

* [vanDam 1972], page 3.

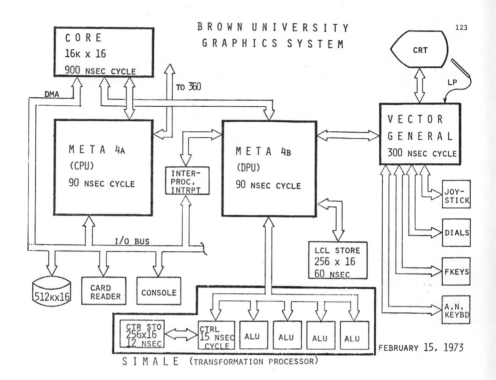

Figure 8.7-1. Brown University Graphics System.

The Brown University Graphics System (BUGS) ([Stabler 1973a,b]) has been developed to investigate "medium cost, microprogrammable, intelligent, graphics terminals and the 'division of labor' trade-offs between a mainframe processor and the intelligent satellite."* The BUGS configuration (see Figure 8.7-1) includes three microprogrammable processors. The META 4A** is a small satellite processor for local processing whose instruction set

* [Stabler 1973a], page 1.
** The META 4 was described in Section 5.3.

(implemented by microprograms) is like that of the System/360 with additions and modifications to enhance the implementation of operating system and graphics applications routines [Anagnostopoulos 1973]. The META 4B micrprograms implement the instruction repertoire used for graphics display. The SIMALE (Super Integral Microprogrammed Arithmetic Logic Expediter) [Webber 1973] is a very high speed (less than 30-n sec instruction time), dynamically microprogrammed, parallel processing computer that is used for real-time picture transformations. The operating system [Stockenberg 1973], which runs primarily on the META 4A, employs many of the concepts discussed in Section 8.5. With these various components, BUGS is an excellent system for studying graphics and other applications of microprogramming.

Other researchers have also investigated the application of microprogramming to graphics systems. Barron and Glorioso [Barron 1973] reported microprogramming a minicomputer to define an instruction set so that the machine could function as a graphics processor unit (GPU). Hartenstein and Mueller [Hartenstein 1973] have discussed a display system which consists of three microprogrammable processors. Bernardy [Bernardy 1973] has used multiple microprocessors in developing a graphic controller.

With its potential advantages, it is not surprising that microprogramming has recently been employed in a commercial graphics system. The Adage GP/400 interactive graphics system [Kerr 1975] was first shipped in March 1974. Its architecture is diagrammed in Figure 8.7-2. A primary objective in using microprogramming in the Adage GP/400 system was to reduce the overhead involved in processing graphic commands. The microprogrammed Graphics Processor uses fifty-six bit horizontal microinstructions that reside in a control store of

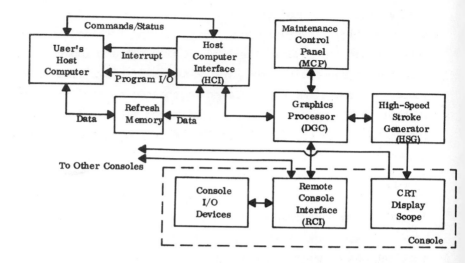

Figure 8.7-2. Adage GP/400 Graphics System.

up to 4K words. Hardware components in the Graphics Processor that are controlled by the microinstructions include

1. a sixteen bit general purpose ALU,

2. a special multiplier-adder that can compute a product and sum in 230 n sec,

3. a register file of 8 sixteen bit words,

4. a scratch pad memory of 256 sixteen bit words, and

5. several additional registers that interface with other system components.

Several graphics functions have been implemented with microprograms, and speed improvements average ten to thirty times better than execution of the the functions by software on

386

the host processor. "The introduction of a microprogrammed processor as the heart of an interactive graphics system has led to enhanced flexibility, superior performance, and more effective maintainability, at a lower cost, compared with previous-generation hybrid graphics systems."*

8.8 Microdiagnostics and Fault Tolerance

Microdiagnostics are microprograms which diagnose system hardware to detect and locate hardware faults. The microdiagnostics for a computer are often broken into two classes - microprograms that are always resident in control store and those which are not. Microdiagnostics may be executed at different times:

1. when the system is started, to facilitate check out,

2. periodically during the day (or week), to ensure proper operation, and

3. when a hardware fault, such as a parity error, occurs.

To initiate the diagnostics, the resident microdiagnostics are executed. Of course some portion of the system must be functioning properly to perform the resident microdiagnostics. These resident microdiagnostics test the data paths, functional units, and storage elements that perform basic operations and that can transfer the nonresident microdiagnostics into control store for execution. When this hardware has been tested, the nonresident microprograms are loaded into control store and executed. They test a larger set of functions which in turn are used to test another set of functions, and so on. Microdiagnostics thus use a hierarchical building-block approach which first tests a hardware kernel and then successively tests additional levels of hardware that depend on

* [Kerr 1975], page 33.

previously tested levels. Such microdiagnostics have been developed for the IBM System/360 Model 30 [Johnson 1971], the IBM System/360 Model 85 [Bartow 1970], and the Standard Computer Corporation MLP-900 [Guffin 1971]. There are many advantages of microdiagnostics over other types of hardware testing:

1. Microdiagnostics provide absolute control of the processor resources; microdiagnostics can generally get at all of the CPU resources.

2. Microdiagnostics can locate a hardware fault with high resolution.

3. Microdiagnostics generally do not require extensive use of main memory.

In addition to these technical advantages, microdiagnostics have the practical advantages of requiring less training and service equipment to use following their development.

In many computer systems, especially real-time systems, it is necessary to continue operation even in the presence of hardware failures. Microdiagnostics may be used in such fault-tolerant systems to locate hardware faults. In addition to the previous advantages of microdiagnostics, they can generally locate faults faster than other methods. Having located a hardware fault, it is necessary to configure the system so that the fault does not affect performance. The ease with which a system can be reconfigured depends on its structure, so fault-tolerant systems require special architectures. The flexibility offered by microprogramming merits its consideration in supporting such a system [Caillouet 1974]. One approach to using microprogramming in a fault-tolerant computer is to provide redundant data paths, registers, and transformation units and let the microprogram choose the working components to use in executing system functions [Miller 1967].

8.9 Other Applications of Microprogramming

In the conventional execution of higher level language programs, compilers translate programs into machine language programs, and the machine language programs are subsequently executed. Many of the algorithms involved in compiling are simple and repetitious, and therefore amenable to improvement through microprogrammed implementation. A lexical analysis scheme [Roberts 1971], for example, breaks a string of characters into symbols and identifies the syntactic class of the symbols. A syntax recognizer [Chu 1973] accepts a string of symbols and determines whether the string conforms to the syntax of a program in the programming language. Another important part of this process is resolving variable names which may be defined in different parts of a program [Habib 1973]. Combining such processes provides an alternative implementation of higher level language programs [Moulton 1974].

In many computer and communications systems, main processors communicate with auxiliary processors through peripheral control units. These control units often perform such functions as providing a proper interface between the processors and performing some data manipulation operations to alleviate the computational load of one of the processors. They are computers with a different type of instruction set. Using microprogramming to implement controllers has several advantages ([Osofsky 1971], [Strout 1971], [Hancock 1971], [Dromard 1971]).

1. Microprogramming is more flexible than hardware, so that a microprogrammed controller can be used in a variety of situations. Using a microprogrammable controller may thus be more cost effective than developing a dedicated hardwired controller.

2. Microprogramming is generally faster than software. Processing speed is an important consideration in handling high data rates.

3. Microdiagnostics may be used to isolate hardware faults.

Attracted by such advantages, some manufactuers have developed microprogrammed controllers.

Monitoring the performance of computer systems has long been a subject of interest, and debates on the relative merits of software and hardware monitors have amused (and bemused) practitioners for years. Investigating the following criteria of measurement techniques suggests implementation via microprogramming [Saal 1972]:

1. The measurement technique should be inexpensive and easy to use.

2. It should be easy to modify.

3. It should be able to measure any program that runs on the unmeasured system.

4. It should not perturb programs being measured.

In systems where microprograms interpret the instructions of the machine programs, microprograms may be added to perform monitoring and measurement functions. There are several advantages of a microprogrammed scheme over hardware and software monitors.

1. Programs will still be interpreted properly, even if they are wrong.

2. Information can be collected very quickly.

3. Any program in a multiprogrammed system can be monitored.

For such reasons, many systems have utilized firmware monitors ([Saal 1972], [Broadbent 1973], [Shriver 1973], [Mattson 1974]).

During the last few years microprogramming has replaced conventional hardwired techniques in implementing control in pocket calculators. Primary reasons for using microprogramming in calculators are flexibility and low cost ([McDermott 1973], [Whitney 1974]). An example is the Hewlett-Packard HP-65, the first fully programmable pocket calculator, in which there is a 3072 word ROM control store. Each control store word contains ten bits which constitute a calculator microinstruction [Stockwell 1974].

In the field of numerical analysis, special considerations arise when implementing algorithms on digital computers. Some of these considerations are the basic architecture to support numerical algorithms, data structures to represent a variety of information types, and the basic operations that manipulate the data structures. Microprogramming can be applied to many areas in connection with these considerations ([Shriver 1971], [Hyder 1974], [Luk 1974]):

1. With a sufficiently general host machine, microprogramming can support a variety of nonstandard arithmetics (extended range, extended precision, interval, significance, etc.) through new data types and operations.

2. Microprogramming can efficiently provide new data structures, e.g., matrices, and operations for manipulating them.

391

3. Approximations to elementary functions could be computed via firmware routines.

Some of the research computers now under development, e.g., the MATHILDA machine described in Section 6.8, provide facilities that can easily be used in numerical analysis investigations.

Annotated Bibliography

A. Emulation

1. G. Frieder and C. Luk, "Emulation of a Ternary Computer," Fifth Annual Workshop on Microprogramming Preprints, ACM, September 1972, pages 86-89.

2. M. J. Lutz and M. J. Manthey, "A Microprogrammed Implementation of a Block Structured Architecture," Fifth Annual Workhop on Microprogramming Preprints, ACM, September 1972, pages 28-41.

3. E. G. Mallach, "Emulation: A Survey," Honeywell Computer Journal, Volume 6 Number 4 (1972), pages 287-297.
   A survey of emulation from the classical point of view.

4. R. F. Rosin, "Contemporary Concepts of Microprogramming and Emulation," see Chapter 1 entry.
   Rosin follows his definition of emulation, which we have reproduced, with the description of an emulator for a simple machine and how it contrasts with a hardwired implementation. Research topics involving emulation are also

392

discussed.

5. S. G. Tucker, "Emulation of Large Systems," Communications
of the ACM, Volume 8 Number 12 (December 1965), pages
753-761.
    The classical concept of emulation is described. The
emulations for the IBM 7074, 7080, and 7090 systems on the
IBM System/360 is described.

B. Correctness

1. A. Birman, "On Proving Correctness of Microprograms," IBM
Journal of Research and Development, May 1974, pages
250-266.

2. W. G. Bouricius, "Procedure for Testing Microprograms,"
Seventh Annual Workshop on Microprogramming Preprints, ACM,
September 1974, pages 235-240.

3. G. B. Leeman, Jr., "Microprogram Certification: the Extended
S-Machine Experiment," Report RC4640, IBM Thomas J. Watson
Research Center, Yorktown Heights, New York, December 4,
1973.

4. G. B. Leeman, Jr., W. C. Carter, and A. Birman, "Some
Techniques for Microprogram Validation," Proceedings of
IFIPS 74, pages 76-80.

5. C. V. Ramamoorthy and K. S. Shankar, "Automatic Testing for
the Correctness and Equivalence of Loopfree Microprograms,"

IEEE Transactions on Computers, Volume C-23 Number 8 (August 1974), pages 768-782.

6. "User Microprogramming - Utopia or Nightmare," SIGMICRO Newsletter, Volume 2 Number 3 (October 1971), pages 18-19.

C. Program Enhancement

1. A. M. Abd-Alla and D. C. Karlgaard, "Heuristic Synthesis of Microprogrammed Computer Architecture," IEEE Transactions on Computers, Volume C-23 Number 8 (August 1974), pages 802-807.
     A study of automatic tuning.

2. J. A. Clapp, "The Application of Microprogramming Technology," SIGMICRO Newsletter, Volume 3 Number 1 (April 1972), pages 8-47.
     This comprehensive paper includes a discussion of when to microprogram and gives examples of possible performance improvements.

3. R. W. Cook and M. J. Flynn, "System Design of a Dynamic Microprocessor," IEEE Transactions on Computers, Volume C-19 Number 3 (March 1970), pages 213-222.
     Proposes the design of a microprogrammable computer and illustrates performance improvement over conventional iinstruction sets by microprogramming several examples.

4. S. S. Husson, Microprogramming Principles and Practices, see Chapter 1 entry.

Section 3.2 describes possible performance improvements through microprogramming and gives statistics for some routines on models of the IBM System/360.

5. E. W. Reigel, U. Faber, and D. A. Fisher, "The Interpreter – A Microprogrammable Building Block System," 1972 Spring Joint Computer Conference Proceedings, AFIPS Press, Montvale, New Jersey, pages 705-723.
E. W. Reigel and H. W. Lawson, "At the Programming Language – Microprogramming Interface," Proceedings of ACM SIGPLAN-SIGMICRO Interface Meeting, May 1973, pages 2-18.
    Included in these papers are descriptions of tuning.

6. A. B. Tucker and M. J. Flynn, "Dynamic Microprogramming: Processor Organization and Programming," Communications of the ACM, Volume 14 Number 4 (April 1971), pages 240-250.
    Describes a dynamically microprogrammable computer and compares microprogrammed execution of several routines to equivalent machine language programs for the IBM System/360 Model 50.

D. Executing Higher Level Language Programs

1. R. Belgard, "BLAISE – 1726," Seventh Annual Workshop on Microprogramming Preprints Supplement, ACM, September 1974, pages S-14 – S-18.
    A microprogrammed implementation of a virtual machine designed to support Johnston's contour model of block structured processes.

2. F. R. Broca and R. E. Merwin, "Direct Microprogrammed

Execution of the Intermediate Text from a High-Level Language Compiler," Proceedings of the ACM 1973 National Conference, pages 57-63.

An interesting study with several statistics.

3. A. Hassitt, J. Lageschulte, and L. E. Lyon, "Implementation of a High Level Language Machine," Communications of the ACM, Volume 16 Number 4 (April 1973), pages 199-212.

A very thorough description of a fully operational machine that executes APL.

4. H. Park, "Fortran Enhancement," Sixth Annual Workshop on Microprogramming Preprints, September 1973, pages 156-159.

A discussion of enhancing the execution of Fortran programs through microprogramming, with emphasis on the HP2100 computer.

5. E. W. Reigel and H. W. Lawson, "At the Programming Language - Microprogramming Interface," see previous entry in this chapter.

Describes microprogrammed implementations of higher level languages and discusses differences between the "translation machine" and the "execution machine".

6. W. T. Wilner, "Design of the Burroughs B1700," 1972 Fall Joint Computer Conference Proceedings, AFIPS Press, Montvale, New Jersey, pages 489-497.

Describes design philosophy and implementation of a system that executes several higher level languages.

7. H. Weber, "A Microprogrammed Implementation of EULER on IBM System/360 Model 30," Communications of the ACM, Volume 10 Number 9 (September 1967), pages 549-558.

This classic article describes one of the first microprogrammed implementations of higher level language programs.

8. R. Zaks, D. Steingart, and J. Moore, "A Firmware APL Time-Sharing System," 1971 Spring Joint Computer Conference Proceedings, AFIPS Press, Montvale, New Jersey, pages 179-190.

A preliminary description of a microprogrammed APL system that discusses system architecture and the interpretation scheme.

9. "MCM/70 Desk Top Computer," Micro Computer Machines Inc., Willowdale, Ontario, Canada.

Description of MCM/70 in executing APL.

E. Operating Systems

1. R. M. Balzer, "An Overview of the ISPL Computer Design System," Communications of the ACM, Volume 16 Number 2 (February 1973), pages 117-122.

An exploration of the advantages of the concurrent design of the language, operating system, and machine architecture via microprogramming to create an interactive programming laboratory.

2. W. H. Burkhardt and R. C. Randel, "Design of Operating Systems with Micro-Programmed Implementation," Report PIT-CS-BU-73-01, Pittsburgh University, September 1973.

A report which identifies different operating system phases, analyzes their capabilities and interrelationships, and suggests how microprogramming could be applied.

3. P. J. Denning, "Third Generation Computer Systems," Computing Surveys, Volume 3 Number 4 (December 1971), pages 175-216.

4. E. W. Dijkstra, "The Structure of the "THE"- Multiprogramming System," Communications of the ACM, Volume 11 Number 5 (May 1968), pages 341-346.

5. B. H. Liskov, "The Design of the Venus Operating System," Communications of the ACM, Volume 15 Number 3 (March 1972), pages 144-149.

A description of a working multiprogramming system supported by a combination of software and microprograms.

6. J. V. Sell, "Microprogramming in an Integrated Hardware/Software System," Computer Design, Volume 14 Number 1 (January 1975), pages 77-84.

An overview of the use of microprogramming to implement a small scale multiprogrammed system.

7. W. G. Sitton and L. L. Wear, "A Virtual Memory System for the Hewlett-Packard 2100A," Seventh Annual Workshop on Microprogramming Preprints, ACM, September 1974, pages 119-121.

A report on the use of microprogramming to implement a paged virtual memory system on a minicomputer not designed to support that feature.

8. A. H. Werkheiser, "Microprogrammed Operating Systems," <u>Third</u> <u>Annual</u> <u>Workshop</u> <u>on</u> <u>Microprogramming</u> <u>Preprints,</u> ACM, October 1970.

    An early but well done discussion of microprogramming applications to operating systems.

F. Signal Processing

1. H. Aiso <u>et</u> <u>al</u>, "A Very High-Speed Microprogrammable Pipeline Signal Processor," <u>Proceedings</u> <u>of</u> <u>IFIPS</u> <u>74,</u> pages 60-64.

2. W. D. Ashcraft, "Microprogramming of Signal Processors," <u>Sixth</u> <u>Annual</u> <u>Workshop</u> <u>on</u> <u>Microprogramming</u> <u>Preprints,</u> ACM, September 1973. Reprinted in <u>SIGMICRO</u> <u>Newsletter,</u> Volume 4 Number 3 (October 1973), pages 22-25.

3. J. R. Fisher, "The SPS-41 and SPS-81 Programmable Digital Signal Processors," <u>Sixth</u> <u>Annual</u> <u>Workshop</u> <u>on</u> <u>Microprogramming</u> <u>Preprints,</u> ACM, September 1973, pages 171-174.

4. J. P. Ihnat <u>et</u> <u>al</u>, "The Use of Two Levels of Parallelism to Implement an Efficient Programmable Signal Processing Computer," <u>Proceedings</u> <u>of</u> <u>the</u> <u>1973</u> <u>Sagamore</u> <u>Computer</u> <u>Conference</u> <u>on</u> <u>Parallel</u> <u>Processing,</u> Syracuse University, August 1973, pages 113-119.

5. G. L. Kratz and Y. S. Wu, "Microprogrammed Interface Processor (MIP) and Its Application to Phased Array Radar," <u>Third</u> <u>Annual</u> <u>Workshop</u> <u>on</u> <u>Microprogramming</u> <u>Preprints,</u> ACM, October 1970.

6. G. L. Kratz et al, "A Microprogrammed Approach to Signal Processing," IEEE Transactions on Computers, Volume C-23 Number 8 (August 1974), pages 808-817.

7. J. C. Murtha, "Architecture Trade-offs in Programmable Signal Processing," Sixth Annual Workshop on Microprogramming Preprints, ACM, September 1973, pages 168-170.

8. B. P. Shay, "Design Considerations of a Programmable Predetection Digital Signal Processor for Radar Applications," Naval Research Laboratory Report 7455, Washington, D. C., December 1972.

9. W. R. Smith et al, "AN/UYK-17 (XB-1) (V) Signal Processing Element Architecture," Naval Research Laboratory Report 7704, Washington, D. C., June 7, 1974.

G. Graphics

1. P. C. Anagnostopoulos et al, "Computer Architecture and Instruction Set Design," 1973 National Computer Conference Proceedings, AFIPS Press, Montvale, New Jersey, pages 519-527.

2. E. T. Barron and R. M. Glorioso, "A Micro Controlled Peripheral Processor," Sixth Annual Workshop on Microprogramming Preprints, ACM, September 1973, pages 122-128.

3. A. Bernardy, "Microprogrammed Multiprocessor Graphic

Controller," Sixth Annual Workshop on Microprogramming Preprints, ACM, September 1973, pages 131-133.

4. R. W. Hartenstein and K. D. Mueller, "A Microprogrammable Display Processor Concept," Sixth Annual Workshop on Microprogramming Preprints, ACM, September 1973, pages 129-130.

5. H. D. Kerr, "A Microprogrammed Processor for Interactive Computer Graphics," Proceedings of the Second Annual Symposium on Computer Architecture, IEEE, January 1975, pages 28-33.

6. G. M. Stabler, "The Brown University Graphics System," Center for Computer and Information Sciences, Brown University, February 1973.

7. G. M. Stabler, I. Carlbom, and K. Magel, "A Microprogrammed Satellite Graphics System," Proceedings of ACM SIGPLAN-SIGMICRO Interface Meeting, May 1973, pages 121-128.

8. J. E. Stockenberg et al, "Operating System Design Considerations for Microprogrammed Mini-Computer Satellite Systems," 1973 National Computer Conference Proceedings, AFIPS Press, Montvale, New Jersey, pages 555-562.

9. A. vanDam, "Microprogramming for Computer Graphics," SIGMICRO Newsletter, Volume 3 Number 1 (April 1972), pages 3-7.

10. H. Webber, Jr., "SIMALE," SIGMICRO Newsletter, Volume 3 Number 4 (January 1973), pages 25-44.

H. Microdiagnostics and Fault Tolerance

1. N. Bartow   and   R. McGuire,   "System/360   Model 85
   Microdiagnostics," <u>1970</u> <u>Spring</u> <u>Joint</u> <u>Computer</u> <u>Conference</u>
   <u>Proceedings</u>, AFIPS   Press,   Montvale,   New   Jersey,   pages
   191-197.

2. L. P. Caillouet, Jr. and B. D. Shriver, Sr., "An Integrated
   Approach to the Design of Fault Tolerant Computing Systems,"
   <u>Seventh</u> <u>Annual</u> <u>Workshop</u> on <u>Microprogramming</u> <u>Preprints</u>, ACM,
   September 1974, pages 12-24.

3. R. M. Guffin, "Microdiagnostics for the Standard Computer
   MLP-900   Processor,"   <u>IEEE</u>   <u>Transactions</u> <u>on</u>   <u>Computers</u>,
   Volume C-20 Number 7 (July 1971), pages 803-808.

4. A. M. Johnson, "The Microdiagnostics for the IBM System/360
   Model 30," <u>IEEE</u>   <u>Transaction</u> <u>on</u>   <u>Computers</u>, Volume C-20
   Number 7 (July 1971), pages 798-803.

5. E. H. Miller,   "Reliability   Aspects   of   the   Variable
   Instruction   Computer," <u>IEEE</u> <u>Transactions</u> <u>on</u> <u>Computers</u>,
   Volume EC-16 Number 5 (October 1967), pages 596-602.

6. C. V. Ramamoorthy and L. C. Chang, "System Modeling and
   Testing Procedures for Microdiagnostics," <u>IEEE</u> <u>Transactions</u>
   <u>on</u> <u>Computers</u>, Volume C-21 Number 11 (November 1972), pages
   1169-1183.

I. Higher Level Language Processing

1. Y. Chu, "Recursive Microprogramming in a Syntax Recognizer," Sixth Annual Workshop on Microprogramming Preprints, ACM, September 1973, pages 91-98.

2. S. Habib, "Name Resolutions Using a Microprogrammed Interpretive Technique," Proceedings of the ACM 1973 National Conference, pages 42-47.

3. P. Moulton, "Microprogrammed Subprocessors for Compilation and Execution of High-Level Languages," Seventh Annual Workshop on Microprogramming Preprints, ACM, September 1974, pages 74-79.

4. P. S. Roberts and C. S. Wallace, "A Microprogrammed Lexical Processor," Proceedings of IFIPS 71, North Holland Publishing Company, 1972, pages 577-581.

J. Microprogrammed Controllers

1. D. Dromard and O. Gibergues, "A Microprogrammed Data Communications Procedure Controller," Sixth Annual Workshop on Microprogramming Preprints, ACM, September 1973, pages 76-79.

2. R. J. Hancock, "Microprogrammed Disk Peripheral Control Units," 1971 IEEE International Computer Society Conference, pages 113-114.

3. H. Osofsky, "The Description and Use of Atron 600 Series Modules," 1971 IEEE International Computer Society Conference, pages 109-110.

4. F. D. Strout, "Microprogramming in the Hierarchy of Peripheral Control," _1971 IEEE International Computer Society Conference_, pages 111-112.

5. R. Zaks, "A Microprogrammed Architecture for Front End Processing," _Proceedings of the First Annual Symposium on Computer Architecture_, IEEE, December 1973, pages 241-246.

K. Perfomance Monitoring and Measurement

1. J. K. Broadbent and G. F. Coulouris, "MEMBERS - A Microprogrammed Experimental Machine with a Basic Executive for Real-Time Systems," _Proceedings of ACM SIGPLAN-SIGMICRO Interface Meeting_, May 1973, pages 154-159.

   This system, in which microprograms interpret a higher level language and operating system, initiates monitoring by calling a microprogrammed system function which marks the descriptor of the function or data structure to be monitored. It then links the descriptor to a monitoring routine which may be implemented either in software or firmware.

2. R. Mattson and A. Salisbury, "The Microprogrammble Multi-Processor (MMP) System for Simultaneous Emulation of Interoperating Computer Systems," _Seventh Annual Workshop on Microprogramming Preprints_, ACM, September 1974, pages 290-296.

   This multiprocessor system, which uses CDC 5600 computers (see Section 5.6), contains a firmware monitoring facility that collects statistics on interrupt processing, instruction usage, core utilization, I/O device utilization, and other system functions.

3. H. J. Saal and L. J. Shustek, "Microprogrammed Implemetation of Computer Measurement Techniques," Fifth Annual Workshop on Microprogramming Preprints, ACM, September 1972, pages 42-50.

One of the early works on the subject, this paper is an excellent tutorial.

4. B. D. Shriver, "A Description of the MATHILDA System," Department of Computer Science Report PB-13, University of Aarhus, Aarhus, Denmark, April 1973.

The MATHILDA system, described in Section 6.8, contains special hardware facilities, the Snooper facilities, to perform monitoring at the microprogram level.

L. Pocket Calculators

1. J. McDermott, "That Lowly Calculator is Turning into a Vest-Pocket Computer," Electronic Design, Volume 21 Number 13 (June 21, 1973), pages 28-34.

2. R. K. Stockwell, "Programming the Personal Computer," Hewlett-Packard Journal, May 1974, pages 8-14.

3. T. M. Whitney, "The Design and Impact of Pocket Calculators," Proceedings of IFIPS 74, pages 39-43.

M. Numerical Analysis

1. S. S. Hyder et al, "A Firmware Organization for Minimal Error Evaluation in Numerical Computations," Seventh Annual Workshop on Microprogramming Preprints, ACM, September 1974, pages 253-261.

2. C. Luk, "Microprogrammed Significance Arithmetic with Tapered Floating Point Representation," Seventh Annual Workshop on Microprogramming Preprints, ACM, September 1974, pages 248-252.

3. B. D. Shriver, Sr., "Microprogramming and Numerical Analysis," IEEE Transactions on Computers, Volume C-20 Number 7 (July 1971), pages 808-811.

CHAPTER 9

PERSPECTIVE

9.1 Overview

In the presentation so far an attempt has been made to avoid reflection of our bias and opinions in the discussions. In this chapter we present our view of the field, where it has been, where it is, and where we feel it may go.

The development of microprogramming systems can be roughly classified as is often done for computer hardware and software. Just as generations of software have lagged behind the generations of hardware, so the generations of firmware have lagged behind those of software as illustrated in Figure 9.1-1. The generations of microprogrammed systems can be classified by the medium used for control store implementation and the facilities provided to users. Generation 0 of microprogramming systems witnessed much discussion and some research but little development of practical systems. Generation 1 of microprogramming systems was characterized by the wide use of microprogramming in commercial systems. Microprograms resided in ROM control stores and were developed by the manufacturers. Facilities for user microprogramming were negligible. In the second generation, writable control stores provided dynamic microprogramming capabilities. User microprogramming followed with facilities for translating, simulating, and debugging microprograms. We are now entering the third generation of firmware systems as evidenced by the development of higher

Year	Generation	Hardware technology	Generation	Control programs	Generation	Control store technology	User facilities
		Hardware		**Software**		**Firmware**	
1944	0	Electro-mechanical					
1947							
	1	Vacuum-tube Williams tube Drum	0	Loaders I/O Sub-routines			
1950							
					0	Initial research	
1953		Core					
1956							
1959	2	Transistors	1	Interruption subroutines Tape-based "monitors" Tape IOCS	1	ROM (capacitive, transformer, etc.)	
1962	3	Hybrid circuits	2	Disk based operating systems Multi-programming supervisors			
1965							
1968			3	General purpose time sharing systems			
1971					2	Writable (Semiconductor)	Assemblers Simulators Debuggers
1974	4	LSI	4	Networks	3		Higher level languages Operating system support
1977							Integrated hardware-firmware-software-systems

Figure 9.1-1. Generations of computer hardware, software, and firmware (chronology only approximate). Hardware and software classifications are adapted from F. P. Brooks, Jr., "Operating System Design," © Copyright 1970, page 6.

level languages for microprogramming, microprogrammed support
of operating systems, microprogrammed support of higher level
languages, etc. We believe the fourth generation will see the
development of integrated hardware–firmware–software systems in
which system functions may be performed at different levels.
The level chosen for implementation of particular functions
will depend on particular applications. Functions may migrate
among levels, and the migration may become transparent to
users.

9.2 The Past

Microprogramming was formulated as a systemtic alternative
to the usual somewhat ad hoc procedure used for designing the
control section of digital computers. Microprogramming was
introduced into commercial systems for its engineering
advantages:

1. low cost – "microprogram control ... is the only method
known by which an extensive instruction set may be economically
realized in a small system."* The number of sequential logic
circuits required to implement instruction sets is too large to
be economically feasible in all but the fastest systems.

2. flexibility – with a microprogrammed organization it is
easier to change the machine language instruction set or modify
the algorithms used to interpret it than in a hardwired system.

3. ease of development and maintenance – microprogramming
provides a systematic approach to design. It modularizes the
implementation of machine language instruction sets.

The primary disadvantage of microprogramming is the time
involved in fetching the microinstructions from control store.

* [Stevens 1964], page 140.

409

Early microprogrammed systems have been described in detail elsewhere (e.g., [Husson 1970]). Here we have mentioned them only in their historical context.

9.3 The Present

The development of dynamically microprogrammable systems in recent years has had some impact on systems capabilities, and users are starting to benefit from this impact through developments by manufacturers. Even though user development of microprograms can lead to transportability problems, more effective use is being made of user microprogramming as users realize its advantages. Even with dynamic and user microprogramming, however, it is still very much the case that the organization and microinstruction design of microprogrammable machines are strongly influenced by the machine language instruction sets they support. As a result such machines may be difficult to use for interpreting arbitrary machine languages and supporting other microprogramming applications. Facilities and philosophies of machines designed for supporting arbitrary machine languages vary greatly. Investigation into a basic or primitive set of facilities for supporting arbitrary machine languages has not been studied in detail. Few general purpose machines utilize microinstructions that can be classified purely horizontal. Further study on the use and scheduling of different functional units is required before parallelism at the microprogramming level can be fully exploited. While the use of writable control store has been increasing, in several machines this capability seems retrofitted and awkward to use. Few machines support multiprogramming at the microprogramming level, however, techniques and tradeoffs involved in control store implementation in such a system have been reported in the literature ([Wilkes 1972], [Thomas 1974]). While there have been studies of the theoretical aspects of micropogramming, as yet they have had little impact.

In deciding whether or not to develop their own microprograms, users should be concerned about the performance improvement that can be achieved. There have, however, been few definitive investigations of the performance of microprogrammed systems. Techniques and results are needed in making quantitative assessments of microprogramming systems. While some preliminary work has been done in this area [Salisbury 1973], the importance of evaluation is often ignored and users proceed blindly to develop their own microprograms without considering the implications of this step. It is sometimes the case that microprogramming projects are undertaken without performing the analysis necessary for a well-designed system. Often one fails to realize the consequences of the following maxim:

Microprogramming an inefficient algorithm does not make it efficient.

Microprogramming an inefficient algorithm may result in faster execution than with a software implementation, however, the algorithm will still be inefficient. Microprogramming is not a substitute for good algorithmic design and analysis.

9.4 The Future

The significant developments in microprogramming so far have been mainly in the area of hardware technology. These technological developments have progressed to the point that future advances are likely to be innovations in

1. architecture – computer systems will have microprogram level architectures that can support a variety of data representations, operations, and performance monitoring techniques,

2. software – higher level language compilers will allow users to write their microprograms in machine-independent representations and will generate efficient microcode, and

3. applications – aided by architecture and software advances, manufacturers will be able to apply microprogramming systematically to the implementation of computer systems (including operating systems and compilers) and other problems.

Microprogramming should be recognized as an important level in the hierarchical structure of computer systems – hardware, firmware, system software (operating system, compilers, etc.), and applications programs. Systems are likely to be designed by considering these levels as synergistic factors. A shift in this direction is becoming evident in the current literature.

topic of significant interest in the computer systems area is the design and implementation of distributed computing networks. In such networks several types of processors may be connected to provide a variety of services to a large community. A technique that may prove cost effective in implementing a distributed network is extending the single system concept to a complex of computers in which each machine is microprogrammed to perform a variety of functions (see, e.g., [Davis 1972] and [Mattson 1974]). Each of the computers in the network could then be configured dynamically to satisfy changing processing requirements.

With the wide availability and acceptance of microprogrammable computers and the flexibility they offer, their use in a large variety of application areas is natural. Some of the current applications have been discussed here. Many more may be just around the corner.

9.5 Concluding Remarks

Within 25 years microprogramming has evolved from a concept for realizing control, to an economical method for maufacturer implementation of machine architecture, to a tool for user application to specific problems. Advances in hardware technology have made possible the development of dynamically user microprogrammable computers. Developments in software support have made user microprogramming viable. The hardware and software aspects of microprogramming are thus synergistic. As new developments in hardware and software continue, so the interest in microprogramming and its applications increases. While hardware developments for supporting microprogramming have been dramatic, developments in software and applications aspects are still in their infancy. Programming language techniques, such as intermediate language design, interpretation, and optimization, need to be applied and extended. Application areas, somewhat hampered by lack of software support, need to adapt microprogramming to specific problems to realize the potential of microprogramming.

Although we have described many developments, applications, and techniques involved in the design and use of micrprogramming systems, the amount of work done on the subject prohibits a complete examination in a single book. Several bibliograhies provide references to additional literature on the subject of microprogramming ([SIGMICRO 1974], [Agrawala 1974], [Davies 1972], [Husson 1970], [Wilkes 1969]).

Annotated Bibliography

A. Perspective

1. R. L. Davis, S. Zucker, and C. M. Campbell, "A Building Block Approach to Multiprocessing," <u>1972</u> <u>Spring</u> <u>Joint</u> <u>Computer</u> <u>Conference</u> <u>Proceedings</u>, AFIPS Press, Montvale, New Jersey, pages 685-703.

   Describes a Switch Interlock which allows an array of Burroughs Interpreters (see Section 6.6) to be connected to form a multiprocessing system.

2. S. S. Husson, <u>Microprogramming</u> <u>Principles</u> <u>and</u> <u>Practices</u>, see Chapter 1 entry.

3. R. Mattson and A. Salisbury, "The Microprogrammable Multi-Processor (MMP) System for Simultaneous Emulation of Interoperating Computer Systems," <u>Seventh</u> <u>Annual</u> <u>Workshop</u> on <u>Microprogramming</u> <u>Preprints</u>, ACM, September 1974, pages 290-296.

   This multiprocessor system uses CDC 5600 computers (see Section 5.6) and was designed both as a tool and test bed for emulation of new computers or systems, evaluation of hardware/software replacements, system integration and interface testing, and other functions.

4. A. B. Salisbury, "The Evaluation of Microprogram Implemented Emulators," Technical Report No. 60, Digital Systems Laboratory, Stanford University, Stanford, California, July 1973.

Following a survey of emulation and performance monitoring and evaluation, this report describes "synthetic emulation", a new technique for estimating the performance of microprogram implemented emulators.

5. W. Y. Stevens, "The Structure of System/360, Part II – System Implementation," IBM Systems Journal, Volume 3 Number 2 (1964), pages 136-143.

This description of the implementations of the various models of the IBM System/360 has an interesting discussion of microprogram control and why it was used in some 360 models.

6. R. T. Thomas, "Organization for Execution of User Microprograms from Main Memory: Synthesis and Analysis," IEEE Transactions on Computers, Volume C-23 Number 8 (August 1974), pages 783-791.

Describes a system design in which user microprograms are executed directly from main memory rather than from a writable control store. This design is analyzed and compared with the use of writable control store for allowing dynamic user microprogramming in a multiprogramming system.

7. M. V. Wilkes, "The Use of a Writable Control Memory in a Multiprogramming Environment," Fifth Annual Workshop on Microprogramming Preprints, ACM, September 1972, pages 62-65.

An excellent paper that discusses design considerations and alternatives involved in multiprogramming microprograms.

B. Bibliographies

1. "Microprogramming Bibliography 1951 - Early 1974," <u>SIGMICRO</u> <u>Special Issue</u>, September 1974.

    This comprehensive bibliography of 554 works on microprogramming is organized by keywords and by authors.

2. A. K. Agrawala and T. G. Rauscher, "Microprogramming: Perspective and Status," <u>IEEE Transactions on Computers</u>, Volume C-23 Number 8 (August 1974), pages 817-837.

    A bibliography of 131 entries that is similar to the bibliographies in this book, but offers slightly more perspective in a more compact form.

3. P. M. Davies, "Readings in Microprogramming," <u>IBM Systems Journal</u>, Volume 11 Number 1 (1972), pages 16-40.

    The bibliography of 53 papers is somewhat IBM oriented but offers interesting historical perspective.

4. S. S. Husson, <u>Microprogramming Principles and Practices</u>, see Chapter 1 entry.

5. M. V. Wilkes, "The Growth of Interest in Microprogramming: A Literature Survey," see Chapter 1 entry.